THE WORDS YOU NEED

B Rudzka, J Channell, Y Putseys, P Ostyn

MACMILLAN
PUBLISHERS

First published 1981
Reprinted 1982, 1983 (twice), 1984 (twice), 1986 (twice),
1987, 1988, 1989 (twice), 1990 (three times), 1991, 1992 (twice)

Published by MACMILLAN PUBLISHERS LTD
London and Basingstoke

ISBN 0-333-27829-1

Printed in Hong Kong

Contents

B Synonymous Pairs

1 range, scope 2 destroy, devastate 3 puzzle, baffle
4 contaminate, pollute 5 prevent, forestall
6 ugly, unsightly 7 effective, efficacious 8 adventurous, reckless
9 distant, remote

A Semantic Fields

1 reach, accomplish, achieve, attain, gain
2 check, examine, inspect, scan, scrutinize
3 cower, crouch, squat
4 break, smash, crush, shatter, crack, chip, snap, burst
5 refuse, reject, turn down, decline, spurn
6 look, gaze, glance, glimpse, peer

B Synonymous Pairs

1 movements, antics 2 chew, munch 3 pay back, retaliate
4 scamper, scurry 5 cut, sever 6 disturb, ruffle
7 mislead, bluff 8 sad, plaintive 9 aggressive, militant
10 dry, arid 11 harmful, pernicious

A Semantic Fields

1 goods, merchandise, wares, commodity
2 (a) shop, chain-store, general stores, department store,
supermarket (b) kiosk, stall, stand
3 advance, further, promote
4 surprise, astonish, amaze, astound, flabbergast ·
5 grin, smirk, giggle, chuckle
6 rich, wealthy, affluent, opulent
7 meagre, scant, scanty, sparse, frugal

B Synonymous Pairs

1 trick, gimmick 2 doll, puppet 3 beginning, onset
4 piece, slice 5 simple, austere 6 intentional, deliberate

A Semantic Field

1 rear, bring up, breed, grow
2 limit, restrict, confine, constrict
3 complain, bellyache, grouse, grumble, moan, whine
4 worry, bother, tease, get on at, nag, pester, plague, harass, harry
5 quarrel, bicker, squabble, wrangle
6 shrewd, sly, cunning, crafty
7 tidy, neat, orderly, shipshape

B Synonymous Pairs

1 attend, frequent 2 keep up, maintain 3 deal with,
cope with 4 change, shift 5 change, alter 6 lenient,
permissive 7 even, steady 8 doubtful, dubious

Unit 6   **Get down to work!**

A   Semantic Fields
1. work, drudgery, grind, labour, toil
2. lawyer, solicitor, barrister
3. dodge, duck, evade, shirk
4. strip, denude, divest
5. fight, combat, struggle
6. false, spurious, counterfeit, fake, bogus, phony, sham, mock, artificial

B   Synonymous Pairs
1. occupation, profession; occupational, professional
2. salary, wages   3 officer, official   4 revive, restore
5. ward off, avert   6 change, amend   7 get, acquire
8. dull, drab   9 fastidious, fussy

Unit 7   **Do you love me?**

A   Semantic Fields
1. sympathy, compassion, pity
2. like, be attached to, be fond of, love, be in love with, feel/have an affection for, be infatuated, adore
3. boast, crow, brag
4. shine, glow, gleam, glisten, shimmer glimmer, twinkle, flash, glitter, sparkle
5. authentic, real, genuine
6. plain, simple, homely
7. secret, clandestine, secretive, furtive, stealthy, underhand, underhanded

B   Synonymous Pairs
1. keep, retain   2 hide, conceal   3 support, bolster
4. wallow, flounder   5 unpleasant, obnoxious

Unit 8   **There is more to it than meets the eye**

A   Semantic Fields
1. affect, influence, impress, sway
2. show, display, exhibit, expose, flaunt
3. announce, declare, pronounce, proclaim
4. protect, shield, defend, guard, safeguard
5. look for, seek, grope, search, comb, scour
6. gather, accumulate, assemble, collect, muster
7. weird, eerie, uncanny, unearthly, mysterious, inscrutable, enigmatic

B   Synonymous Pairs
1. conduct, transmit   2 flow, emanate   3 receive, pick up
4. have an accident, crash   5 strange, odd   6 shiny, luminous
7. lost, stray

Preface

The importance of words in verbal communication hardly needs stressing, yet no other language component has been more neglected in foreign language teaching than the lexicon. While a great deal of energy and imagination is going into the teaching of grammar, comparatively little is being done to teach words, and students of foreign languages, even after several years of strenuous effort, often know many grammatical frames but have very little to put into them.

The Words You Need sets out specifically to organise the acquisition of language skills within the context of a structured approach to vocabulary teaching.

The inspiration for our book came directly from the work on semantic fields and lexical structure of Adrienne Lehrer from the University of Arizona, and we owe her a particular debt for her encouragement, and continued interest.

The approach used is a completely new one, adapting insights from theoretical linguistics and psycholinguistics to the service of the language learner.

A teacher's book accompanies this student's book. In it we explain the teaching methods used and give practical guidance on the many and varied uses to which the material can be put.

Acknowledgements

We are most grateful to Sandra Colen, René Dirven, Roger Flavell, John Green, Adrienne Lehrer, Jacques van Roey, Emma Vorlat, and Don. Young, who read, reviewed and criticised sections of the manuscript. We would also like to express our thanks to the following people, who provided examples, comments, suggestions and the opportunity to discuss recalcitrant points: Alessandra Bini, the Channell family, Patrick Griffiths, Peter Kelly, Androulla Kyriacou, Mary Ann Martin, Maryam Mathis, Conny Templeman, Margie Thomas, Ludolph van Hasselt, June Wickboldt. The following people arranged or took part in tests and trials of the material: René Dirven and his seminar students at the University of Trier, Germany; students of English at the Katholieke Universiteit te Leuven, Belgium; and students at York Advanced English Summer School, summer 1978.

To the student

You may not have seen analyses of vocabulary like those in the Word-Study sections before. In Unit 1 you will find explanations of how to understand the grids and the terminology. Here are a few tips on how to use the book:

Once you have read the texts in any unit, go through the Word-Study section. You are not expected to learn the contents of the componental grids (analysis of meanings) by heart – rather you should start working through the exercises and keep going back to the Word-Study section or the texts when you find something you can't answer. You should aim to be able to give the answers to the exercises instantaneously when asked to do so in class, as this will be a similar situation to spontaneous speech. In this connection you are advised to pay special attention to the collocational grids (which words go with which) and example sentences. You will find the Word-Study slow at first but as you become more familiar with the method you will speed up. In addition you will learn a way of looking at words which you can apply to any vocabulary items you come across on your own.

American and British English

This book teaches standard British English. Yet much written English is American, and you should be able to recognize and understand American English. Where we include American texts, we note differences of meaning and usage in the glosses. Differences of spelling are all noted below, and are not mentioned in the units. You will see that most of the differences are systematic.

AMERICAN	BRITISH
I CONSONANT DOUBLING	
l → ll	
counseling	counselling
counselor	counsellor
grueling	gruelling
labeled	labelled
marvelous	marvellous
refueling	refuelling
traveler	traveller
others	
focusing	focussing
kidnapers	kidnappers
program	programme

2 . . . . . or → . . . . . our

arbor	arbour
behavior	behaviour
color	colour
enamored	enamoured
endeavor	endeavour
favor	favour
favoritism	favouritism
harbor	harbour
humor	humour
labor	labour
neighbor	neighbour
vapor	vapour
vigor	vigour

3 . . . . . er → . . . . . re

center	centre
fiber	fibre
meter	metre
theater	theatre

4 s → c

defense	defence
offense	offence

5 others

check	cheque
esthetic	aesthetic
mold	mould
plow	plough

Abbreviations

abbr	abbreviation	*of*	old-fashioned
Am	American	*sb*	somebody
Br	British	*sl*	slang
coll	colloquial	*sth*	something
esp	especially	*US*	United States of America
fig	figurative	usu	usually
lit	literally	*vulg*	vulgar

Symbols

★   indicates that the word or phrase used is considered incorrect

⇒   indicates the figurative sense of the word

{ }   used to enclose features which apply to more than one word

---

Stylistic distinctions

Where a word's use is limited to one particular style, we have pointed this out. We have also noted when a word should **not** be used in a certain style. The descriptions used in this connection should be understood in the following way:

slang   not accepted as correct English, not used in writing except personal letters. Used between close friends or members of a social group to express intimacy or sense of community eg criminals, students

colloquial   used between close friends, or people of equal age and social standing eg relations, work colleagues

informal   used between friends and acquaintances in informal settings eg parties, meals, classroom situations and in some publications eg popular newspapers

formal   used between people of unequal age or social standing, or people meeting for the first time. Also used, for example, in lectures, conferences, legal proceedings, academic writing, official documents and reports, and in business correspondence

literary   used in creative writing, novels, poetry, etc

These stylistic distinctions are intended as a general guide and are in no way definitive or exhaustive.

Dictionaries consulted

The Barnhart Dictionary of New English 1963–72, London: Longman, 1973

Britannica World Language Dictionary, Edition of Funk and Wagnalls Standard Dictionary, Volumes 1 and 2

Cassell's English Dictionary, London: Cassell, 1975

The Compact Edition of the Oxford English Dictionary, Volumes 1 and 2, London: Oxford University Press, 1971

A Dictionary of Slang and Unconventional English, Volumes 1 and 2, London: Routledge and Kegan, 1970

Oxford Advanced Learner's Dictionary of Current English, A S Hornby, E V Gatenby and H Wakefield, London: Oxford University Press, 1975

Longman Dictionary of Contemporary English, London: Longman, 1978

Oxford Dictionary of Current Idiomatic English, Volume 1, London: Oxford University Press, 1975

The Oxford Illustrated Dictionary, Oxford: Clarendon Press, 1976

The Penguin English Dictionary, Harmondsworth: Penguin Books, 1973

Roget's Thesaurus, Harmondsworth: Penguin Books, 1973

Webster's New Students Dictionary, New York: American Book Company, 1964

Webster's New World Dictionary of the American Language, Cleveland and New York: The World Publishing Company, 1968

Webster's Third New International Dictionary of the English Language, Unabridged, Springfield, Mass.: GC Merriam Company, 1976

Unit 1

Beauty isn't only skin deep

Body Image

The Happy American Body: A Survey Report by Ellen Berscheid, Elaine Walster, and George Bohmstedt

More than 62,000 'Psychology Today' readers answered a questionnaire about their attitudes towards their bodies. Overall, most of us like what we see in the mirror quite a bit.

'No one is free who is a slave to the body', wrote Seneca some 1,900 years ago. Judging from the advertisements, products, and best sellers that **deluge**[1] us daily, we are a nation of slaves. We are obsessed with being thin, beautiful, young, and sexy, and we will go to extraordinary lengths to approach those ideals.

In a recent issue of *Psychology Today*, we offered readers the opportunity to express their thoughts and feelings about the body. The topic was **timely**[2] and the response

overwhelming[3]: more than 62,000 readers returned the 109-item 'Body Image' questionnaire. But they were divided and **ambivalent**[4] on the matter of how important attractiveness and physical looks are — or should be.

A good number of people wrote letters to protest a 'whole survey' on the body. Some said that appearance is a superficial matter, not worthy of undue discussion: 'Perhaps if I thought I were ugly or beautiful I would pay more attention to my appearance', wrote one

woman. 'But as it is, this is a topic **of little concern for myself**[5]. There are just many more important matters in my life.' Nevertheless, she filled out the whole questionnaire.

Another woman summarized the views of many: 'There's a lot more to me than my looks. I know I'm attractive, but I don't want to be attractive to someone only because of physical appearance. That would be **ghastly**[6].'

By contrast, other respondents acknowledged, some **reluctantly**[7], the importance of one's appearance. 'Your questionnaire made me feel as though I have **floated**[8] through life ignoring my body. You have made me **dissect**[9] myself and realize that I do think it's important. Now I must learn to connect my body with the rest of myself.' 'The questionnaire was extremely thought-provoking,' **seconded**[10] an older woman. 'My long-held belief that our bodies are un-important was **shattered**[11].' One honest soul confessed, with some shame, that 'I discriminate against beautiful people, probably out of jealousy, and tend to label them **shallow**[12] and egotistical.'

Good Looks and Self-Esteem

In their studies of body image done in the 1950s, Paul Secord and Sidney Jourard found that college students who had negative body images also tended to have low **self-esteem**[13]. Our survey gave us the opportunity to test this relationship on a more diverse group of people.

We used 10 questions such as, *How often do you dislike yourself?*, *How sure of yourself do you feel among strangers?*, *How often do you feel self-conscious?*, and *Overall, how confident do you feel about your abilities?*

We found that for both sexes, body image is strongly related to self-esteem. Only 11 percent of those with a below-average body image (compared to 50 percent of those with an above-average body image) had an above-average level of self-esteem. We also looked at the **links**[14] between satisfaction with various parts of the body and self-esteem, and found that, for both sexes, the face makes the difference. People who are satisfied with their faces are more self-confident.

Most psychologists have **over-looked**[15] the connection between body image and self-esteem. Obviously, body image is only one **component**[16] of self-esteem; a person's **assessment**[17] of his or her abilities and other attributes is equally important. Some respondents felt that other sources of self-esteem can **supersede**[18] the relevance of body image; looks don't matter, **runs**[19] this view, since I'm **bright**[20]/talented/charming or whatever.

'I was quite self-conscious when I was younger, even though I was probably **average**[21] in looks, now I am less worried and embarrassed about my looks — I think because I feel more intelligent and intellectually interesting.'

But others clearly distinguished their body image from their personal **traits**[22].

'No problems with self-confidence, **fellers**[23]. There's never been any doubt that my intellectual (and lately, **sensitivity**[24]-type) abilities have always been **at the top of the ladder**[25]. But that doesn't mean I have a good, or even accurate, body-image picture.'

Of course, one trouble with survey findings is that we cannot determine cause and effect. A positive body image may increase a person's self-esteem, or basic self-esteem may lead a person to feel good about his or her body.

Self-esteem — the general feeling that one is competent and confident — **spills over**[26] into other areas of personality. Respondents who have above average positive body images also consider themselves to be more likeable, **assertive**[27], conscientious and even more intelligent than the 'average person'. For example, of those who **rate**[28] their body images as above average, 69 percent also indicate that they're more likeable than the average person, compared to 40 percent of those who rate their body images below average.

People who are happy with their bodies may actually be more assertive and likeable than those who have negative body images. Or they *think* they are. One young man explained that in the last year his body image has changed very much for the better, as a result of his personal development: 'I've gone from considering myself some sort of **asshole**[29] to believing that I'm a **charismatic**[30] individual nearly impossible to dislike . . . I have more friends than I know what to do with.'

Psychology Today

BODY IMAGE

1 flood, overwhelm
2 opportune, occurring at just the right time
3 overpowering, crushing
4 containing contradictory and opposing tendencies
5 which does not interest me much
6 very unpleasant
7 unwilling
8 moved about freely and aimlessly
9 take a living organism to pieces to examine how it works
10 supported a proposal
11 smashed, broken into pieces

12 not capable of feeling deep affection, *lit* not deep
13 well-balanced judgement of, and respect for, oneself
14 relationships, connections
15 failed to see or notice
16 part of a whole
17 evaluation
18 take the place of because better or more important
19 goes
20 cheerful and happy, clever
21 the same as the majority
22 characteristics

23 *coll* fellows
24 the state or quality of being sensitive, quick to receive mental impressions, easily affected
25 very good
26 flows over, *lit* falls out accidentally
27 positive, in the habit of insisting on one's rights
28 evaluate, assess
29 *Am vulg* person unworthy of esteem, *lit* vulgar way to refer to anus
30 having very strong appeal, charm, attractiveness

Pretty Pleases

by Peter L Benson, Stuart A Karabenick, Richard M Lerner

The effects of physical attractiveness, race and sex in receiving help.

PRETTY PLEASES

1 starting signals for specific actions, eg in a play
2 appointments with a member of the opposite sex, the member of the opposite sex with whom one has such an appointment
3 scenery, surroundings
4 grades, marks
5 force
6 importance
7 outcome of an enquiry or research
8 questionnaires using scales
9 open, explicit
10 profitable, bringing in money
11 *Am* division of a university offering courses higher than first degree level. There is no *Br* equivalent.
12 written request

A rapidly increasing body of literature indicates that physical attractiveness **cues**[1] generate specific evaluations and impressions. The physically attractive benefit from this process. In comparison to the less attractive, persons with good looks are liked more, are desired more as **dates**[2], are attributed more socially desirable characteristics, are expected to achieve more in educational **settings**[3] and receive more favorable task performance **ratings**[4]. This preference for the physically attractive appears to be of such **strength**[5] that even those who associate with beautiful persons gain in **stature**[6].

These **findings**[7], however, are based almost exclusively on studies which ask subjects to rate persons of varying attractiveness on **paper and pencil measures**[8]. Hence, it is not known if physical effects generalize to nonreactive situations in naturalistic settings where subjects are not aware of their roles.

Besides, ratings are measures of attitudes, and it remains to be demonstrated in which areas, if any, these attitudes will translate into **overt**[9] behavioral responses that will favor the physically attractive. If preferential attitudes do translate into preferential behaviors, we might expect, for example, that the physically attractive will receive more **lucrative**[10] court settlements, better jobs, higher grades, more votes in an election, and be helped more in comparison to the unattractive.

The present study investigated the effects of physical attractiveness on helping behavior in a naturalistic setting which was that of helping to deliver a **graduate school**[11] **application**[12] lost by a traveler at an airport. A picture attached to the application varied the attractiveness

13 *lit* object to be aimed at (in shooting)
14 fastened with a paper clip
15 a board fitted into a cupboard or bookcase, etc
16 *Br* telephone box/kiosk
17 found out, realised
18 *Br* posting
19 passing on, handing to
20 advantages, favour
21 make more certain, strengthen, agree with
22 draw out, cause to come out
23 always the same, unoriginal
24 conclusions
25 Intelligence Quotients
26 professional
27 deserving disapproval
28 concerned with, about
29 all the time, invariably
30 bad condition

of the person needing help (**target**[13]). The race and sex of both the subjects and the targets were varied to determine the generality of physical attractiveness cues. The completed application form with the picture, **paper clipped**[14] to the outside of a stamped addressed envelope, was placed on a small **shelf**[15] in a **phone booth**[16] in such a way as to be unavoidable to anyone entering the booth. A person was used as a subject if he or she entered a phone booth, handled the materials, and read the personal note, whose function was to make sure that subjects **ascertained**[17] that helping would consist of **mailing**[18] the application (or **turning it over to**[19] an official to mail) and that leaving it in the phone booth would be unhelpful. The note read: 'Dear Dad, have a nice trip. Please remember to mail this application before you leave Detroit on your flight to New York. Love, Linda (Bob).'

As predicted, the target's physical attractiveness influenced helping behavior, independently of sex of subject and sex and race of target. The attractive, then, appear to receive the **benefits**[20] of assistance regardless of these other major stimulus characteristics. The present results thus demonstrate that favoritism for the physically attractive, previously found with rating scale measures, generalizes to overt helping behavior in a naturalistic setting. Since no significant interactions were found, the findings do not **corroborate**[21] studies which show that the effect of physical attractiveness is modified by the sex of the subject and/or the sex of the target.

Three possible explanations for why physical attractiveness influences helping responses are as follows: First, attractiveness cues may **elicit**[22] **stereotyped**[23] **inferences**[24] such as 'what is beautiful is good' and 'what is ugly is bad'. In the present study the target persons are applying to graduate school. Accordingly, inferences about the academic competence and potential of the candidate could influence the amount of help given. Studies have shown that the physically attractive are perceived to have higher **IQs**[25] and educational potential and be better writers. From these studies, one might conclude that attractive applicants were considered more qualified and, therefore, more deserving of help in pursuing their **vocational**[26] goals. Thus, subjects faced with the unattractive target may feel less **blameworthy**[27] for neglecting to give help.

Second, studies **dealing with**[28] liking may also provide clues for explaining the relationship between appearance and being helped. Several authors have found that helping is positively associated with the degree of liking for the target. Also, it has been **consistently**[29] shown that the attractive are liked more than the unattractive. Therefore attractive people are likely to be helped more.

Finally, even though all subjects handled the stimulus materials and read the note to the father, those who saw physically attractive pictures may have been led to pay more attention to the stimulus materials than those who saw unattractive pictures. Such a difference in attention may have produced an increased sensitivity to the **plight**[30] of the 'victim' and/or an increased desire to give help.

Condensed from *Journal of Experimental Social Psychology*

Beautiful people

If you're **fed up with**[1] people **propositioning**[2] you, asking directions or even just **bumping into**[3] you on the street, don't call a policeman – brush your hair. Two American psychologists have discovered that people on the street keep at least three **inches**[4] farther away from an attractive woman than from an ordinary-looking one, and never **mutter**[5] dirty things at her or ask for help. For those unsure of their charm, the psychologists' research offers a further test: **edge up close to**[6] a man on a crowded rush hour bus. If you're attractive he'll look uneasily up, down and out of the window. But if he just stands there . . . oh dear!

Honey

Image-builder

One Saturday morning my wife and I were **grimy**[1] from decorating when a new colleague and his wife called to invite us to dinner that evening. As my wife was getting ready, she **donned**[2] **wig**[3] and false **eyelashes**[4], **applied**[5] eyebrow pencil, eyeshadow, lipstick and **nail varnish**[6] and said triumphantly: 'There, now they'll see the real me!' – L S Haslemere, Surrey.

Woman's Own

WINNING WAYS

My friend was horrified to hear that her two children had entered their rather **scruffy**[1] **mongrel**[2] in a dog show. But they returned triumphantly, the dog **sporting**[3] a large **rosette**[4] on its collar.

It had won the prize for the dog with the happiest face.
Mrs M B, Co. Tyrone.

Weekend

BEAUTIFUL PEOPLE

1 *coll* tired of, bored with
2 making an improper suggestion to
3 meet accidentally; strike against or knock into
4 *Br* and *Am* non-metric measure =2.5 cm
5 speak in a low indistinct voice
6 move slowly and carefully closer to

IMAGE BUILDER

1 dirty
2 put on
3 an artificial covering of hair for the head
4 hairs on the edge of the eyelids
5 put on
6 liquid which dries to form a hard, glossy surface, usually coloured for the nails and clear for wood, stone, etc

WINNING WAYS

1 not smart
2 a dog of no special breed or of mixed breed
3 wearing, displaying
4 a small ornament in the shape of a rose, usually marking an animal which has won a prize in a competition

Discussion

1 Do you agree with the survey respondents who said that beauty is a superficial matter, not worthy of discussion? How far is this disproved by these articles?
2 In your experience, have you noticed that physically attractive people have an advantage professionally or socially? Give some examples.
3 What criteria do you think we use to measure our own 'body image'? Are they the same criteria which we use to judge other people? Are these criteria valid?
4 Is it harder for people who are beautiful when they are young to come to terms with growing older and aging physically?

5 In the survey referred to, women were more likely than men to agree that physical appearance is very important. Would you have expected this result, and if so, why?

6 'People who are satisfied with their faces are more self-confident.' But is it true that those who are not so satisfied can compensate by feeling themselves to be intelligent, talented, or charming? Don't they really always care about how their faces look?

Word Study

This first Word Study contains guidance notes. All the other Word Study sections work in the same way as this one, and you will be able to study them by yourself. You can always refer back to the notes in this unit if you need to.

A   Semantic Fields

A Semantic Field is a group of words which are similar in meaning. For example the words printed in **heavy black type** in the COMPONENTIAL GRID below all describe a person having a good opinion of himself:

1 **Opinions of oneself**

	good opinion of oneself or what one has done		desire that others praise you to your face
	exaggerated	*or* justified	
conceit	+		
pride	+	+	
self–esteem		+	
vanity	+		+

The differences and similarities between the words are shown by the *semantic features* at the top of this grid. If there is a + against a word this means that the feature is part of the meaning of the word, so here, **conceit** and **pride** both include in their meaning [+ exaggerated good opinion of oneself]. (Note that when we write features outside a grid we put them in square brackets with a + sign.) If there is no +, either the feature is not part of the meaning of the word, or the feature does not help us to know the difference between this word and others in the field.

Or between two features can mean two things:
If a word is marked for both the features, then both of them are part of its meaning, although not necessarily at the same time. **Pride** is such a word – in certain contexts it means that the 'good opinion of oneself' is 'exaggerated' and in others that it is 'justified'.

If a word is marked for only one feature, the other one is *not* part of its meaning.

This scale shows how good or bad the qualities expressed by these words are:

good   bad

$\longleftrightarrow$

self-esteem   pride   vanity   conceit

This is not exact, of course, but it shows you that **vanity** is usually regarded as worse than **pride** which can have both a good and a bad sense.

The following adjectives are derived from these nouns, **conceited**, **proud** and **vain**. **Self-esteem** does not produce an adjective.

EXAMPLES

conceited   He is so **conceited** he can't imagine he might fail the exam.

proud   I am very **proud** of my garden this year. (positive sense)
He is too **proud** to mix with the ordinary people in the village. (negative sense)

vain   **Vain** people like to be told nice things about themselves.

2 Counting up the worth

	count up the worth of	implies precise analysis	implies temporary judgement	always implies positive judgement	by placing or as if by placing on a numerical scale
assess	+	+			
estimate	+		+		
evaluate	+				
value	+			+	
rate	+				+

This grid shows features working in two different ways. All the words in the field are marked for [+ count up the worth of], so it is helping to distinguish one field from another. The other features distinguish the different words in the field from each other.

All the above verbs, except **evaluate**, can appear in expressions of the type, **to ..... sth at.**

EXAMPLES

I would **estimate** my losses at $200.
His IQ is **rated** at 110.
The value of the house has been **assessed** at £25,000.
Only **estimate** can be followed by a that-clause.

EXAMPLE

We **estimated** that the work would take us two hours.

Rate is colloquial except when it is being used with reference to statistical enquiry or analysis.

The next grid is a COLLOCATIONAL GRID. It gives examples of the most typical ways in which the words in the field are used. Of course it does not give all the possible uses, but if you know these examples, it will help you to decide whether the word is suitable in another situation. If there is a + against a word printed in bold this means that the word collocates with the word or expression at the top of this grid. In this case **assess damages** is a good collocation, whereas ★**evaluate damages** is not. (+) means that the collocation does not seem correct to all speakers, although many would use it.

	sb's income for tax purposes	damages	the cost of sth (at)	the importance of sth	the evidence	sb's performance	sb's contribution to the debate	sb's ability	sb as very competent, highly capable, highly gifted	sb's property (at)	sb as a leader	sb's advice
assess	+	+	+	+	(+)	+	+	+				
estimate		+	+	+								
evaluate				+	+	+	+					
rate			(+)		+		(+)	+		+		
value						+	+			+	+	+

3 Forming judgements

	hint —or— form an opinion (about)	by imaginative deduction from given information	usu by careful and critical examination of facts	stresses idea of finality
conclude	+			+
infer	+	+	+	
judge	+		+	

These verbs are all transitive and can occur with the preposition **from** and a **that-**clause.

Verbal classification The categories *transitive* and *intransitive* are used differently in different books. We have adopted the following distinctions: If a verb can be used with no object of any kind, it is described as *intransitive*.

EXAMPLES

He is running.
She cried.

She goes out.
We will go there tomorrow.

If it takes an object—noun, pronoun, participle, infinitive, object introduced by a preposition, sentential object—it is said to be *transitive*.

EXAMPLES

He bought a book.
He said nothing.
I like her.
I like swimming.
I like to swim.

I thought of my sister.
I threw out all my old letters.
He asked when we would come back.
He said that he would come with us.

In cases where the nature of the verbs is obvious, no comment is given.

EXAMPLES

conclude   Am I to **conclude** from your criticism that you intend to leave your job?

infer   They **inferrèd** from his behaviour that he no longer wished to be friends with them.

judge   From all I know of her, I would **judge** that she will make an excellent mother.

Judge is more common, however, with a direct object followed by an adjective and/or a **to**-infinitive.

EXAMPLES

I would **judge** him to be a first-rate linguist.
Would you **judge** it necessary to read all the books on the reading list?
They will **judge** him overqualified for the job, I am afraid.

4 **Being dirty**

dirty		
filthy	grimy	grubby

These words are related to each other in a way which can be explained by a diagram. The word at the top is more general, and the ones below are different kinds of **dirty**.

	covered with dust, soil, mud, etc	disgusting	dirt covering surface	dirt rubbed onto or into surface	result of human contact
dirty	+				
filthy	+	+			
grimy	+		+		
grubby	+		+	+	+

The words also differ in the amount of dirt implied:

not very   very

←——→

dirty   **grimy**   **filthy**
                             grubby

	man	family	dog	house	windows	clothes	hands	face	streets	water	language	joke	mind	trick	business
dirty	+	+	+	+	+	+	+	+	+	+	+	+	+	+	+
filthy		+		+	+			+	+	+	+	+			
grimy			(+)	+	+	(+)	+								
grubby					+	+	+								

Notice that **dirty** and **filthy** are frequently employed figuratively to mean 'vulgar' or 'immoral'.

5 Being attractive

	making a pleasant impression on the senses	close to an ideal	worthy of being loved	suggest relative smallness	suggests feminity or delicacy	arousing interest	causing pleasure	or suggests lightness and grace	suggests having good manners	may suggest sexual attraction	having well proportioned features	well made or of good quality	often suggests strength	often suggests dignity	or result of great generosity
beautiful	+	+													
lovely	+		+												
pretty	+			+	+										
charming	+				+	+	+	+							
attractive	+				+				+						
good looking	+								+						
handsome	+									+	+	+	+		+

> In this grid, *or* occurs alone in a box. It introduces a feature which is not in contrast with the one immediately before it. It is in contrast with an earlier feature presenting a basic sense. For example, [+ result of great generosity] is in contrast with [+ making a pleasant impression on the senses] and *not* with [+ often suggests dignity].

When qualifying people, **good-looking** and **handsome** are more often used for men, and **lovely, beautiful** and **pretty** for women. **Attractive** may be used for either. When qualifying inanimate and abstract nouns, there is often little semantic distinction between **beautiful, lovely, charming** and **attractive**.

	woman	man	child	dog	bird	flower	weather	landscape	view	day	village	house	furniture	bed	picture	dress	present	voice	proposal
beautiful	+		+	+	+	+	+	+	+	+	+	+	+	+	+	+	+		
lovely	+		+	(+)		+	+		+	+	+	+	+	(+)	+	+	+		
pretty	+		+		+	+		+			+	+		+	+	+			
charming	+	+	+								+	+					+		
attractive	+	+									+	+			+			+	+
good-looking	+	+	+	+															
handsome	+	+													+				

In speech, **beautiful, lovely, charming** and **attractive** are often used for situations in which their real meaning would be too strong, in order to express enthusiasm.

EXAMPLES

The walls were covered with a most $\left\{\begin{array}{l}\textbf{beautiful}\\ \textbf{lovely}\\ \textbf{charming}\\ \textbf{attractive}\end{array}\right\}$ wall paper.

I'll come to see you about seven – will you be there? **Beautiful** – okay – see you later.

She does really **lovely** things for people like bringing them their favourite flowers on their birthday.

Bacon and eggs for breakfast! **Lovely!**

6 Having a good appearance

	graceful	formal and fashionable	showing good taste	fashionable	formally dressed	clean and tidy	showing great attention to small details of one's appearance	usu of women only
elegant	+	+	+					
smart				+	+	+		
well-dressed			+	+				
well-groomed						+	+	+

Note that it is not necessary for all the words in a semantic field to share a single feature. In such cases, it is the similarity of features which brings the words together.

Smart, when it means [+ clean and tidy] or [+ formally dressed], is colloquial.

EXAMPLES

elegant She dismissed him with an **elegant** wave of her hand.
The most **elegant** clothes are often the most simple, but usually also the most expensive.
Fiona manages to look **elegant** even in riding clothes.

Clothes by a new young designer are suddenly to be seen at all the season's most **elegant** occasions.

smart   One of my favourite amusements is to sit in a **smart** restaurant in the centre of town and watch the famous and **elegant** people one sees there.

Should I put on something **smart** to go out to the Browns'?

Judith always looks so **smart**, she makes me feel very untidy.

well-dressed   You can always tell a really **well-dressed** man by his shoes.

It is important to be **well-dressed** when one goes for a job interview.

well-groomed   No **well-groomed** woman ever goes out without checking her make-up in the mirror.

What I tend to notice about a woman is whether or not she is **well-groomed**.

B   Synonymous Pairs

In this section, you will find pairs of words similar in meaning, with an explanation of the difference between them.

1   **work**
    task   [+ piece of] [+ usu assigned]

When one member of a pair can be explained in terms of the other, we mention the features of the more specific word which make it different from the more general word. For example, here, a **task** is a 'piece of work, usually assigned'.

	a task	work	some/one's work
to do		+	+
to perform	+		
to set	+	+	

2   **situation**
    plight   [+ bad]

EXAMPLE
With no documents and no money in a country where she didn't speak the language, she was in a terrible **plight**.

3   **to produce**
    to generate   [+ energy, force] ⇒ [+ be the cause of]
                       [+ usu a state of mind]

⇒ indicates the figurative sense. For example, the literal sense of **generate** is 'to produce energy', as in:
The hydro-electric scheme **generates** enough power for the whole city.
Used figuratively, it means 'to cause' as in:
The government's policy towards immigrants has **generated** a lot of hostility.

	electricity	wrong attitudes	hostility	heat	ideas	milk	food	plays	films	effects
produce				+	+	+	+	+	+	+
generate	+	+	+	+	+					

4 **to speak**
  to mutter | [+in a low voice] [+indistinctly]

EXAMPLE
He came home in a bad mood, **muttered** something about coming back later, and I haven't seen him since.

5 **unpleasant, unattractive**
  ghastly | [+intensely]; often used in colloquial speech and writing to express strong dislike. It is not used in this sense in formal speech and writing.

EXAMPLES

a	**ghastly**	job
		dinner party
		film
		dress
		book
		lecture
		boyfriend

6 **unwilling**
  reluctant

Unwilling and **reluctant** are synonymous when used attributively; for instance, both **an unwilling helper** and **a reluctant helper** denote someone who helps but does not want to.
    When used predicatively, however, **unwilling** means 'not doing' and **reluctantly** means 'not wanting to do'.
EXAMPLES
He was **unwilling** to give any information. (This means that he did not give any information.)
He was **reluctant** to give any information. (This implies that he did give information but without wanting to.)

7   **open**
    overt   [+ of actions, attitudes] [+ to be noticed]

	person	house	window	letter	hostility	hatred	threat	declaration	proposal	beliefs
open	+	+	+	+	+	(+)	+	+		
overt					+	+	+	+	+	+

8   **profitable**
    lucrative   [+ bringing in a lot of money]

	arrangement	experience	discovery	business	deal	profession	trade	occupation
profitable	+	+	+	+	+			
lucrative				+	+	+	+	+

9   **carefully**
    conscientiously   [+ guided by one's sense of what is right]

	carefully	conscientiously
to drive	+	
to observe the rules	+	
to describe sth	+	
to work	+	+
to look after one's children	+	+
to inspect sth	+	+
to care for one's patients	+	+
to fulfil one's obligations		+

Exercises

1 Give the opposite of the following:

EXAMPLE: to decrease   *to increase*
1 to take care of (one's children)   2 to look up to   3 arrival
4 deep   5 beautiful   6 relevant   7 sure   8 willingly

2 Match appropriate features with each of the following words. Notice that not all of the features mentioned are relevant.

EXAMPLE: assess   [+ *decide the value of*]
1 competent   2 conceit   3 handsome   4 to mutter   5 assertive
6 grimy   7 to rate   8 dates   9 conscientious   10 self-conscious

[+ guided by one's sense of what is right] [+ fast]
[+ having ability, knowledge or skill] [+ of men]
[+ over-high opinion of oneself] [+ decide the value of]

[+of women] [+place on a numerical scale] [+voice]
[+insisting on one's rights] [+with members of the opposite sex]
[+clean] [+indistinct] [+shy] [+covered with dirt]
[+appointments]

3 Explain in your own words the meaning of the following words and expressions:

EXAMPLE: questionnaire   *a series of questions used eg in an opinion poll or in psychological or sociological research*
1 stranger   2 ladder   3 (phone) booth   4 eyebrows   5 airport
6 plight   7 is of little concern   8 to gain in stature   9 rush hour

4 What can you . . . . .?

EXAMPLE: fill out/in   *a form, a questionnaire, an application, a cheque*
1 shatter   2 label   3 mail   4 clip   5 elicit   6 post   7 achieve
8 be aware of   9 stamp   10 brush   11 predict   12 spill
13 generate

5 Which nouns can be derived from the following words? (All these words appeared in the texts.)

EXAMPLE: to question   *questionnaire, question*
1 to advertise   2 to relate   3 to find   4 to settle   5 to appear
6 to interact   7 to apply to/for   8 to respond   9 to assess
10 to depart   11 to assist   12 to infer

6 Who or what can you . . . . .?

EXAMPLE: be fed up with?   *your work, your family, bad food, bad weather*
1 look down upon   2 be horrified by   3 overlook
4 acknowledge   5 discriminate against   6 be obsessed with
7 believe in   8 bump into   9 benefit from   10 be sensitive to
11 pursue

7 What are the similarities and/or differences between the following pairs?

EXAMPLE: to meet sb/to bump into sb
Similar: both mean 'to meet' Different: 'bump into' applies only to accidental meeting
1 to see/to look at   2 to summarize a text/to copy a text
3 to take the place of/to supersede   4 to pour tea/to spill tea
5 to dissect/to analyse   6 to wait for/to expect
7 a stranger/a foreigner   8 a plight/a situation   9 a picture/ a painting

8 Find words to fit the following descriptions:

EXAMPLE: object to be aimed at: *target*
1 well-balanced judgement of, and respect for, oneself
2 take a living organism to pieces to examine how it works
3 hairs on the edge of the eyelids
4 outcome of an enquiry or research
5 smash, break into pieces
6 clever; cheerful and happy
7 move slowly and carefully closer to
8 replace because better or more important
9 artificial covering of hair for the head

9 Complete the following:

EXAMPLE: a thought-. . . . . questionnaire   *a thought-provoking questionnaire*
1 a . . . . . envelope   2 to fill out/in an application . . . . .   3 to

pursue one's . . . . . 4 to be at the top of the . . . . . 5 to conclude
. . . . . the study   6 it was neither above nor . . . . . average   7 it's
a change for the . . . . .   8 these are paper and . . . . . measures
9 poor man, his belief was . . . . .   10 he felt . . . . . about the
accident   11 they finally . . . . . a reply/the truth

10 What differences and/or similarities are there between the following:

EXAMPLE: paint/varnish
Similar: both are liquids for covering surfaces
Different: 'paint' is coloured, 'varnish' is clear
1 inch/metre/yard   2 eyeshadow/eyelashes   3 task/duty
4 link/connection   5 shelf/cupboard   6 ability/skill
7 collar/neck   8 target/goal   9 scruffy/dirty

11 Explain the meaning of each of the following. Your explanations may include mime, descriptions, enumerations of uses, or examples.

EXAMPLE: timely   *occurring just when it is wanted*
1 plight   2 to mutter   3 lucrative   4 mongrel   5 collar
6 ambivalent   7 traits   8 ghastly   9 reluctant   10 ascertain
11 overt

12 Guess the right word. The first letter(s) of the missing item should help you.

1 I suggested that we help those poor people but nobody se . . . . .
   my proposal.
2 She put on her make-up in front of the m . . . . . .
3 The proposal received o . . . . . support from the committee.
4 The girl was always j . . . . . of her pretty little sister.
5 The mother was e . . . . . by her child's bad behaviour.
6 Two good character t . . . . . are honesty and generosity.
7 The president's plans for social reform were the t . . . . . of a
   great deal of criticism.
8 He is b . . . . . in the sense that he did not try to avoid the
   accident.
9 Really, you never think of others! You are so eg . . . . . .
10 University selection panels are generally felt to f . . . . .
   applicants from certain schools which have good academic
   reputations.

13 Body Image Questionnaire

Make up a 'Body Image' questionnaire and give it to your
class-mates to answer.

Unit 2   What is the earth coming to?

NUCLEAR ENERGY

1 self-satisfaction, not seeing need for action
2 the act of splitting or breaking apart the nucleus of a radioactive atom leading to the release of energy
3 risk, danger
4 an insurance which covers damage or injury caused by the thing or person insured to another thing or person
5 responsibility for a possible or actual loss, damage, etc
6 *lit* the state of being a slave

Nuclear Energy – Salvation or Damnation?

The main cause of the **complacency**[1] – now gradually diminishing – about future energy supplies was undoubtedly the emergence of nuclear energy, which, people felt, had arrived just in time. Little did they bother to inquire precisely *what* it was that had arrived. It was new, it was astonishing, it was progress, and promises were freely given that it would be cheap. Since a new source of energy would be needed sooner or later, why not have it at once?

The fact that nuclear **fission**[2] represents an incredible, incomparable, and unique **hazard**[3] for human life does not enter any calculation and is never mentioned. People whose business it is to judge hazards, the insurance companies, are reluctant to insure nuclear power stations anywhere in the world for **third party risk**[4], with the result that special legislation has had to be passed whereby the State accepts big **liabilities**[5]. Yet, insured or not, the hazard remains, and such is the **enslavement**[6] to the religion of economics that the only question that appears to interest either governments or the public is whether 'it pays'.

It is not as if there were any lack of authoritative voices to warn us. The effects of alpha, beta, and gamma rays on living tissues are perfectly well known: the radiation particles are like bullets tearing into an organism, and the damage they do depends primarily on the dosage and the type of cells they hit. As long ago as 1927, the American biologist, H J Muller, published his famous paper on genetic **mutations**[7] produced by X-ray bombardment, and since the early 1930s the genetic hazard of exposure has been recognised also by non-geneticists. It is clear that here is a hazard with a hitherto unexperienced 'dimension', endangering not only those who might be directly affected by this radiation but their **offspring**[8] as well.

A new 'dimension' is given also by the fact that while man now can – and does – create radioactive elements, there is nothing he can do to reduce their radioactivity once he has created them. No chemical reaction, no physical interference, only the passage of time reduces the intensity of radiation once it has been set going. Carbon-14 has a half-life of 5,900 years, which means that it takes nearly 6,000 years for its radioactivity to decline to one-half of what it was before. The half-life of strontium-90 is twenty-eight years. But whatever the length of the half-life, some radiation continues almost indefinitely, and there is nothing that can be done about it, except to try and put the radioactive substance into a safe place.

But what is a safe place, let us say, for the enormous amounts of radioactive waste products created by nuclear reactors? No place on earth can be shown to be safe. It was thought at one time that these wastes could safely be dumped into the deepest parts of the oceans, on the assumption that no life could subsist at such depths. But this has since been disproved by Soviet deep-sea exploration. Wherever there is life, radioactive substances are **absorbed**[9] into the **biological cycle**[10].

The most massive wastes are, of course, the nuclear reactors themselves after they have become **unserviceable**[11]. There is a lot of discussion on the trivial economic question of whether they will last for twenty, twenty-five, or thirty years. No-one discusses the humanly vital point that they cannot be **dismantled**[12] and cannot be **shifted**[13] but have to be left standing where they are, probably for centuries, perhaps for thousands of years, an active **menace**[14] to all life, silently **leaking**[15] radioactivity into air, water and soil. No-one has considered that their number and location will **relentlessly**[16] accumulate. Earthquakes, of course, are not supposed to happen, nor wars, nor civil disturbances, nor riots like those that **infest**[17] American cities. Disused nuclear power stations will stand as **unsightly**[18] monuments to man's assumption that nothing but tranquillity, from now on, stretches before him, or else – that the future counts as nothing compared with the slightest economic gain now.

E F Schumacher, *Small is Beautiful.*
A Study of Economics as if People Mattered.

7 change or alteration in the structure of the genes, ie chemically complex units which are assumed to be the carriers of specific physical characteristics from parents to offspring
8 descendants, child or children, young
9 taken in
10 recurring series of biological operations
11 no longer suited for use
12 taken to pieces
13 moved from one place to another
14 threat, something capable of doing damage
15 accidentally letting out (through a leak or crack)
16 without pity, mercilessly
17 be present in large numbers, especially so as to render unpleasant or unsafe
18 ugly, displeasing to the sight

The Population Bomb

I. TOO MANY PEOPLE

Figures[1] and **numerous**[2] facts prove that there are already, and certainly that there will be, too many people. Simply calculating the lengths of time necessary to double the world's population is **enlightening**[3]. **Impressively**[4], the time **required**[5] grows ever shorter: 6,000 years before Christ, 1,000,000 years were necessary to double the population, then about 1,650 years after Christ only 1,000, around the 1850's 200 years, in 1930 80 years. **Currently**[6], the world's population doubles every 37 years.

What would happen if the population were to continue doubling in volume every 37 years?

According to recent calculations, maintaining such a rhythm of growth would result in 60 million **billion**[7]

people on the earth in 900 years, which represents 120 inhabitants per square meter.

Optimists believe and often **assert**[8] that science will indeed find solutions to the problem of **overcrowding**[9], namely by providing the means to immigrate to other planets. But this solution is totally **utopian**[10]. In effect, even if it should become possible, ·50 years would be sufficient for the 60 million billion persons to multiply to the point of populating Venus, Mercury, Mars, the Moon and the satellites of Jupiter and Saturn with a **density**[11] equal to that of the Earth.

II. FOOD SHORTAGE

Today, a good part of humanity suffers from **malnutrition**[12] or from **under-nourishment**[13].

Some think that recent scientific discoveries applied to agriculture and known under the name of 'green revolution' will resolve the problem. Nothing is less certain. Promoters of the revolution themselves believe that it can offer only a **respite**[14] of ten or twenty years.

In underdeveloped countries, although **predominantly**[15] agricultural, the **lag**[16] in food production in relation to demographic growth increases more and more. As the crisis **worsens**[17] these countries will have to import food. But from where?

III. A DYING PLANET

The world's population explosion is the source of a whole series of **environmental**[18] **deteriorations**[19], which in time can have **disastrous**[20] consequences.

THE POPULATION BOMB

1 numbers, quantities, statistics
2 great in number, very many
3 instructive, giving more knowledge
4 importantly and noticeably, in a way that makes a deep impression on the mind and feelings
5 necessary
6 at present
7 *Br* a million million, *Am* a thousand millions
8 declare, put forward an idea

9 over-population
10 attractive and desirable but impracticable
11 the number of persons (families, dwellings, etc) per given surface area of the earth
12 faulty and unbalanced nourishment or food
13 nourishment insufficient in amount or quality for proper health and growth

14 temporary relief, short period of rest
15 mostly
16 slowing down, delay
17 becomes worse, less good
18 ecological, concerning the physical conditions in which life takes place
19 decline, worsening of condition
20 catastrophic, calamitous, having a severe effect

Because the population-food **imbalance**[21] necessitates 'at any price' a growth of agricultural production, methods often **harmful**[22] to the environment are used without judgment. Examples **abound**[23]. The construction of **colossal**[24] dams to **irrigate**[25] hundreds of thousands of **acres**[26] can in fact provoke catastrophes. Thus, the Aswan Dam currently prevents the **deposit**[27] of **fertile**[28] **silts**[29] brought each year by the flooding of the Nile. The result will obviously be a decrease in the fertility of the Delta lands. Damming the Mekong risks the same consequences for Vietnam and neighbouring countries.

Fertilizers, **synthetic**[30] pesticides, **DDT**[31] can be **devastating**[32], transforming complex **ecosystems**[33], necessary for the conservation of the environment, into simple ecosystems. **Monocultures**[34] are a case of such **mutation**[35].

Certain situations are **perceived**[36] as dangerous only when they become critical enough to cause numerous deaths. **Smog**[37] is an example. In London in 1952 it caused some 4,000 deaths. This incident provoked an awakening of conscience and resulted in decisions which have **proven**[38] **efficacious**[39]. But smog presents still other dangers: namely, it destroys plants which offer little resistance, and whose oxygen production is indispensable to us, and it changes the earth's **thermal**[40] **equilibrium**[41].

For these forms of **pollution**[42] as for all the others, the **destructive**[43] chain of cause and effect goes back to a prime cause: 'too many cars, too many factories, too many **detergents**[44], too many pesticides, more and more trails left by supersonic jets, inadequate methods for **disinfecting**[45] **sewers**[46], too little water, too much **carbon monoxide**[47]. The cause is always the same: too many people on the earth.'

Paul Ehrlich. *The Population Bomb.* Condensed from a summary in *Prospective*

21 lack of balance or equilibrium, the fact of not being of equal weight, force or influence
22 bad for, causing damage, injury
23 are numérous
24 immense, enormous
25 supply (land, crops) with water (by means of rivers, water channels, etc)
26 *Br* and *Am* non-metric measure of land = about 4000 square metres
27 act of putting down or dropping
28 producing or capable of producing abundantly
29 sand, mud, etc carried by moving water and left, eg at the mouth of a river
30 artificial, man-made
31 substances used to destroy pests which damage crops, such as insects, mice, snails, etc
32 causing destruction or ravage
33 ecological system, a system of species of plants and animals highly adapted to its habitat
34 the use of a piece of land for the intensive cultivation of only one crop or product
35 change, alteration
36 understood
37 mixture of smoke and exhaust fumes from motor-vehicles
38 *Br* usu proved
39 producing good results, effective
40 of heat
41 balance
42 being made dirty, arrival in an environment of harmful waste-products
43 damaging, breaking
44 chemical substances that remove dirt
45 cleaning, making free from infection by bacteria
46 underground channels to carry off sewage (waste, foul liquid material)
47 poisonous gas present in the exhaust gas of petrol engines

Fire and Ice

Some say the world will end in fire,
Some say in ice.
From what I've tasted of desire
I hold with those who favor fire.
But if it had to **perish**[1] twice,
I think I know enough of hate
To say that for destruction ice
Is also great
And would **suffice**[2].
Robert Frost

FIRE AND ICE

1 (literary) stop existing, die
2 be enough, sufficient

MAKING US QUAKE

Since the birth of Christ it is estimated that 75,000,000 people have died in earthquakes. The quake in Rumania that killed more than 1,000 people shook the ground with the energy of 10 A-bombs. And the ferocity of earth tremors is on the increase, according to Professor Bernhard Ernst, of Tubingen University, West Germany.

Last year was one of the worst in earthquake history. Ten major quakes killed more than 1,000,000 people and the professor believes that underground tests of nuclear weapons are causing greater earth movements.

Every year there are around 100,000 earth tremors, but most are so minor that they do not register on anything other than seismic test-apparatus.

Prof Ernst fears that unless A-bomb tests are abandoned, more people will die in earthquakes such explosions trigger off.

Weekend

Is there any future in futurism?

"Off with her head!" – an uncertain future for Alice? from Alice's Adventures in Wonderland by Lewis Carroll

IS THERE ANY FUTURE IN FUTURISM?

1 *lit* prevent air arriving at nose and mouth by use of a soft object
2 rapid multiplication, reproduction
3 too rapid using up of food, energy, materials, etc
4 existing as a natural and permanent part or quality of
5 factories
6 supersonic transport
7 risky
8 secondary or indirect effect
9 quick, imperfect view
10 enlarged view of sth
11 marked to show what something is, where it is to go, etc
12 exact, free from error
13 not valid, not sound, not well-based
14 of new fashion (generally pejorative)
15 reaching an opinion about a possibility beyond the strict evidence of facts, events
16 research team
17 inconsistent, opposed in character, unable to exist in harmony
18 *lit* extreme scarcity of food for a group of people
19 prospering, well and active
20 showing sound judgement and common sense, astute
21 twelfth sign of the Zodiac, Latin for 'Fish'
22 assess, evaluate
23 prominent article in a newspaper or magazine
24 buying and selling of stocks and shares
25 looking forward a long way in the future
26 programme or timetable

Biologist Paul Ehrlich (*The Population Bomb*) tours campuses warning of a planet **smothered**[1] by **proliferation**[2] and **overconsumption**[3]; Barry Commoner's new volume, *The Poverty of Power*, sees capitalism as an irresponsible, even destructive force in global affairs. Nuclear physicists describe the radiation catastrophes **inherent**[4] in nuclear power **plants**[5]; meteorologists calculate the insults to the ozone present in every flight of the **SST**[6]; biochemists estimate the brain cells destroyed with every martini. Even the Pill, once announced as the answer to population control, now appears to have **hazardous**[7] side **effects**[8].

Such perceptions may be **glimpses**[9] of tomorrow, or they may be **magnifications**[10] of the present – shadows thrown upon a screen **labeled**[11] AD 2000. They may be **accurate**[12], or they may be as **invalid**[13] as the predictions of almost a century ago that saw city dwellers transported everywhere by that **new-fangled**[14] invention, the balloon. Forecasters have a habit of **extrapolating**[15] from their surroundings: the scientist from the laboratory, the statistician from his calculator, the administrator from his **think tank**[16].

Such predictions rise, in Lewis Mumford's phrase, from a mind 'operating with its own conceptual apparatus, in its own restrictive field . . . determined to make the world over in its own oversimplified terms, willfully rejecting interests and values **incompatible**[17] with its own assumptions'.

Does this mean that prediction has no future? Hardly.

In an epoch of uncertainties, the hunger for prediction is rising to the **famine**[18] level. Never before has speculative fiction been so popular. Thirty-five science-fiction books were published in 1945; in 1975, 900 such books were published. Even the pseudo sciences are **flourishing**[19]. **Shrewdly**[20] unspecific astrological charts can be found in most major newspapers (**PISCES**[21]: *Do your work despite passing moments of stress*). The *National Enquirer*'s annual contest to **gauge**[22] readers' psychic ability is among the weekly's most popular **features**[23] In fact, it has become impossible to lead a modern life without some form of prophecy. Every **stock market**[24] letter, every **long-range**[25] weather report and baseball **schedule**[26] is a prediction; every garden and every child is an expressed belief in the future. As Toffler observes, 'Under conditions of high-speed change, a democracy without the ability to anticipate condemns itself to death.'

But just how much can it anticipate? How deeply into the future can it **peer**[27]? Unhappily, not very far at all. No matter how **sophisticated**[28] the **devices**[29] or **demographics**[30], certain events and event makers will always lie outside the **scope**[31] of **seers**[32]. The maniac, the genius, the **random**[33] event are unpredictable, yet they have formed much of this century's history. There is no reason to suspect that they may not form the history of the next.

Futurists can help **to forestall**[34] these troubles. Or they can press for changes in some **remote**[35] **purgatory**[36] or Eden. Examining Herman Kahn's thesis, Adam Yarmolinsky. University of Massachusetts professor, asks a series of rhetorical questions: 'How do we get from here to there? What is the best mind set to move us in that direction? Are we more likely to succeed if we keep our eyes firmly on the target centuries away? Or ought we to be more concerned about **pitfalls**[37], obstacles, difficulties we seem to be encountering in the immediate future?'

All responsible seers know the answers. The future of futurism lies **rooted**[38] in the current human condition – the saving of cities, the administration of foreign policy, the **forestalling** of war and famine and natural catastrophe. Given decent **underpinnings**[39], tomorrow may yet take care of itself. What Novelist Antoine de Saint-Exupéry wrote three decades ago must remain the moral force behind all truly prophetic workers: 'As for the future, your task is not to foresee, but to enable it.'

Stefan Kanfer, *Time*

DEMOCRACY VS. THE ATOM

TECHNOLOGICAL EUPHORIA

Formerly, rulers were blamed by their subjects for endless wars, exploitation and cruelty. But the rulers of today's industrial democracies are suspected of sins no less grave: **levity**[1], irresponsibility, even **recklessness**[2]. They have, their subjects fear, **fallen prey to**[3] technological **euphoria**[4]. Parliaments either do not decide these matters or do not know what they are talking about; posterity, to whom we will **bequeath**[5] the poisonous, **carcinogenic**[6], perhaps **mutagenic**[7] **garbage**[8] of our nuclear civilization, is not represented in the councils of state; the level of acceptable risk is decided for our societies by technocratic **fiat**[9] rather than by decisions democratically arrived at.

Admittedly, the nuclear issue is complex. At a recent international conference, this **baffling**[10] complexity led to the somewhat helpless summary: 'For every expert who says mankind cannot live with nuclear energy, there is at least one more who says mankind cannot live without it.' **Primordial**[11] fears of the atom, a democratic horror of **inscrutable**[12] decision making processes and, perhaps, the **lure**[13] of yet another cause worth demonstrating, protesting and fighting about – these make up a **potent**[14] mixture. And the whole issue undeniably poses a serious challenge to democracy. How do we define technological problems in a democratic system? How do we clear up misunderstandings, **disperse**[15] doubts, handle the manifestations of objectors? How can we **harness**[16] the planners and make them responsible, or at least responsive, to the people? These questions must be answered **lest**[17] democracy be **trampled underfoot**[18] as technology marches on.

Newsweek

Discussion

1 From these articles, does it seem to you that man is racing towards his own destruction? Are they much too pessimistic?
2 Nuclear energy can, and has already been, used for destructive purposes. Why do you think most countries want to possess nuclear weapons, even when they know that if they used them they could precipitate a conflict that might destroy the world?
3 What methods can we use for controlling the population? Should these methods be imposed on people by the Government of each country?
4 What do you think of the idea that population control proposals are a racist plot by the rich countries to keep the developing nations weak and powerless?
5 What factors account for the present imbalance in the distribution of the world's food resources? Should countries who have enough food share it with those who have less? Practically, how could they do this?
6 What is the use of being able to predict the future? What are the advantages and disadvantages of predictions which are very pessimistic?

Word Study

A   Semantic Fields

1 Misfortunes

great misfortune			
cataclysm	catastrophe	disaster	calamity

DISASTER — a road accident, a plane crash

the loss of all one's money

CALAMITY — the loss of one's job

becoming blind

an earthquake, a flood, a fire, a war

a political or social revolution

CATASTROPHE

CATACLYSM

The distinctions made here are not absolute and may vary from speaker to speaker. The following may be taken as a general guide:

cataclysm   includes in its meaning [+always widespread], and [+sudden and violent change (often social and political)]

catastrophe   stresses the feature [+ fatal outcome]

disaster   implies [+ loss of life] or [+ loss of property, status, or certain abilities]

Calamity stresses the amount of upset or disruption caused by the event. Its use has been extended to include more personal misfortunes, when it emphasises the features [+ brings personal sorrow] and [+ greatly complicates one's situation].

Notice also that all these terms, except **cataclysm**, can be used figuratively.

EXAMPLES

catastrophe   The unexpected arrival of all my aunts in the middle of our nude bathing party was a **catastrophe**.

disaster   The absence of audience for the concert made it a total **disaster**.

calamity   **Calamity**! The washing machine overflowed while I was on the telephone.

2 Damaging

	partially destroy	cause loss of value	with inanimate objects	or with abstract objects	cause physical pain	or cause mental suffering	have a bad effect on	cause wounds, bruises, broken limbs	make worse, less, weaker	in function or quality	make less than perfect	by doing or giving too much	or completely ruin
damage	+	+	+	+									
harm							+						
hurt					+	+							
injure							+	+					
impair									+	+			
mar				+							+		
spoil							+					+	+

Here are a few examples illustrating the major senses of the verbs:

damage   The storm **damaged** the house.
Smoking can **damage** your health.

harm   You will **harm** the baby if you give him too many sweets.
His jealousy **harmed** their relationship.

hurt   The climber was **hurt** by the falling rock.
She was **hurt** by her friend's critical remarks.

impair   Loud noise can **impair** your hearing.
My sense of time has been greatly **impaired** by working at night.

injure   The horse's legs were **injured** when it jumped over the fence.

Brain damage is often caused by head **injuries**.

mar The beauty of the summer afternoon was only **marred** by one shower of rain.

My aunt's presence **marred** the enjoyment of my stay at the sea.

spoil Constant quarrelling is **spoiling** the happy family atmosphere.

This year's apple crop was **spoiled** by long periods of drought.

	sb's car	a painting	the environment	one's health	sb's reputation	children	one's legs	sb's feelings	sb's pride	sb's speech	sb's enjoyment	sb's happiness
damage	+	+	+	+	+							
harm		(+)	+	+	+	+						
impair			+	+					+	+		
hurt						+	+	+	+			
injure				+	+	+						
mar			(+)	+							+	+
spoil		(+)	+	(+)				+			+	

3 Shaking

shake				
tremble	quake	quiver	shiver	shudder

	move from side to side or up and down				often because of		
	with quick, short motions	rather violently	slightly	momentarily	fear or excitement	weakness or anger	cold or disgust
shake	+			+			
tremble	+			+	+	+	
quake	+	+		+			
quiver	+		+	+	+		+
shiver	+		+	+		+	
shudder	+			+	+		+

All the above verbs, except **shake**, are intransitive. **Shake** can be used either transitively or intransitively.

EXAMPLES

The explosion **shook** the whole village.

Why is the dog **shaking**?

As a transitive verb, **shake** can also be used figuratively.

EXAMPLE

The news of the crime **shook** my faith in the goodness of humanity.

Moreover, all these verbs, except **shiver**, can take either an animate or inanimate subject. The subject of **shiver** must be animate.

EXAMPLES

shake   Before entering the examination room, the candidate was **shaking** with fear.

The branches of the tree **shook** in the wind.

tremble   She **trembled** as he took her in his arms for the first time.

The old bridge **trembled** under the train.

quake   The child **quaked** with fear as he told us about the accident he had seen.

As they climbed the volcano, the ground **quaked** under their feet.

quiver   He **quivered** with emotion at the sight of his long-lost son.

The rabbit's ears **quivered** when it heard the hunter.

shiver   She **shivered** at the very thought of seeing a ghost.

shudder   On seeing the blood-stained knife, she **shuddered** and screamed.

The whole ship **shuddered** with the vibrations of the engines.

When taking an animate subject, all these verbs can – and **quake** must – be followed by the preposition **with**.

	with cold	with fear	with fright	with anger	with rage	with horror	with emotion	with excitement	with laughter	with disgust
shake			+	+			+	+	+	
tremble		+		+			+			
quake		+	+					+		
quiver			+		+		+	(+)		
shiver	+									
shudder						+				+

4 Knowing and telling in advance

	predict	**forecast**	**foretell**	**prophesy**
tell of some future event	+	+	+	+
only for events having large-scale effects		+		+
without a sound factual basis			+	+
imply mystic inspiration				+

	forecast	predicted	foretold	prophesied	
Meteorologists	+				stormy weather with bright periods.
Biologists	+	+			a decrease in the bird population due to pollution.
Politicians	+	+			that another war would break out.
Agriculturalists	+	+			a bad harvest.
Economists	+	+			massive unemployment.
The old farmer	+	+	+	(+)	a dry summer.
Mme Soleil, the French clairvoyant		+	+		Nixon's downfall.
The gypsy		+	+		that we would have a daughter.
Their religious leaders		+	+	+	the end of the world for April 1, 1969.
The prophet Isaiah			+	+	Jesus' death on the cross.
The astrologer			+		his rise to stardom.
The old lady			+		the death of their son.

5 Causing danger

dangerous		
hazardous	perilous	risky

Perilous is more literary than the other words and has the feature [+serious], whereas **hazardous** and **risky** suggest [+chance]. **Risky** collocates with nouns that denote action.

	dangerous	hazardous	risky	perilous
Our situation is	+	+	+	+
His journey was	+	+	+	+
Their escape was	+		+	+
Mountain climbing can be	+	+	+	
This operation is	+	+	+	
This road is	+	+		
This person is	+			
This animal is	+			
Smallpox can be	+			
Books can be	+			

6 Being strong

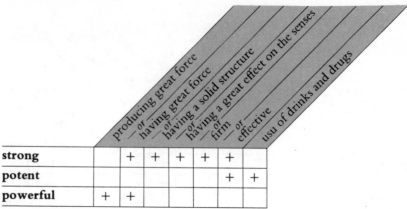

	producing great force	having great force	having a solid structure	having a great effect on the senses	firm	effective	usu of drinks and drugs
strong		+	+	+	+	+	
potent						+	+
powerful	+	+					

	wind	smell	beliefs	desire	horse	tea	drink	drug	influence	argument	man	leader	weapon	car	effect	generator
strong	+	+	+	+	+	+	+	+	+	+	+					
potent							+	+								
powerful							+	+	+	+	+	+	+	+	+	

B   Synonymous Pairs

range	[+ measurable or countable]
scope	[+ not measurable or countable]

	books	colours	10 miles	mountains	one's voice	a book	an article	sb's knowledge	sb's ability	sb's research
range of	+	+	+	+	+					
scope of						+	+	+	+	+

Unlike **range**, **scope** can take the preposition **for**.

EXAMPLE
The course doesn't offer much **scope** for development.

2   **to destroy**
    to devastate | [+ area of land, city, village] [+ leaving nothing that can be used]

EXAMPLES
The town was **devastated** by a series of particularly violent hurricanes.
The country was **devastated** by the invading army.

3   **to puzzle**
    to baffle | [+ confuse] [+ cause to have difficulty in understanding]

EXAMPLES

The clues left by the murderer **baffled** the detectives who were trying to solve the case.

Regular sightings of unidentified flying objects continue to **baffle** astronomers.

4 **to contaminate** | [+make impure or poisonous] [+by contact with harmful matter] [+ esp with harmful bacteria, poison-gas, or radioactivity]

to pollute | [+make dirty] [+by introduction of harmful waste-products]

EXAMPLES

The well was **contaminated** by dead rats.

One bag of mouldy flour was responsible for **contaminating** a whole day's bread production.

The air in big cities is heavily **polluted** by carbon monoxide.

Waste from the chemical factory has **polluted** the lake and killed all the fish.

5 **to prevent**
  to forestall | [+by doing sth before the action intended by another even starts]

	a marriage	an explosion	sb from doing sth	an accident	sb's action	a surprise attack	an attempt	sb's intention
prevent	+	+	+	+	+	+		
forestall			(+)	+	+	+	+	

EXAMPLES

The guards **prevented** him from escaping.

The guards **forestalled** his attempt to escape.

6 **ugly**
  unsightly

The two words differ mainly in their collocational properties.

	man	face	furniture	building	surroundings	blocks of flats and car parks
ugly	+	+	+	+	+	(+)
unsightly				+	+	+

7 **effective**   ⎰ [+capable of bringing ⎱
                          about, or bringing   ⎱ [+beneficial]
   efficacious   ⎱ about, definite results] ⎰ [+often to health]

Notice that the ⎰⎱ brackets enclose features that apply to both
words. ⎱⎰

	teaching methods	measures to combat inflation	defence systems	cure for cancer	drug	decision	solution
effective	+	+	+	+	+		
efficacious				+	+	+	+

8 **adventurous**   [+eager to explore the unknown] [+positive]
   reckless   [+not worrying about possible bad
                        consequences] [+negative]

	trip	person	character	driving	investment	attempt to escape	spender
adventurous	+	+	+				
reckless		+	+	+	+	+	+

9 **distant**   ⎰ [+far away] [+in space] or [+in time] or ⇒[+in⎱
   remote   ⎱ manner]   ⎰

	view of the tower	cousin of ours	future	past	possibility	little town
distant	+	+	+	+		
remote				+	+	+

Figuratively, **distant** and **remote** are more common as predicative
adjuncts.
EXAMPLES
He is very **distant** towards his students.
It's difficult to communicate with the Browns because they are so
remote.

Exercises

1 Give the opposite of the following:

1 a responsible act   2 a simple device   3 an adequate description   4 an industrialized country   5 a valid statement   6 an increasing birth rate   7 a well nourished child   8 an incredible story

2 Which nouns can be derived from the following words?

1 complacent   2 deep   3 ferocious   4 short   5 to nourish   6 to fertilize   7 to pollute   8 to consume   9 to dwell   10 to assume   11 to perceive   12 democratic   13 to grow   14 cruel

3 Match the appropriate features with each of the following words:

1 hazardous   2 to lure   3 ferocity   4 valid   5 reckless   6 inherent   7 to suffice   8 tranquillity   9 to disperse

[+dangerous] [+cruel] [+sound] [+be enough] [+peace] [+attract] [+well based] [+permanent quality of] [+not worry about consequences] [+chance] [+calm] [+cause to disappear]

4 What are the things that can .....?

1 flourish   2 worsen   3 leak   4 taste   5 smother   6 baffle   7 quake   8 endanger   9 infest   10 clear up   11 perish   12 last

5 Which verbs correspond to the following nouns?

1 success   2 announcement   3 extrapolation   4 destruction   5 observation   6 application   7 danger   8 reduction   9 assertion

6 Guess the missing word.

1 I was sitting right at the back of the cinema, and I couldn't see the s . . . . . properly.
2 Two years of bad harvests provoked a food shortage which caused widespread f . . . . ..
3 We are taking part in a new research project on the environment whose s . . . . . should be wider than any yet undertaken.
4 The new d . . . . . which has been built across the river will create a large lake.
5 Now that we have had some rain the flowers and vegetables are f . . . . ..
6 A thorough inspection will be necessary before we can ga . . . . . exactly the extent of the damage.
7 Once he had told her he thought she was too fat their relationship d . . . . . rapidly, and within a few weeks they separated.
8 A survey made of a r . . . . . selection of students shows that over fifty percent prefer to study at night and sleep during the day.
9 Most of the country's food is grown in its most f . . . . . region.
10 You have both taken up such extreme points of view that I cannot see how to r . . . . . your conflict.

7 Which adjectives and adverbs can be derived from the following?

1 poison   2 truth   3 shrewdness   4 concept   5 hazard
6 efficacy   7 impression   8 end   9 comparison   10 doubt
11 number   12 utopia

8 Choose the word that best fits the context. Modify its form where necessary.

EXAMPLE
I don't like this coffee.   It's far too *strong*.   (powerful, strong, potent).

1 The killing of two students . . . . . a violent rebellion. (cause, trigger off)
2 If you don't like washing up, you could . . . . . into the possibility of buying a washing-up machine. (inquire, ask)
3 The witness was . . . . . to tell us anything, but in the end he agreed. (unwilling, reluctant)
4 The father vowed he would . . . . . his daughter marrying the man. (forestall, prevent)
5 Exactly how children learn to speak is a problem which . . . . . linguists no less now than twenty years ago. (baffle, astonish)
6 A most . . . . . argument about who should go and fetch the bread from the kitchen was going on between Martin and Paul when I came in. (trivial, unimportant)
7 In spite of all attempts to elicit information, mother remained quite . . . . . about the promised surprise. (inscrutable, mysterious)
8 Most of the people questioned in the survey were far more . . . . . than we hoped, and gave very full answers to our questions. (sensitive, responsive)
9 The . . . . . fashion for women to have their hair short is most unfeminine. (current, present)
10 The accident . . . . . his confidence in his driving ability. (shatter, break)

9 What can you . . . . .?

1 dismantle   2 trigger off   3 absorb   4 fear   5 harness
6 irrigate   7 destroy   8 publish   9 gauge   10 forestall

10 What are the similarities and/or differences between the following pairs?

1 propeller-driven plane/jet   2 schedule/time-table   3 hunger/famine   4 city/town/village   5 misfortune/catastrophe
6 smog/fog/mist   7 weapon/gun/bomb/bullet   8 happiness/euphoria   9 self-confidence/complacency   10 one's children/one's offspring   11 responsibility/liability   12 war/riot   13 look/glimpse   14 forecast/prediction/prophecy   15 lag/gap
16 fertilizer/manure   17 ground/soil

11 Give some nouns with which the following could collocate:

1 (a) gradual . . .   2 (a) safe . . .   3 a carcinogenic . . .   4 a harmful . . .   5 a hazardous . . .   6 two incompatible . . .   7 (a) long-range . . .   8 a sophisticated . . .   9 a random . . .   10 an inadequate . . .   11 an irresponsible . . .   12 a shrewd . . .

12 Summarize, orally or in writing, Schumacher's 'Nuclear Energy' using the following words:

radioactive, radiation, damage, cells, hazardous, nuclear, exposure, wastes, reactors, to dismantle, to dump

Revision Exercises

R1 In what way are the following words or phrases negative?

1 complacency   2 a hazardous experiment   3 vanity   4 damage
5 overcrowding   6 waste(s)   7 insult   8 reckless driving
9 horror   10 earthquake   11 shortage   12 undernourished
13 side effects (of a medication)   14 devastating   15 pitfalls
16 maniac   17 to smother   18 conceit

R2 Find words to fit the following definitions/ descriptions:

1 bringing in a lot of money   2 never finishing, ceaseless
3 unable to exist together in harmony   4 showing sound
judgment and common sense   5 unsystematic, unplanned
6 far away, distant   7 artificial, man-made   8 written request
9 a necessary part of a whole   10 move about freely and
aimlessly   11 a piece of work, usually assigned   12 containing
contradictory features

R3 Match appropriate features with each of the following words: Notice that not all of the features mentioned are relevant.

1 stature   2 plight   3 overt   4 conscientious   5 eyelashes
6 bump into   7 grimy

[+dirt rubbed into surface] [+bad] [+closed] [+glosses] [+meet]
[+importance] [+dirt covering surface] [+hairs] [+to be noticed]
[+to be done slowly] [+accidentally] [+guided by one's sense of
what is right] [+privilege] [+condition]

R4 Test your collocational competence by filling in this chart. It took a native speaker 1½ minutes to identify the 33 collocations in this table. Time yourself while completing the chart. Notice that the order of the items has been changed.

	woman	man	child	dog	bird	flower	weather	landscape	view	house	furniture	bed	picture	dress	present	voice
handsome																
pretty																
charming																
lovely																

R5 And now try these:

1 Native-speaker time 45 sec.

	electricity	effects	hostility	plays	heat	food	films
produce							
generate							

2 Native-speaker time 1 min.
and 25 sec.

	smell	weapon	beliefs	leader	man	argument	desire	horse	tea	drink	influence	drug	wind	car	effect
strong															
potent															
powerful															

R6 Choose the word that best fits the context. Modify its form where necessary.

1 He does not . . . . . money. (to rate, to assess, to value)
2 The surveyor . . . . . the damage to the houses at £100,000. (to estimate, to evaluate, to assess, to value)
3 What a . . . . . man! (pretty, lovely, handsome)
4 What a pity that her manners are not as . . . . . as her face! (lovely, pretty, charming)
5 The cleaner looked at the list of . . . . . to be done in the house and groaned inwardly. (task, chore, work)
6 His homework was a . . . . . that lasted two hours each night. (work, chore, task)
7 . . . . . is overestimating your own worth! (vanity, conceit, self-esteem)
8 Vultures live on . . . . ., decaying carcasses. (grimy, filthy, grubby)
9 She's a . . . . . student, never failing to turn up to lectures. (honest, conscientious, careful)
10 We felt as . . . . . as the wind, now that the long term was over. (careless, reckless, carefree)
11 He was very . . . . . with the children, looking after them as though they were his own. (conscientious, careful, honest)
12 The chances of finding him were so . . . . . that they gave up the search. (remote, distant, far away)

R7 Produce a logical and coherent story by filling in the blanks with appropriate words from the list, modifying their form where necessary. Notice that not all of the words listed are relevant.

scruffy, filthy, effective, unsightly, strong, powerful, potent, reckless, remote, dissect, kill, harm, spoil, ruin, injure, hurt, damage, impair, cut, replace, supersede, matter, forestall, assess, evaluate, estimate, value, rate, calamity, cataclysm, range, scope

The motorcyclist 1 . . . . . a pedestrian when he collided with him, and as a result the pedestrian's health was 2 . . . . . for several weeks. The motor-cycle itself was not 3 . . . . ., however, and the motor-cyclist was not 4 . . . . . . 'This has 5 . . . . . my day!' 6 . . . . . the cyclist. The pedestrian, a rather 7 . . . . . individual at the best of times, now looked positively 8 . . . . . as he picked himself up out of the mud. 'My motorbike's a bit too 9 . . . . . .' apologised the cyclist, mentally 10 . . . . . ing the man, who bore a 11 . . . . . resemblance to a well-known film actor. He handed the pedestrian a rather 12 . . . . . drink from a small bottle, like a doctor giving out medicine. Indeed one could well imagine the cyclist in this role, or sitting white-coated in a laboratory 13 . . . . . ing specimens. . . .

In actual fact the cyclist had once been a champion boxer but had
eventually been 14 . . . . . by a younger rival. By that time anyway
he was fed up with such 15 . . . . . things as bleeding mouths and
broken noses, and had decided to go in for motorcycle racing. He
had imagined that there would be plenty of 16 . . . . . in this field
for someone of his capabilities, and besides, the 17 . . . . . of
competitions each year was unlimited. 18 . . . . . ing the value of the
prizes to be won had set his head spinning, and it was in this
19 . . . . . moment that he had put his foot on the accelerator and
the 20 . . . . . had occurred. He tried to 21 . . . . . the collision with
the pedestrian, but alas, his brakes, all too 22 . . . . ., had set the bike
spinning.

Unit 3   The human animal

The social order of Japanese macaques

JAPANESE MACAQUES

1 a variety of monkey
2 very noticeable, attracting attention
3 groups of people or animals – often when moving together, or, for animals living together
4 return the same ill treatment
5 menace, communicate one's attention to be aggressive
6 drive away, run after to capture or kill
7 structure with graded ranks
8 similar, corresponding
9 a hierarchy of social privilege and status among the members of a flock of chickens
10 position relative to other individuals or things in the same group
11 one after the other, in lines
12 changes of direction towards point of origin
13 in the same way

Among Japanese **macaques**[1] are these **striking**[2] features: a few males dominate the **troop**[3], several old females attack others of their sex without **retaliation**[4] and many adult females **threaten**[5] and **chase**[6] males. There is clearly a rigid dominance **hierarchy**[7], **analogous**[8] to a **pecking order**[9].

Aggressiveness is not important in determining **rank**[10]. The higher a monkey's status, the fewer the attacks made on him. (Dominance rank is basically **linear**[11] but there are occasional **reversals**[12].) **By the same token**[13], high rank does not necessarily **entail**[14] highly aggressive behaviour. Having **attained**[15] his position, the leader, secure and confident, does not need to attack others as much as lower-ranking males.

Nor does size play a vital role. One leader observed was small, had no **canine teeth**[16] and only one eye. Yet there was never any **challenge**[17] to his authority.

Ethologists[18] believe an animal's dominance rank is closely **correlated**[19] with its mother's. Sons of high-ranking females

14 make necessary, carry with it as a necessary consequence
15 reached
16 the four pointed teeth
17 disagreement with sb; signal that one wishes to fight with sb
18 those who study natural animal behaviour
19 connected, related to
20 the boundary line, the outside or outer surface
21 continue to be present
22 contests to deceive others by pretending to be strong or by threatening to do something that one cannot really do
23 probably
24 beasts of prey which kill and eat others
25 the highest order of animals, including man, apes and monkeys

may remain at the centre of the troop while others are driven to the **periphery**[20]. Probably the mother's influence **carries over**[21] and this is seen in many macaques fights which turn out to be **bluffing matches**[22]. Here, as usual, the deciding factor is the monkey's status. **Presumably**[23] the higher the rank of the combattant's mother, the more self-confident he is and the more certain of victory.

Also important in determining the social order is the functional role of each animal, ranging from watching for **predators**[24] to rearing a family.

The study of such **primate**[25] societies may help us to better understand human social behaviour.

an abstract from 'The Social Order of Japanese Macaques' by G Gray Eaton, *Scientific American*

Jackdaws in love

JACKDAWS IN LOVE

1 trying to attract sexually, courting (*of* if used of people)
2 a European bird, something like a crow, but smaller
3 object of sexual pursuit
4 warm, passionate quick turnings of the eyes to show feeling
5 *of* one who tries to persuade a woman to marry him
6 grotesque movements, sometimes ridiculous
7 honestly, really
8 *of* boyfriend
9 consent, agreement
10 crouching close to the ground
11 shaking, trembling, making quick, small uncontrollable movements
12 future wife
13 *of* engagement or promise to marry
14 make necessary, carries with it as a necessary consequence
15 not married

Remarkable and exceedingly comical is the difference in eloquence between the eye-play of the **wooing**[1] male **jackdaw**[2] and that of the **courted**[3] female: the male casts **glowing glances**[4] straight into his loved one's eyes, while she apparently turns her eyes in all directions other than that of her ardent **suitor**[5]. In reality, of course, she is watching him all the time, and her quick glances of a fraction of a second are quite long enough to make her realize that all his **antics**[6] are calculated to inspire her admiration; long enough to let 'him' know that 'she' knows. If she is **genuinely**[7] not interested, and will not look at him at all, then the young jackdaw male gives up his vain efforts as quickly as, well – any other young fellow. To her **swain**[8], now proudly advancing in all his glory, the young jackdaw lady finally gives her **assent**[9] by **squatting**[10] before him and **quivering**[11], in a typical way, with her wings and tail. These movements of both partners symbolize a ritual mating invitation, though they do not lead to actual union, but are purely a greeting ceremony. From the moment that the **bride-to-be**[12] has submitted to her male, she becomes self-possessed and aggressive towards all the other members of the colony. For a female, the **betrothal**[13] **entails**[14] a high promotion in the colony, for being, on the average, smaller and weaker than the male, she stands much lower in rank than he as long as she is **single**[15].

The betrothed pair form a heart-felt mutual defence league, each of the partners supporting the other most loyally. This is essential, because they have to

16 fight, struggle
17 actively engaged in supporting a
   cause
18 *lit* watch
19 walk up and down
20 slowly, heavily
21 not lying flat
22 mournful, sorrowful, sad
23 asking in a humble way
24 low, soft tones of voice
25 a bird's beak
26 keeping clean, usually for horses
27 at a stretch, without interruption
28 smooths and arranges its feathers
   with its beak
29 appealing to the senses, or
   conscious of one's body and its
   effect on others
30 extends, makes longer or larger
31 eager, anxious to help, or take care
   of, sb
32 trembling, shaking

contend[16] with the competition of older and higher standing couples in the struggle to take and hold a nesting cavity. This militant[17] love is fascinating to behold[18]. Constantly in an attitude of maximum self-display, and hardly ever separated by more than a yard, the two make their way through life. They seem tremendously proud of each other, as they pace[19] ponderously[20] side by side, with their head feathers ruffled[21] to emphasize their black velvet caps and light grey silken necks. And it is really touching to see how affectionate these two wild creatures are with each other. Every delicacy that the male finds is given to his bride and she accepts it with the plaintive[22] begging[23] gestures and notes otherwise typical of baby birds. In fact, the love-whispers[24] of the couple consist chiefly of infantile sounds, reserved by adult jackdaws for these occasions. Again, how strangely human!

The male jackdaw's habit of feeding his wife is a charming gesture which appeals directly to our human understanding, and the chief expression of tenderness shown by the female is no less attractive to our minds. It consists in her cleaning those parts of his head feathers which he cannot reach with his own bill[25]. Friendly jackdaws, as also many other social birds and animals, often perform mutually the duty of 'social grooming[26]', without any ulterior erotic motive. But I know of no other being which so throws its heart into the process as a love-sick jackdaw lady! For minutes on end[27] – and that is a long time for such a quick-silvery creature – she preens[28] her husband's beautiful, long, silken neck feathers, and he, with sensuous[29] expression and half-shut eyes, stretches[30] his neck towards her. The most appealing part of their relationship is that their affection increases with the years instead of diminishing. Jackdaws are long-lived birds and become nearly as old as human beings. Furthermore, they become betrothed in their first year, and marry in their second, so their union lasts long, perhaps longer than that of human beings. But even after many years, the male still feeds his wife with the same solicitous[31] care, and finds for her the same low tones of love, tremulous[32] with inward emotion, that he whispered in his first spring of betrothal and of love.

Konrad Z Lorenz, *King Solomon's Ring*

Instinct or Intelligence?

Of all the **crutch-words**[1] that modern scientists use to describe what they do not understand, 'instinct' is probably the most **pernicious**[2]. To Austrian ethologist Karl von Frisch, however, the mysteries of nature are not so easily explained, and he finds evidence in the behavior of insects, birds and other creatures suggesting that learning and individual experience play a greater role in the life of animals than **evolutionary**[3] **hard-liners**[4] care to admit. In 'Animal Architecture' von Frisch explores, with an **alert**[5] eye for **craftsmanship**[6], the details of animal construction from the **pebble-lined**[7] homes of the tropical jawfish to the simple tree-nests of apes. In his view, termites are the animal world's master architects and civil engineers. Some species build towering homes nearly 25 feet high — the equivalent, on a human scale, of a mile-high **apartment building**[8]. In rainy climates, termites add roofs with overhanging **eaves**[9] to protect their homes against torrential storms. In **arid**[10] regions of the Australian **outback**[11], compass termites construct termitaries in the shape of **axheads**[12]; the thin sides always point north and south so that the broad sides can catch the warming rays of the rising and setting sun. For water, some desert termites in Africa bore holes down to water tables at a depth of 130 feet — 'a truly **prodigious feat**[13] of civil engineering', von Frisch **marvels**[14], for such small animals working in such **loosely packed**[15] soil.

Equally impressive, though less complex, are the hanging nests of the **penduline titmice**[16], whose homes are so **sturdily**[17] built that they are sometimes used as purses by the Masai of East Africa and even worn as **slippers**[18] by children in eastern Europe. The nest of the knot-tying **weaverbird**[19] is at once more delicate and more loosely **plaited**[20] — and for a very good reason. The female of the species, it appears, is very **fastidious**[21]. If she finds her mate's workmanship **shoddy**[22], she will **spurn**[23] his sexual **overtures**[24], forcing him to unweave his **handiwork**[25] and begin all over again. Obviously, von Frisch argues, the male is learning from his **rebuff**[26], not operating by instinct alone. Through repeated experience, individual birds learn how to build better nests, and through trial and error, they may also discover that some grasses make better materials

INSTINCT OR INTELLIGENCE

1 word used as a false support for an idea, crutches *lit* supports to help a lame person to walk
2 destructive, injurious, harmful
3 who believe in the gradual development of more complicated forms of life (plants, animals) from earlier and simpler forms
4 fanatics
5 keen, watchful
6 skilled handiwork
7 lined with small, round stones worn smooth by water
8 *Br* block of flats
9 the overhanging edges of a roof
10 dry, barren
11 unsettled inland country in Australia, the bush
12 metal head, sharp at one edge, of heavy instrument to cut wood
13 amazing, enormous act showing great ability
14 wonders greatly
15 not dense or compact, not close or pressed together
16 a variety of bird
17 strongly, firmly
18 light, comfortable shoes worn indoors
19 birds so named because they construct elaborate nests of interlaced grass and other vegetation
20 interlaced
21 difficult to please, a perfectionist
22 of poor quality
23 treat with contempt
24 advances
25 work that is done by hand
26 unexpected and direct refusal, rejection
27 Australian birds that build a bower or playhouse to attract the female
28 *of* meeting for romantic purposes
29 decorated with chains of flowers, ribbons, leaves
30 brilliant, brightly-coloured, showy things used only for decoration
31 a shady place in the garden, in a wood or forest
32 pressed together in order to break
33 examining with great thoroughness
34 moves smoothly and quickly
35 unite for the purpose of producing young
36 insects with powerful sting
37 anything made by human work or art

Australian termite towers: Master architects and civil engineers

for weaving than others.

Close observation of **bowerbirds**[27] indicates to von Frisch that these amorous creatures exercise distinct esthetic judgments in pursuit of sexual conquest. Unlike other birds, the males build their bowers exclusively for **trysting**[28], and they spare no effort in decorating their love nests. The bower is **festooned**[29] with brightly colored flowers, berries and parrots' feathers, plus any bottle tops, bits of glass or other glittering **baubles**[30] the male can steal from human habitation. As a finishing touch, a bowerbird may actually paint the inside of his **arbor**[31] with the juice of blueberries that he has **crushed**[32] in his beak. When all is ready, he stands back like a painter, **scrutinizing**[33] his display. He will not hesitate to rearrange a blossom or a berry if the pattern does not please him. Courtship ends when a female **slips**[34] into the bower and **mates**[35] with her 'decorator'. Later, she builds a separate nest for the homely business of raising children.

In fact, von Frisch suggests, the bird's activities — like those of other animals — actually anticipated 'human behavior in comparable circumstances'. Indeed, 'Animal Architecture' offers several examples in which the birds and bees — not to mention whole colonies of **wasps**[36] — have anticipated by thousands of years some of man's most useful **artifacts**[37].

Newsweek

The Language of Parrots

The well-known Berlin **ornithologist**[1], Colonel von Lukanus, possessed a grey parrot which became famous through a **feat**[2] of memory. Von Lukanus kept, among other birds, a tame **hoopoe**[3] named 'Hopfchen'. The parrot, which could talk well, soon mastered this word. Hoopoes unfortunately do not live long in captivity, though grey parrots do: so, after a time, 'Hopfchen' **went the way of all flesh**[4] and the parrot appeared to have forgotten his name, at any rate, he did not say it any more. Nine years later, Colonel von Lukanus acquired another hoopoe and, as the parrot **set eyes**[5] on him for the first time, he said at once, and then repeatedly, 'Hopfchen' . . . 'Hopfchen'. . . .

Konrad Z Lorenz,
King Solomon's Ring

1 a student of birds and bird life
2 an act showing great ability
3 a kind of bird (with a long, pointed, curved bill)
4 *coll* died
5 *coll* noticed, saw

KOALA EXPLOSION

1 charming
2 lovable
3 good to cuddle, hold close and lovingly
4 lots, *lit* a score = 20
5 pleasant-natured
6 killed, butchered
7 the thick, soft hair that covers some animals
8 *Br* was on its way
9 surrounded by a fence, barrier of wood and/or wire
10 sit, stand, or lie in a lazy and relaxed way
11 eating with much movement of the jaws
12 going through process of producing young
13 with joy, enthusiasm
14 leave, *lit* of liquid or substance too plentiful for its container and which comes over the top
15 worried
16 hurrying off, with much agitation

The Koala Explosion

There is probably no animal on earth more **winsome**[1], **endearing**[2] and **cuddly**[3] than Australia's gentle koala bear. It was precisely these attributes that made the koalas one of the first species in the world to be protected by law. That was back in 1927, after **scores**[4] of millions of the **amiable**[5] creatures had been **slaughtered**[6] for **fur**[7] to be used in coats, hats and handbags, and conservationists had come to fear that the koala was **headed**[8] for extinction.

Now, a half century later, the koala bear is flourishing so vigorously that some Australians think there may be more koalas on their continent than there are Australians. In the special **fenced**[9] preserves the government built for them, the koalas **lounge**[10] happily in eucalyptus trees, **munching**[11] the leaves by night (eucalyptus leaves provide them with both food and water), sleeping undisturbed by day, and **procreating**[12] with **gusto**[13] in between.

Recently, the koalas have begun to **spill out**[14] of their special preserves. In one suburb of Sydney, the creatures are so numerous that special signs have been posted along the streets: CAUTION, KOALAS CROSSING. Other koalas have taken to moving into eucalyptus trees in backyards. This can sometimes create confusion. The cry of a young koala left temporarily alone by its mother is remarkably like that of a human baby — so much so that **harried**[15] mothers have occasionally found themselves **bustling off**[16] toward their backyard eucalyptus tree, instead of to the nursery.

Newsweek

CAUTION!
KOALAS CROSSING

THE VALUE OF THE DOG

1 useful
2 similar
3 a large, black bird resembling a crow
4 the common wild grey goose
5 make active, gay and cheerful
6 link, feeling of being in contact
7 all powerful, knowing everything
8 cutting off
9 strong longing, feeling of desire for
10 broken by twisting or bursting
11 link between two or more separate things
12 dull, gloomy, not cheerful
13 got, obtained
14 view, sight of
15 moving lightly and quickly from place to place
16 moving at a steady pace a little faster than walk, running slowly

The Value of the Dog

In these days, the value of the dog to man is purely a psychological one, except in the few cases where the animal has a **utilitarian**[1] purpose, as for sportsmen or policemen. The pleasure which I derive from my dog is closely **akin**[2] to the joy accorded to me by the **raven**[3], the **greylag goose**[4] or other wild animals that **enliven**[5] my walks through the countryside; it seems like a re-establishment of the immediate **bond**[6] with that unconscious **omniscience**[7] that we call nature. The price which man had to pay for his culture and civilization was the **severing**[8] of this bond which had to be torn to give him his specific freedom of will. But our infinite longing for paradise lost is nothing other than a half-conscious **yearning**[9] for our **ruptured**[10] **ties**[11]. Therefore, I need a dog.

Let us not lie to ourselves that we need the dog as a protection for our house. We *do* need him, but not as a watch-dog. I, at least in **dreary**[12] foreign towns, have certainly stood in need of my dog's company and I have **derived**[13], from the mere fact of his existence, a great sense of inward security, such as one finds in a childhood memory or in the **prospect**[14] of the scenery of one's own home country. In the almost film-like **flitting-by**[15] of modern life, a man needs something to tell him, from time to time, that he is still himself, and nothing can give him this assurance in so comforting a manner as the 'four feet **trotting**[16] behind.'

Konrad Z Lorenz,
King Solomon's Ring

A rare sight

Steven Pritchard of Probus, near Truro, in Cornwall, is a very lucky man. He has **witnessed**[1] a rare event in the Animal Kingdom.

It happened early one morning last week when Steven, a tractor-driver, was walking to work through the woods near his home. A movement on a grassy bank behind some trees attracted his attention, and **crouching**[2] behind a treetrunk he watched amazed as eight stoats walked in **single file**[3] down the bank, **making for**[4] a large beech tree at the bottom. At first they were on all **fours**[5]. Then they reared on their **hind**[6] legs, making high whistling noises and **gazing**[7] from side to side. Each one took his turn at pushing an object like a furry ball towards the beech tree. Once there, the stoats **scraped**[8] a hole between the roots and pushed the furry ball into it, covering it with earth.

All eight then formed a circle around the tree and ran nose to tail, making the same high whistling noises as before. Finally they **scampered**[9] away leaving a puzzled Steven still looking on.

In fact he had a **sneaking**[10] suspicion about this event. He went to the beech and carefully dug up the furry ball. As he expected, it was the body of an old stoat.

What Steven had seen was the **burial**[11] of the leader of a **pack**[12] of stoats. When the leader, or 'King' stoat dies, the other stoats bury it with the **touching**[13] ritual which Steven had been lucky enough to see.

The Tuesday Mail

A RARE SIGHT

1 be present at a significant or important event
2 lowering himself
3 in one line, one behind the other
4 went in the direction of, headed for
5 of mammals – resting on all four limbs
6 of parts of animal's body – back, rear
7 look fixedly and intently
8 made, by digging with their paws
9 ran quickly
10 *coll* vague but persistent
11 placing of a dead body in its final resting place, usu with some ceremony
12 group of animals of the same species
13 emotionally moving, arousing sympathy

CAT THAT WAS TOO BIG
FOR A FLAT

1 *Br* non-metric measure = 14 pounds/
1 stone
2 flat built and owned by a city,
county, etc, *usu* for low-income
families
3 representative
4 *Br* and *Am* non-metric measure of
land = about 4000 square metres

Cat that was too big for a flat . . .

A lion has been banned from its owner's home.

In Manchester, corporation officials ruled that Elsa, a **9st**[1] lioness, was not a suitable pet to be kept in a **council flat**[2].

'No permission is needed to keep a cat – but not one this size,' said a Housing Department **spokesman**[3].

Since the decision last month, Elsa has moved to a private house with a third-of-an-**acre**[4] grounds.

Daily Express

Discussion

1 In what ways is man like the other animals? In what ways is he different? Do you prefer to think of yourself as a kind of animal, or as something different from them?
2 'Since a moral capacity is not found in the lower animals in the reflective self-conscious sense, it constitutes one of the earmarks of man's essential humanity.' (A Munk, 'The Moral Factor', *Intellect*) Do you think this is true? Why doesn't moral capacity prevent men from sometimes treating each other in a more cruel way than animals could ever do?
3 Why do men like to keep animals as pets? Is it because they are his friends, or his enemies?
4 Two groups of animals mentioned here live in wild life reserves. Does man have an obligation to preserve species of animals which are threatened with extinction? Why might he want to do so?
5 'To survive is to adapt, and man's understanding of the macaques' successful adaptation to many different environments may ultimately contribute to his own survival.' What might we learn from animals which might help us to understand ourselves better and solve some of our current problems?

Word Study

A   Semantic Fields

1 Arriving at some goal

reach			
accomplish	achieve	attain	gain

There is a considerable overlap between the semantic components of these words. We can, however, distinguish them as follows:
reach usually means [+ come to the limit or end of]
attain usually suggests [+ reach sth above the average]
gain often implies [+ much effort]
achieve stresses [+ use of skill] and
accomplish [+ success in completing task].

	the top of a mountain	the shore	land	London	the end of a book	unexpected proportions	a speed of 150 m.p.h.	perfection	great riches	power	prestige	distinction in public life	victory	a great success	one's goals	what one set out to do	one's ambitions	one's hopes	a great deal
reach	+	+	+	+	+	+	+												
attain					+	+	+	+	+	+	+	(+)	+						
gain			(+)							+	+	(+)	+						+
achieve						+					-		+	+	+	+	+	+	+
accomplish															+	+	+	+

2 Looking over

	look at/over					
	manner		*purpose*			
	usu closely, carefully	usu quickly, superficially	make sure of a fact or detect errors	or determine condition, quality	that rules are observed	often searching for one specific thing
check			+	+		+
examine				+		
inspect			+	+	+	
scan		+				+
scrutinize	+		+			

All these verbs can be followed by a direct object and a **to**-infinitive indicating purpose or, less frequently, the preposition **for**.

EXAMPLES

check   I am **checking** the text **for** printing errors.
Could you **check** the timetable **to** see if there is a train at 5 o'clock?

examine   They are **examining** the furniture **for** damage.
The doctor **examined** the patient **to** see if he was injured.

inspect   The safety officer was **inspecting** the pipes **for** leaks.
The teacher **inspected** the pupils' hands **to** make sure they were clean before lunch.

scan   The captain **scanned** the horizon **for** approaching ships.
Matthew **scanned** the article **to** see if there was anything of interest.

scrutinize   The policeman **scrutinized** the gun **for** fingerprints.
The immigration officer **scrutinized** my passport **to** make sure it was in order.

	a bill	some figures	sb's entry permit	the records	the instructions	sb's statement	the meaning in the dictionary	the headlines in the morning papers	the situation	a building for fire hazards	a school	sb's chest	a patient	a student	the horizon
check	+	+	+	+	+	+	+	+							
inspect	(+)	(+)	+	+					(+)	+	+				
scrutinize	+	+	+	+	+										
examine		+	+						+			+	+	+	
scan								+							+

3 Lowering one's body

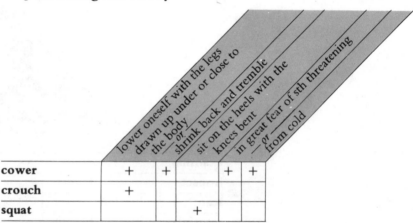

	lower oneself with the legs drawn up under or close to the body	*or* shrink back and tremble	sit on the heels with the knees bent	in great fear of sth threatening	*or* from cold
cower	+	+		+	+
crouch	+				
squat			+		

Squat and **crouch** are often followed by **down**.

EXAMPLES

cower   The child **cowered** in a corner as his pursuers approached.
The dogs were terrified by the thunderstorm and **cowered** under
the table till it was over.

crouch   **Crouch down** behind the hedge so as not to be seen
from the house!

squat   **Squatting down** on all fours, he tried to see if his watch
had fallen under the bed.

In informal style, **squat** is often used figuratively.

EXAMPLE

If there are no chairs left, I'll just **squat** on the floor.

4 Breaking

	suddenly and quickly	with or resulting from force or violence	usu with noise	by application of pressure	into very many small pieces	so that irregular lines or fissures appear on surface	or open an object enclosing sth	off a small piece or pieces from the whole	usu at the edge	completely apart	usu of thin, brittle objects	apart because too full, or from internal pressure	usu results in contents diffusing over wide area
smash	+	+	+										
crush				+									
shatter	+	+			+								
crack						+	+						
chip								+	+				
snap										+	+		
burst												+	+

All the verbs, except **crush**, are both transitive and intransitive; **crush** is transitive only.

Notice also that all, except **chip**, can be used figuratively and that **snap** then means [+speak sharply and abruptly] and **crack** means [+decode] or [+begin to understand]. **Crack**, **snap** and **burst** are informal when figurative.

EXAMPLES

break I think it really **broke** her heart to see her own son accused of murder.

smash Losing that match today will **smash** any hopes the team had of getting somewhere in the national championships.

crush He started to protest, but was **crushed** by an acid comment from the Chairman.

shatter Six months of working in a shop have completely **shattered** any illusions I had about the tradition of good manners still being alive.

crack It took several months for the Police to **crack** the system used by a ring of car-thieves operating from London airport.

snap Jones is in a bad mood – I only asked him how he was and he practically **snapped** my head off!

burst Father came home **bursting** with indignation that new regulations stop him from parking his car outside his own office.

	break (broke) (broken)	smash(ed)	crush(ed) (ing)	shatter(ed)	crack(ed)	chip(ped)	snap(ped)	burst	
I'm afraid her leg is	+								in two places.
The wrecked ship will	+								up on the rocks if the wind gets any stronger.
The cat knocked over a cup and	+	+							it.
The angry crowd	(+)	+							all the windows in the street as they passed.
The glass fell on the stone floor and		+		+					into a hundred tiny pieces.
The brittle rock				+					under the force of the explosion.
Juice may be extracted from fruit by			+						it.
Someone sat on my flowers and			+						them.
I can never					+				Brazil nuts because they are so hard.
The plate isn't broken, only					+	+			.
The ice was tight-packed around the door and had to be						+			away a little at a time.
The wind was so strong that several branches	+						+		clean off the big oak tree.
He	+						+		the twigs in two so that they would fit into the fire.
I had my shopping in a plastic bag which	+							+	under the weight just as I was getting onto the bus.
The nasty boys								+	all the pretty balloons we had blown up for the party.
The river has								+	its banks and flooded a wide area.

5 Saying 'No'

	not allow sth to happen	express unwillingness to do sth or to accept sth	esp requests	esp applications	esp offers	esp invitations	definitely and completely	politely	suggests contempt
refuse	+	+	+						
reject		+		+	+		+		
turn down		+	+	+	+	+			
decline		+			+	+		+	
spurn		+			+		+		+

All the verbs are transitive. **Refuse** and **decline** may be followed by a **to**-infinitive.

EXAMPLES

The witness **refused to** tell us anything.

I **declined to** accompany him to the theatre.

Turn down, while correct in speech, is not used in formal writing.
Refuse and **reject** are often used in the passive.

EXAMPLES

refuse My brother was **refused** admission to the restaurant because he was so badly dressed.

reject 'Did you get into university?' 'No, I was **rejected**.'

turn down Those fools on the Selection Committee **turned down** my application again.

decline I am sorry that I have to **decline** your very kind invitation to come and stay.

spurn He **spurned** all offers of help because he is so proud.

	a lover	sb's attentions	sb's offer	a request	an invitation	sb's proposal	an application	a candidate	a gift	sb admittance	sb permission	sb's money
spurn	+	+	+									
decline			+	+	+							
turn down			+	+	+	+	+	+				
reject			+			+	+	+	+			
refuse			+	+	+				+	+	+	+

6 Looking

look			
gaze	glance	glimpse	peer

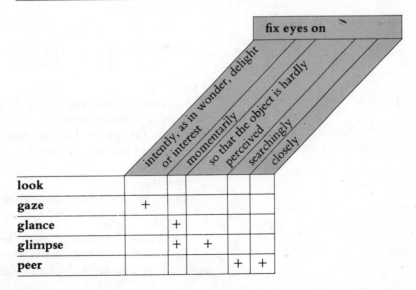

	intently, as in wonder, delight or interest	momentarily	so that the object is hardly perceived	searchingly	closely
look					
gaze	+				
glance		+			
glimpse		+	+		
peer				+	+

Glimpse must take a direct object, while the other verbs require a preposition – often **at**, but also **into**, **over**, and others.

EXAMPLES

glimpse   I just **glimpsed** the house through the trees as we drew near to it.

look   **Look** at that monkey stealing an apple!

gaze   As he **gazed** lovingly into her eyes, she felt she would always love him.

glance   Could you just **glance** over this letter to make sure there are no mistakes in it?

peer   We **peered** uncertainly into the darkness, trying to distinguish the route through the forest.

B   Synonymous Pairs

1   **movements/steps**
     antics | [+grotesque] [+often funny, amusing]

EXAMPLE

Children visiting the zoo love to watch the monkeys' **antics**.

2   **to chew**
     to munch | [+bigger movement of the jaw] [+usu of hard or crisp things]

EXAMPLE

The twins were each **munching** a large, crisp, juicy apple.

3   **to pay back**
     to retaliate | [+return the same sort of ill treatment]

EXAMPLE

My noisy neighbours kept me awake again last night, so I **retaliated** by playing the trumpet outside their bedroom at 6.30 a.m.

4   **to scamper**   [+run]   [+usu of small or young animals or children] [+sometimes playfully]
     to scurry   [+with short, quick steps] [+as if in a hurry]

EXAMPLES

The puppies **scampered** round the garden.
The children **scampered** off across the sand.
When the cat appeared, all the mice **scurried** away into their holes.
The rain sent everyone **scurrying** back to their cars.

5   **to cut**
     to sever | [+completely detach one part from another]

EXAMPLES

He accidentally **severed** a vein in his arm with the axe.
All communication links between the island and the mainland were **severed** for two weeks by bad weather.

6 **to disturb**
 to ruffle $\quad$ [+surface] $\Rightarrow \left\{ \begin{array}{c} \text{[+upset]} \end{array} \right\}$ [+slightly]

EXAMPLES

Only the movements of a lone swimmer **ruffled** the smooth surface of the swimming pool.

She is usually very calm, but this morning she seemed a bit **ruffled**, probably because she was not confident that her research project would be acceptable to the Board of Studies.

7 **to mislead**
 to bluff $\quad$ [+on purpose] [+by presenting false information]

EXAMPLE

I was stopped by the police and I didn't have my papers with me, but I **bluffed** my way out of it by pretending not to speak the language.

8 **sad**
 plaintive $\quad$ [+sounding sorrowful or melancholy]

	voice	cry	request	person	book
sad	+	+	+	+	+
plaintive	+	+	+		

9 **aggressive**

 militant $\quad$ [+ wanting to fight] [+ for a cause] $\left. \right\}$ or [+ for oneself] [+ often organize

	man	people	tone	voice	disposition	workers	students	supporters of equal rights	extremist group	action
aggressive	+	+	+	+	+	+	+	+		
militant						+	+	+	+	+

10 **dry**
 arid $\quad$ [+abnormal] [+intense] [+often without life] [+large area]

	river bed	climate	weather	region	country	soil	land
dry	+	+	+	+	+	+	+
arid				+	+	+	(+)

11 **harmful**
   pernicious | [+ working in a hidden way] [+ often serious]

	disease	books	habits	anaemia
harmful	+	+	+	
pernicious			+	+

Exercises

1 What do you need to make the following?

1 a knot   2 slippers   3 a hole   4 a coat   5 a nest   6 a roof
7 a handbag   8 a fence

2 Fill in the missing words.

1 the trial and . . . . . approach
2 the . . . . . sun
3 to tie a . . . . .
4 to play an important . . . . .
5 to . . . . . a high rank
6 by the . . . . . token
7 to stretch one's . . . . .
8 for minutes on . . . . .
9 to pay a high . . . . .
10 from the . . . . . fact
11 to . . . . . slippers
12 to spare no . . . . .

3 Match appropriate features with each of the following words:

1 arid   2 alert   3 pernicious   4 dreary   5 plaintive   6 shoddy
7 genuine   8 utilitarian   9 winsome   10 rigid   11 prodigious
12 rebuff   13 predator

[+ charming] [+ direct refusal] [+ dull] [+ harmful] [+ poor quality]
[+ useful] [+ gloomy] [+ watchful] [+ enormous] [+ dry]
[+ sorrowful] [+ honest] [+ firm] [+ beast of prey] [+ true]
[+ strict] [+ kills and eats others]

4 Find words to fit the following descriptions:

1 supports to help a lame person to walk
2 small, round stones worn smooth by water
3 a structure with graded ranks
4 anything made by human work or act
5 the thick, soft hair that covers some animals
6 reject or refuse contemptuously
7 strong longing, feeling or desire for
8 make from threads (eg into cloth)
9 small insect that produces honey
10 cut off completely (eg one's connections with sb)

5 Find two adjectives which could collocate with each of the following nouns. Try not to use the same adjective twice.

1 pattern   2 display   3 feat   4 soil   5 shape   6 experience
7 movement   8 explosion

6 What is the meaning of the following?

1 to retaliate   2 to glitter   3 to crush   4 to procreate   5 to spill (out)   6 to slaughter   7 to explore   8 to cross   9 to marvel   10 to peck

7 Add appropriate nouns to the following adjectives.

1 shoddy   2 fastidious   3 delicate   4 rainy   5 gentle   6 harried   7 tame   8 utilitarian   9 genuine   10 rigid   11 straight   12 plaintive   13 solicitous   14 militant

8 Which adjectives and adverbs can be derived from the following?

1 depth   2 delicacy   3 affection   4 separation   5 torrent   6 vigour   7 repetition   8 touch   9 rigidity   10 comfort   11 pride   12 extinction

9 What are the differences between the following?

1 to quake/to quiver   2 to reach/to attain   3 to scrutinize/to inspect   4 to refuse/to reject   5 to glance/to look   6 to sit down/to squat down

10 Choose the word that best fits the given context, modify its form where necessary.

1 Dogs like to . . . . . rabbits. (to chase, to run)
2 We . . . . . by the swimming pool in the sun the whole afternoon. (to lounge, to sit)
3 The monkey which was caught in the trap . . . . . to get free. (to struggle, to fight)
4 I . . . . . finishing the job tomorrow. (anticipate, expect)
5 I can't find any logical . . . . . between these two sentences. (tie, bond, link)
6 He . . . . . backwards and forwards across the room like a caged animal. (to pace, to trot)
7 I . . . . . him not to go on such a dangerous journey, but nothing I could say would stop him. (to beg, to request)
8 Children must learn to be . . . . . with small animals. (gentle, delicate)
9 Some trees . . . . . their leaves in winter. (to shed, to throw)
10 I was in bed, but still . . . . ., when I heard a car arrive outside the house. (alert, awake, watchful)

11 What are the differences between the following pairs?

1 to whisper/to talk   2 to glow/to glitter   3 to cry/to shout   4 to fight/to struggle   5 to tear/to destroy   6 to fly/to move   7 mature/old   8 infantile/young   9 sensuous/sensitive   10 a bond/a knot   11 arid/dry

12 Explain the meaning of the following in your own words:

1 feathers   2 berries   3 eaves   4 backyard   5 suburb   6 bower   7 hard-liner   8 beak   9 nest   10 bottle tops   11 desert   12 crutches

13 Choose the word that best fits the context. Modify its form where necessary.

1 Artificial sweeteners have been . . . . . in many States of the USA (to ban, to forbid)
2 The journey through the mountains was most . . . . . . (amiable, pleasant)
3 The skin of the ripe tomatoes has . . . . . in the intense heat. (to sever, to cut, to rupture)

4 He . . . . . the day when he would see his home again.
(to long for, to miss)

5 The defending armies achieved a great . . . . . over the
aggressors. (conquest, victory)

6 Our visit was rendered more pleasant by the . . . . . care of our
friends. (solicitous, anxious, ready)

7 Ever . . . . . energy resources will soon pose serious problems on a
world-wide scale. (to go down, to diminish, to decrease)

8 New research is producing theories, which . . . . . long-held
views about animals. (disagree, provide, challenge)

**14 What are the differences
and/or similarities between
the following pairs?**

1 group/society   2 hierarchy/pecking order   3 to enter/to slip
into   4 to scrutinize/to look at   5 to crush/to crash   6 to kill/
to slaughter   7 to groom/to clean   8 to take/to steal   9 to chase/
to hunt   10 to bustle off/to leave

15 Write a short report.

Imagine you arrive from another planet and have to write a short
report on the 'social order of humans'. Try to use the same kind of
words as you find in these articles.

Revision Exercises

**R1 Fill in the collocational
grids.**

a

	one's back	sb's reputation	sb's pride	sb's car	somebody
damage					
harm					
hurt					

b

	damages	sb's income	sb's performance	the importance of sth	the evidence
assess					
estimate					
evaluate					

**R2 Which of the given
semantic features are
relevant to the following
words?**

1 conceit   2 cataclysm   3 filth   4 self-esteem   5 shudder
6 predict   7 rate

[+ misfortune] [+ move] [+ know] [+ over-high] [+ from horror]
[+ justified] [+ causing disgust] [+ pride in oneself] [+ dirt]
[+ widespread] [+ from side to side] [+ judge] [+ future event]
[+ tell] [+ place on a numerical scale]

**R3 Which nouns can be
derived from the following
verbs?**

1 assess   2 prophesy   3 rate   4 respond   5 fertilize   6 apply
7 expose   8 perceive   9 destroy   10 predict   11 find   12 infer
13 estimate   14 solve   15 assume   16 acknowledge

R4 Guess the right word.

1 Now that fewer pesticides are used on the land, many species of birds and insects are again fl . . . . . .
2 New le . . . . . has been passed by the government, to control the deposit of noxious wastes.
3 I always wear sc . . . . . old clothes when I am painting the house.
4 While we were out, the cows broke into the garden and tra . . . . . on my beautiful tomato plants.
5 I thought she had dark hair, but today she has covered it with a blonde w . . . . . .
6 Being co . . . . . is half of what is necessary to succeed.
7 Martin knocked the bottle over and s . . . . . wine all over the floor.
8 The Americans sent up a sa . . . . . to survey meteorological conditions.
9 To solve the energy crisis we need to ha . . . . . the vast potential resources of water power.
10 Large de . . . . . of waste material are blocking the mouth of the river.

R5 Match appropriate features with each of the following words:

1 supersede 2 scan 3 decline 4 accomplish 5 shiver 6 peer 7 gaze 8 militant 9 retaliate 10 inscrutable 11 infest 12 respite 13 sewer 14 target

[+ object to be aimed at] [+ take the place of because better] [+ examine] [+ cannot be understood] [+ politely] [+ superficially] [+ say 'no'] [+ succeed in completing] [+ from cold] [+ be present in large numbers] [+ want to fight] [+ tremble] [+ look] [+ underground channel] [+ as in wonder] [+ intently] [+ carries off waste] [+ short period of rest] [+ return the same sort of ill treatment] [+ for a cause]

R6 What differences and/or similarities are there between the following:

1 to value/to rate/to assess 2 to mar/to impair/to injure 3 to conclude/to infer/to judge 4 to generate/to produce 5 condition/plight 6 effective/efficacious

R7 What other verbs can be used in the following phrases?

1 to rate something at 2 to conclude from sth that 3 to inspect something for 4 to shake with

R8 What can you . . . . . ?

1 dump 2 abandon 3 forestall 4 condemn 5 resolve 6 suffer from 7 shake 8 inquire about 9 forecast 10 assess 11 oversimplify 12 restrict 13 acknowledge 14 benefit from

R9 Explain the meaning of each of the following. Your explanations may include mime, descriptions, enumerations of uses, or examples.

1 mongrel 2 court 3 stock market 4 to clip 5 to trigger off 6 to elicit 7 to disprove 8 to mutter 9 relentless 10 carcinogenic 11 random 12 ambivalent

R10 In each case provide three or four words that can collocate with the following:

1 grimy   2 conscientious   3 distant   4 reckless   5 to forecast   6 to forestall   7 to value

R11 Choose the word that best fits the context. Modify its form where necessary.

1 We are constantly . . . . . of the serious consequences of changing the balance of nature, but still we do not do anything about it. (to threaten, to menace, to warn)
2 Two thousand acres of previously arid land are now . . . . . and produce the greater part of the country's food requirements. (to irrigate, to water)
3 More than half the forest was . . . . . by a fire which raged incontrollably for two days. (to devastate, to ruin, to destroy)
4 It is . . . . . that students will have doubled their vocabulary in six months. (to foresee, to anticipate)
5 I'm sorry, but I don't see the . . . . . of this point to the rest of your argument. (connection, relevance)
6 The . . . . . along the road to understanding one's fellow men are many and various. (pitfalls, dangers)
7 His mother has always . . . . . all his attempts to get married. (to stop, to forestall, to prevent)
8 The professor is a(n) . . . . . supporter of open-book exams. (public, open, overt)
9 Spending six months in England was a very . . . . . experience for me. (profitable, lucrative)
10 My new job gives me a lot of . . . . . to use my languages. (range, scope)

R12 Solve the crossword puzzle.

Across

1 a time-gap between two events (3)
3 temporary relief, short period of rest (7)
5 People who predict the future give us g . . . . . s of tomorrow's world. (8)
12 great achievement, sounds like part of the body you walk with (4)
13 Why do you . . . . . so many questions? (3)
15 E . . . . . to nuclear radiation has been shown to be very dangerous to humans. (8)
18 provide water to a dry region so that it can be used for growing crops (8)
19 If you . . . . . too many chocolates you will get fat. (3)
20 not stopping for any reason, mercilessly continuing (10)
22 By the window was a plant in a . . . . .. (3)
23 order or decree of a government (4)
25 existing since the beginning of life on earth (10)
27 bones attached to the spine, and enclosing the chest, heart, lungs (4)
28 chemicals used to kill insects which eat crops (10)
31 The company plans to enlarge the s . . . . . of its operations in the Far East. (5)
32 substances used to change the colour of sth (4)

Down

2 makes sure, checks (10)
4 be present in large numbers, so as to be dangerous or unpleasant (6)
6 cannot be understood or known about (11)
7 Nothing will . . . . . his belief in capitalism. (5)
8 The magazine sent out a questionnaire designed to g . . . . . readers' ability to see in the dark. (5)
9 faster than the speed of sound (10)
10 She looked . . . . . him in surprise. (2)
11 The bower-bird builds a beautiful bower to . . . . . the female inside. (4)
14 something for which one is legally responsible (9)
16 eliminate, get rid of, doubts or problems (8)
17 look closely and attentively at (4)
21 top which fits on a box or pan (3)
24 I can't wait to see her face when she . . . . . the paper off her present and sees what is inside. (5)
25 small seeds inside fruit (4)
26 My watch has disappeared and I reported its . . . . . to the police. (4)
29 This crossword . . . . . easy! (2)
30 Help me . . . . . do my homework. (2)

Unit 4

Exclusively for you

Equality before the object

The **quest**[1] for happiness through the objects one possesses **haunts**[2] modern civilization in much the same way that the quest for **salvation**[3] did in the past. And the ideological force of this new image of happiness comes from the fact that in modern societies it picks up and embodies the myth of Equality. The 'revolution of well-being' is the **heir**[4] of the 'middle class revolution'. Having failed to realize the objectives of democratic equality in social relationships, society seeks equality before the Object. This is the 'democracy of status'. The whole political game in consumer society consists in making people believe that comfort and well-being will make conflicts disappear and assure the equality of destiny for all.

However, despite appearances, an abundance of things does not transform unequal social relationships. In fact, it is only the manifestation of an enlarged sphere of production. Consumption is the morality of our time. Everything can be sacrificed to it.

Men of the **opulent**[5] **era**[6] are surrounded more by objects than by other men. Their daily interaction has less to do with their fellow men than with receiving and manipulating goods and messages. In this regard the **drugstore**[7] or the shopping center are a sort of symbol. There the synthesis of consumer activities – flirting with objects and the **ludicrous**[8] **roaming**[9] induced by the **amalgam**[10] of signs – is carried out. The possession of goods and objects is the language, the code by which the whole society communicates and speaks to itself. For consumption is an active and collective behavior. It is a **constraint**[11], a morality. It is a whole system of values. As Galbraith says: 'the individual serves the industrial system not by giving it his savings and providing it with capital, but by consuming its products. Moreover, there is no other religious, political or moral activity for which he is prepared in so complete, knowledgeable and costly a manner.'

Jean Baudrillard. *Théorie de la consommation*. Summarised in *Prospective*.

Advertising can sell you anything

Like everyone else in this country, you are an advertising expert. Why not? You have been brought up with advertising. The first words you ever read were probably written on a **billboard**[1] or the front of a box of cereal. The first sounds you ever heard were probably **emanating**[2] from a radio or a television set. Before you knew who daddy was, you knew that Wheaties was the breakfast of champions. Before you could tell a Republican from a Democrat, you could tell a **Bufferin**[3] from a plain aspirin. Naturally, you're an advertising expert, and as such you know two things for sure.

First, you know what you like and what you don't like. You know which commercials make you laugh, which ones make you **giggle**[4], which ones raise **a lump in your throat**[5], and which ones **bore**[6] **you to tears**[7]. In short, you react emotionally to each one of them, and are able instantly to identify these emotions. Indeed, advertising is the art form of the common man, making just about all of us react just about the same way, just about all the time. Preplanned? **You bet it is**[8]. We know what will make you feel happy or sad or calm or **mad**[9]. And we **elicit**[10] those emotions from you through the highly skilled use of this art form called advertising. Yet, they are your emotions, your reactions, and you do know how you feel. And that makes you an expert.

The second thing you think you know for sure is the conscious decisions you make concerning products you see advertised. The chances are that you have never made a deliberate decision to buy a product based on an ad you have seen. As a matter of fact, I have heard only quotes to the contrary, **ranging**[11] from 'I would never buy a product that I have seen advertised' to the more basic 'Come on, who do they think they're **kidding**?'[12]. Well, we're not kidding anyone. It's you who are kidding yourself. Because every day, in hundreds of ways, we are selling you products on a logical, intellectual, factual basis. And you are being persuaded.

There is a great mythology in America that advertising has, at best, a negligible influence on you. Nothing could be further from the truth. Today's advertising industry is the most potent and powerful mass marketing and merchandising instrument ever devised by man.

The truth of it is, advertising can sell you anything.

Advertising tells you what to buy, how to buy, and why to buy any particular **brand**[13] or product. The thing that amazes me is that it continues to work. You'd think that, after all these years of the same old line people would have become **immune**[14] to it. But not so. You are continually **hanged, drawn, and quartered**[15] by somebody's **commercial**[16]. So the real ques-

ADVERTISING CAN SELL YOU ANYTHING

1 a board intended for the display of posters, *Br* hoarding
2 come from, flow from, proceed from
3 brand-name of pain-killing tablet sold in US
4 laugh in a nervous and silly way
5 a feeling of pressure caused by strong emotion
6 make tired by talking too much or by being dull and uninteresting
7 *coll* bore you so much that you feel you could cry
8 *coll* you may be quite certain
9 *Br* angry, cross
10 draw out, cause to come out
11 varying within definite limits
12 joking
13 a particular type of goods
14 safe, secure or protected, not susceptible
15 captured, destroyed, *lit* (archaic) to kill, draw out entrails and cut in four
16 advertisement inserted in a TV or radio programme

tion is, how come? **How come**[17] people keep believing? How come you keep buying things you know won't do what they're supposed to do? How come advertising works?

Several years ago a friend of mine was working on Pampers, the disposable **diapers**[18]. Now, Pampers was so drastically different from anything else in its category that the agency decided to play it straight. They set up a legitimate test situation, and went about showing, without any tricks or gimmickry, that this product was clearly superior. Then they put the thing into a test market (a small area of the country in which Pampers also ran advertising) and the product **proceeded to die**[19]. **Flopped on its ass**[20]. Lay there like a dead **mackerel**[21]. Within a few weeks the manufacturer was getting phone calls from the grocers and super-market chains, demanding that the product be removed from the **stores**[22], as it was taking up valuable shelf space. The agency panicked, so **they fell back on**[23] the old **standby**[24], the so-called '**slice of life**'[25] commercial. The all-knowing mother, the **bumbling**[26], insignificant father, and the bright but uninformed next-door neighbor. They did a commercial, and then showed it to a group of ladies. Well, the ladies laughed at it. 'Nobody talks that way', they said. 'Do you think we're stupid?' Guess what the **punch line**[27] of this story is? The commercial went on the air, and the product **went through the roof**[28]. Couldn't make it fast enough. Within a matter of a few months, Pampers was responsible for more than 90 percent of all sales in its category. **Blame**[29] the advertising. Blame its effect on people. It contained, as a matter of fact, less information, less fact in the slice of life than in the straight, honest approach, yet everyone **responded**[30] to it. Was it because the advertising was reflecting life, or changing life styles? Was it that the group of ladies lied; that, indeed, people really do talk that way? Probably it was a combination of all of them. The point is, people were **affected**[31], motivated to go out and buy something. That's how deeply advertising affects us, and our lives. So the next time someone says to you, 'Hey, you sound like a commercial', don't be alarmed. Don't be surprised. You probably do.

Carl O Wrighter,
I Can Sell You Anything

17 *Br* why
18 *Br* baby's napkins, nappies
19 *coll* did not sell at all
20 *coll* did not sell at all, *lit* fell on its behind, *Br* fell flat on its face
21 a sea fish used as food
22 *Am*, British uses 'store' for large shops and 'shop' for small ones
23 went back to, relied on, made use of some thing one had used before when the first failed
24 a person or thing that can be relied on in time of stress or emergency
25 realistic, as if representing a real scene
26 bungling, confused, slow
27 last line of story or joke which makes the point of the whole thing
28 *informal* was a big success
29 say that something is the cause of something bad
30 reacted, were influenced by and acted accordingly
31 influenced

YARDLEY

1 cosmetic preparations tinted blue, green, black, etc applied to the eyelids
2 cosmetic preparations used to darken the eyelashes, usually black, brown, or blue
3 cosmetic preparation which helps to keep eyelashes healthy
4 small tray of colours, *lit* for painting

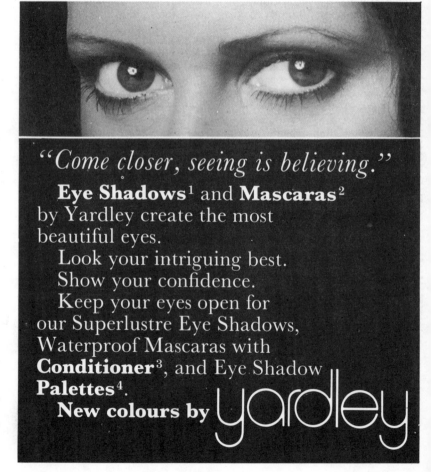

Cosmopolitan

CONSUMER RESISTANCE

1 harsh, very strict, very simple, without ornament
2 is in conflict with
3 good judgement and common sense, knowledge
4 start, beginning
5 shortage, insufficiency, lack
6 religious men living in a monastery
7 with very little of anything in it
8 economical, careful not to waste
9 should
10 against
11 obey
12 returning, going back to
13 inflated or empty speech, rubbish, something which is untrue
14 cause to move faster, increase the speed of

Caught Napping[1]

An Aberdeen butcher bought some top-quality lambs cheap.

He decided to **pass on**[2] the saving to customers, and labelled the lamb at **bargain prices**[3].

Despite a 'Best Quality' label, housewives barely gave it a second glance.

So the butcher marked up the lamb to top price and sold it as fast as he could **wrap** it **up**[4]!

Wake up, Mum!

The Sunday Post

Consumer resistance to austere life style

The fact that American buyers are returning to big car preference plus the rate of economic recovery demonstrate clearly that the consumer is still king and is still unwilling to buy the arguments that we must conserve and live an **austere**[1] life, according to Ross Willhelm, Graduate School of Business Administration, University of Michigan. 'The high demand for big cars comes as a shock to the auto makers since they had over the past two years invested huge amounts of money for the production and promotion of small cars. The growing demand for big cars **flies in the face of**[2] all of the conventional **wisdom**[3] that we hear from environmentalists and others that the American people are in the process of changing their life styles and wants because of the **onset**[4] of a world of **scarcity**[5] and rapidly diminishing resources. The American people obviously are not buying the argument that we have to turn into a nation of **monks**[6] who live **sparse**[7] and **frugal**[8] lives. And obviously, if the American people do not buy the austerity life style argument, politicians in Washington **had better**[9] reexamine their own positions vis-à-vis expansion of energy supplies **versus**[10] greater conservation.'

'For years, we have heard that we are all puppets who **do the bidding of**[11] the manufacturers. We are, according to these people, manipulated by the producers who want the products the producers offer us and not to want the products we really need and should have. The huge companies with their advertising and marketing efforts are supposed to be able to push us into buying things we do not want. Yet, if this is the case, why is it the consumers are **swinging back to**[12] buying big cars when the auto makers have been going all out to build and promote small cars? The argument that the consumer is not king and he is just a manipulated puppet is a lot of **bunk**[13] and is not demonstrable in consumer behavior.'

Prof Wilhelm concludes that business and advertisers do not have anything resembling the power that their critics say they have. 'Advertising doesn't manipulate consumers into spending and saving more than they want. It is obvious, based on last year's recession, that advertising and marketing cannot prevent recessions by stimulating consumer spending any more than it can **speed up**[14] recovery.'

Intellect

CAUGHT NAPPING

1 *coll* caught unawares, *lit* nap(n) short sleep during the day
2 give something one has received from somebody else
3 price below the real value
4 roll or fold around, cover

FRIGHTENING

1 a glossy coating for nails
2 not credible, not believable, unlikely

Frightening

A nine-year-old girl is getting ready for school. She carefully applies her eyeshadow, powder, &c., while her **nail varnish**[1] 'dries'.

Far-fetched?[2] Well, a survey says 28 per cent of girls between nine and ten use some form of skin conditioner. By the age of 14, more than half are using cosmetics.

So next year, the big cosmetic firms are to turn some of their attention to little girls.

Frankly, we hope they stick to their dolls.

The Sunday Post

Make the most of life.

Veuve du Vernay.

The light dry **sparkling**[1] wine of France.
It's life.

VEUVE DU VERNAY

1 containing bubbles of gas

Cosmopolitan

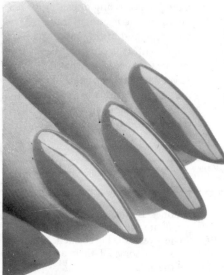

Hands. Seen almost as soon as your face.
On show[1]. Touching. Holding. Loving.
Nail polish is as important as make-up.
That's why we call Cutex the make-up for nails.
Thirty different colours. Some dramatic.
Some soft. Some vivid. Some gentle.
More than nail polish. It's make-up
for nails.

**Thirty colours. Some so spectacular
they send messages.**

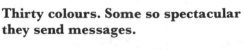

CUTEX

1 exhibited, displayed

She

From verse to worse

Liberty belle

A more personalised form of advert appeared **gummed**[1] on the window of a Midlands bus in the 1960s. The anonymous authoress airs her views on the **iniquities**[2] of Women's Lib!

> I often think when, in a bus,
> I balance on my **weary**[3] feet,
> That sex equality for us
> Won the vote but lost the seat!

No doubt penned by a **winsome**[4] **lass**[5] – and a resigned loser!

Divine write!

A Dorset reader gave us a nice advertising **jingle**[1] for the Bible which first appeared in a newspaper in 1850:

> Holy Scripture, **Writ Divine**[2],
> Leather-bound at **one and nine**[3].
> Satan trembles when he sees
> Bibles sold as cheap as these.

Well, we always thought the Good Book was a Good Buy!

Old Codgers, *The Daily Mirror*

FROM VERSE TO WORSE

Liberty belle
1 stuck with gum
2 great injustices
3 tired
4 attractive, charming
5 girl (slightly old-fashioned)

Divine write!
1 simple poetry
2 Holy Writ, the Bible
3 1 shilling 9 pence in old money, 9 pence approximately in new money

ADS
1 *Br* sweets
2 covered with chocolate
3 easy to chew
4 sweets in the shape of a cylinder or ball
5 brand-name of a gun
6 beer
7 a soft, partially transparent, semisolid food usu made of fruit juice and sugar (by Kraft)
8 fruit which has been preserved (by Kraft)
9 *coll* grandmother's
10 *Br* petrol

Discussion

1 If advertising is so powerful, is it wrong that we are subjected to so much of it? Should there be some controls?
2 What effect does advertising have on you? Does it tell you about products, or does it persuade you to buy? Are you sure?
3 What evidence can you find to support Baudrillard's observation that men's daily interaction has 'less to do with their fellow men than with receiving and manipulating goods and messages'?
4 Baudrillard and Wrighter both claim that we are far less free than we think we are. Do you think you are free? What do you think freedom is?
5 Why do people continue to want large cars, even in an energy crisis? Are they demonstrating their freedom of choice? Or are they unable to avoid the temptation of being one better than their neighbour?

Word Study

A   Semantic Fields

1 Things sold and/or bought

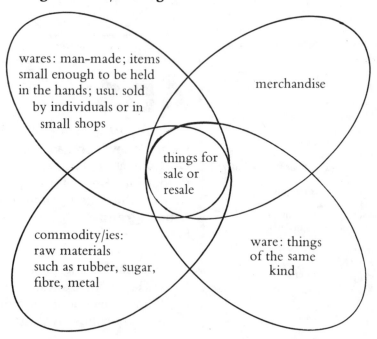

wares: man-made; items small enough to be held in the hands; usu. sold by individuals or in small shops

merchandise

things for sale or resale

commodity/ies: raw materials such as rubber, sugar, fibre, metal

ware: things of the same kind

In this sense, **goods** never appears in the singular and cannot take a numeral as a modifier; **merchandise** does not form a plural, **ware**, in the singular, is always part of a compound, and **commodity** may be singular or plural.

EXAMPLES

goods The **goods** that they have on display are far inferior to those I have seen in other shops.

merchandise We regret to inform you that the **goods/merchandise** that you delivered to our factory last Thursday are faulty.

The store is expanding and hopes to be able to offer a larger range of **merchandise** in the near future.

wares A travelling salesman sells his **wares** from door to door. Every stall holder tries to display his **wares** to better advantage than the one next to him.

commodity The rising price of coffee makes it a much sought after **commodity**.

Developing countries are now demanding higher prices on the world market for the **commodities** they produce.

Goods and **ware** often appear in set phrases or compounds.

household goods: eg pots and pans, china, plastic bowls

consumer goods: eg washing machines, record players, cars, cameras

leather goods: eg gloves, handbags, suitcases

perishable goods: things that can decay, eg food

hardware: eg tools, nails, screws, locks, keys, paint, wood

silverware: items made of silver used in the house, eg knives and forks, teapots

glassware

ironware

2 Shops

shop			
chain-store	general stores	department store	supermarket

The words are distinguished by the following features:

chain-store [+one of many] [+owned by the same company]

general stores [+ usu small] [+ selling a wide range of goods], often found in villages;

department store [+large] [+divided into sections according to the type of merchandise] [+selling a wide range of goods]

supermarket [+selfservice] [+selling mostly food]

Open fronted structures from which things are sold

kiosk often found in parks, streets and railway-stations for the sale of newspapers, sweets, cigarettes

stand usu at trade exhibitions for displaying or selling merchandise or giving information; also used in the compound **news-stand**

stall usu moveable, sometimes just a table found in markets, streets, railway-stations; often used in compounds eg **book-stall, flower-stall, antique-stall**

3 Helping to move forward

	make progress _or_	contribute to progress of sth or sb	by giving higher rank, station, or position _or_	by publicising _or_	by giving financial or other support	stresses the movement forward	stresses the effort involved
advance	+	+				+	
further		+					+
promote		+	+	+	+		

All the verbs are transitive and **advance** may also be intransitive.

EXAMPLE

Our understanding of the brain has **advanced** very rapidly in the last ten years.

Since they have no intransitive sense, **further** and **promote** occur frequently in the passive.

EXAMPLES

Our interests have not been **furthered** by the recent bad publicity we have received.

She has been **promoted** twice this year, and is now head of the department.

	scientific knowledge	human understanding	psychological research	one's interests	economic recovery	a cause	a project	sb's plans	the cause of freedom	good relations between two countries	good will between our two parties	a worker to a higher position	sb to the rank of general	a new product	the sale of sth
advance	+	+	+	+	+	+			+						
further	+	+	+	+	+	+	+	+	+						
promote				+	+				+	+	+	+	+	+	+

4 Being surprised

	because unexpected	because difficult to believe	so as to cause confusion	affect with wonder — so as to leave one helpless to act or think
surprise	+			
astonish		+		
amaze			+	
astound				+
flabbergast				+

These verbs are most common in their participial forms.
In the **-ed** form, they can all be followed by a **to** infinitive or the preposition **at**. They can also take a **that** clause.

They differ in the degree of wonderment implied:

least   greatest

←———————————————————————————————→

surprise   astonish   amaze   astound   flabbergast

	surprised	astonished	amazed	astounded	flabbergasted	
I was	+					to receive so many presents on my birthday.
She was clearly	+					at our sudden arrival.
I am	+					that you can't speak English. It's so useful.
Everybody was	+	+				that our best student didn't get the job.
I was		+				at his overt preference for attractive female students.
We were		+				to see a girl piloting the plane.
We were		+	+			at the two-year-old's ability to sing.
The tropical Islanders were		+				to see snow the first time they came to Europe.
You shouldn't be	+		+			that I am leaving home; after all, I am 25 years old.
I am	+			+		that my otherwise conscientious secretary offered no explanation for her failure to do this work.
Even the professor was				+		at the result of the experiment.
Her parents were				+	+	to learn that their shy little Lucy had robbed a bank and blown up a railway line.
I was					+	to hear that my grandparents had sold their house and gone round the world.
I was					+	at the committee's decision to close the psychology department.

5 Smiling and laughing

	smile	laugh	broadly	in an affected or conceited manner	often at sb else's misfortune	nervously or	in a silly way	with a low-pitched sound	as if to oneself	of short duration
grin	+		+							
smirk	+			+	+					
giggle		+				+	+			
chuckle		+						+	+	+

All the verbs can be used either transitively or intransitively and all collocate with the preposition **at**.

EXAMPLES

grin   I knew he had good news as soon as I saw how he was **grinning** at me.

smirk   He could not help **smirking** when he was told how few votes his opponent had received.

giggle   The girl **giggled** nervously to cover her embarrassment.

chuckle   I must say **I chuckled** to myself as I remembered how silly we both looked when we went swimming and those monkeys stole our clothes!

6 Being rich

rich	wealthy	affluent	opulent

Rich and **wealthy** are synonymous when referring to material possessions and money, but **rich** seems to be more common. In its extended sense, **rich** often includes the features [+full of nutritious or choice ingredients] or [+having an abundance of good constituents] or [+deep or full]. **Affluent** often implies [+spending a lot]; **opulent** means [+displaying great riches] and usually refers to the external signs of being rich.

	residence	mansion	house	furniture	car	gift	style	existence	society	family	man	banker	country	food	cake	tones	voice
rich									+	+	+	+	+	+	+	+	
wealthy									+	+	+						
affluent									+	+	+						
opulent	+	+	+	+	+	+	+	+									

The adjectives or corresponding nouns are quite common in the following expressions: **to grow rich**, **to become rich**, **to get rich** (*coll*), **to acquire great wealth** (*more formal*), **to live in great opulence**. **To acquire great wealth** suggests the wealth is the result of eg large-scale business enterprises.

7 Being insufficient, inadequate or thinly distributed

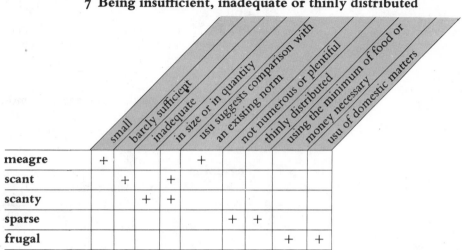

	small	barely sufficient	inadequate	in size or in quantity	usu suggests comparison with an existing norm	not numerous or plentiful	thinly distributed	using the minimum of food or money necessary	usu of domestic matters
meagre	+				+				
scant		+		+					
scanty			+	+					
sparse						+	+		
frugal								+	+

Scant is not normally used predicatively.

EXAMPLES

meagre   The country suffers economically from its very **meagre** natural resources.

People are discouraged by having to work so hard for such **meagre** salaries.

scant   From your poor performance in the test it is quite evident that you were paying **scant** attention to what was being said in the lesson.

A **scant** 50% of the population turned out to vote.

scanty   A girl whose ample figure was scarcely concealed by her **scanty** bathing suit caused a great stir on the beach.

The claims being made for the success of this drug are really based on the most **scanty** evidence.

sparse   We felt his conviction was unfair because the evidence against him was so **sparse**.

We saw in front of us a flat plain whose uniformity was broken only by a **sparse** covering of vegetation.

frugal   A **frugal** meal of bread and apples was all they could afford.

He seems to prefer a **frugal** existence, isolated from people and comforts.

B Synonymous Pairs

1 **trick**
gimmick   [+in selling situations] [+for publicity purposes] [+often derogatory]

Gimmick is not used in formal style.

EXAMPLES
To claim that these chocolates actually make you thinner is nothing but an absurd sales **gimmick**.
Their latest **gimmick** to promote the sale of fresh vegetables is to give a bunch of flowers to each customer who buys at least two different kinds.

2 **doll**
  puppet | [+ moved by strings or by hand inside] [+ used in shows] ⇒ [+ person] [+ whose acts are completely controlled by another]

EXAMPLES
The children watching the puppet show almost believed the **puppets** were alive.
The so-called head of state is nothing but a **puppet** in the hands of the army.

3 **beginning**
  onset | [+ of things not wanted]

	a journey	a long lasting friendship	spring	winter	hostilities	an argument	the disease
beginning of	+	+	+	+	+	+	
onset				+	+	+	+

4 **piece**
  slice | [+ flat]

EXAMPLE
Please cut the meat into thin **slices**.

5 **simple** ⎰ [+ without luxury or ornament] ⎱
  austere   or [+ imposing lack of luxury] or [+ imposing strict moral standards]

	diet	man	way of life	room	conditions	upbringing	treatment	regime
simple	+	+	+	+				
austere		+	+	+	+	+	+	+

6 **intentional**
  deliberate | [+ result of consideration]

Deliberate is usually used attributively, whereas **intentional** is preferred as a predicate.
Compare:

a **deliberate** ⎰ lie / attempt / insult / deception ⎱

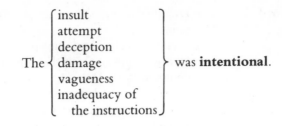

The
{
insult
attempt
deception
damage
vagueness
inadequacy of
the instructions
}
was **intentional**.

Exercises

1 How would you explain the following?

1 It fell flat on its face.   2 Play it straight!   3 The product went through the roof.   4 You must be kidding!   5 What is the punch line of the story?   6 The ad went on the air.   7 Try to get the most out of it.   8 That's far-fetched.   9 We had to fall back on this method.

2 What is the use of the following?

1 a commercial   2 hoarding   3 nappy   4 skin conditioner   5 mascara   6 eye-shadow   7 nail varnish   8 puppet

3 Give the opposite of the following:

1 tiny   2 hard   3 humid   4 slow down   5 negligible   6 abundance   7 wake up   8 cheap   9 superior   10 responsible

4 In each case provide three or four nouns that can collocate with the following adjectives:

1 daily   2 emotional   3 deliberate   4 drastic   5 legitimate   6 insignificant   7 top-quality   8 frugal   9 vivid   10 spectacular   11 sparkling   12 stimulating

5 What nouns can be derived from the following words?

1 to save   2 to constrain   3 to prefer   4 to condition   5 to promote   6 to abound   7 to resist   8 true   9 wise   10 scarce

6 What differences/similarities are there between the following pairs?

1 to haunt/to follow   2 to roam/to walk   3 to flop down/to sit down   4 to wake up/to get up   5 to mark up/to raise   6 a consumer/a user   7 middle class/working class   8 an ad/a poster   9 meagre/scanty   10 straight/direct

7 Complete the following sentences:

1 He couldn't even . . . . . a cow from a horse.
2 They were bored to . . . . . .
3 I . . . . . £10 that he's wrong.
4 They will never . . . . . rich.
5 The prices . . . . . from £1 to £50.
6 I don't . . . . . your argument.
7 The desk will . . . . . too much space.
8 I don't know how they have . . . . . such great wealth.
9 As a . . . . . of fact, you are right.
10 Try to make the . . . . . of it.

8 Guess the right word.

1 Despite its v . . . . . colours, the painting remained lifeless and uninteresting.
2 A taxi screeched by in hot p . . . . . of the car in front.
3 Her neat appearance is the result of choosing s . . . ., well designed clothes.
4 Having once had chicken-pox, one is i . . . . . to it for life.
5 The cost of shipping raw materials and other c . . . . . from their country of origin to Europe is rising at an alarming rate.
6 All the g . . . . . for sale in this store have been tested by our quality department.
7 The s . . . . . on which we laid out our wares was made of wood.
8 Having had a poor childhood, he remained a f . . . . . man despite his new wealth.
9 We could tell he was speaking the p . . . . . truth.
10 The children were completely am . . . . . by all that they'd seen at the circus.

9 What verbs are derivationally related to the following?

1 body   2 reception   3 response   4 fright   5 persuasion
6 investment   7 drought   8 usage   9 wrapping   10 device

10 Give a few examples of:

1 commodities   2 consumer goods   3 leather goods   4 hardware
5 silverware   6 ironware

11 In each case provide a few adjectives or nouns which can collocate with the following:

1 a(n) . . . . . style   2 a(n) . . . . . skin   3 a(n) . . . . . brand
4 . . . . . art   5 a(n) . . . . . nail polish   6 a(n) . . . . . experience
7 a(n) . . . . . recovery   8 a(n) . . . . . story   9 a(n) . . . . . trick
10 a(n) . . . . . reaction

12 What differences and/or similarities are there between the following:

1 to laugh/to smile   2 to answer/to respond   3 to wrap/to pack
4 to grin/to smirk   5 to giggle/to chuckle   6 kiosk/stall/stand
7 shelf/board   8 trick/gimmick   9 purchase/bargain
10 beginning/onset   11 scant/scanty   12 affluent/opulent
13 big/huge   14 scanty/frugal

13 Choose the word that best fits the context. Modify its form where necessary.

1 The magician's next . . . . . was to produce a rabbit from his ear. (gimmick, device, trick)
2 The house looked . . . . . in the falling evening light. (strict, severe, austere)
3 Because of its abundance of consumer products, Western society is known as the . . . . . society. (opulent, wealthy, affluent)
4 The Palace offered a variety of . . . . . riches: Persian rugs, marble tables, etc. (wealthy, opulent, affluent)
5 In London you'll see tramps . . . . . the streets, looking for something or looking for nothing. (roam, walk, go)
6 His . . . . . was loud and very infectious. (smile, laugh, giggle)
7 There was a . . . . . of welcome on her lips. (laugh, giggle, smile)
8 Everyday he would take a . . . . . after lunch before returning to the office. (sleep, nap)

9 They say our . . . . . is written in the stars! (destination, destiny)
10 The . . . . . of the play was warmly applauded by the audience. (manufacturer, producer)

14 Look at the sample advertising slogans and analyse what each one is trying to make us believe.

Most of these advertising slogans either tell us nothing useful about the product, or claim something which cannot possibly be true. Explain how this is done.

You may like to make a collection of advertisements yourselves and analyse them in the same way.

Revision Exercises

R1 What can cause or lead to the following?

1 retaliation   2 a rebuff   3 boredom   4 the extinction of a species   5 competition   6 promotion to a higher position
7 use of crutches   8 pecking   9 malnutrition   10 smog
11 famine   12 genetic mutations

R2 What adjectives are derivationally related to the following?

1 opulence   2 day   3 knowledge   4 potency   5 response
6 fact   7 cost   8 consciousness   9 austerity   10 infant
11 analogy   12 line   13 gene   14 vanity   15 pride   16 touch
17 hazard   18 restriction   19 fertility   20 assertion   21 grime
22 affluence

R3 Fill in the following collocational grids:

1

	a bill	the horizon	sb's entry permit	the records	a patient	sb's statement	the meaning in the dictionary	the headlines in the morning papers	sb's chest	a building for fire hazards	a school
check											
inspect											
scrutinize											
examine											
scan											

2

	sb's offer	sb's attention	sb permission	an invitation	a request	a lover
spurn						
decline						
refuse						

R4 Guess the right word.

1 His view through the window was m . . . . . by condensation on the glass.
2 The radio f . . . . . good weather today.
3 I managed to b . . . . . the police and thus make my escape.
4 My cough was cured by an e . . . . . remedy suggested by my mother.
5 Walking past the wooden fence he g . . . . . through one of its cracks a girl on the other side.
6 'You must c . . . . . your clothes, you can't go like that!'
7 They dropped food into the water to l . . . . . the fish to a place where they could easily be netted.
8 It was a r . . . . . decision, but as it turned out, the right one.
9 What a c . . . . . when the house burnt down and we were not insured against fire!
10 One of the most difficult things is to e . . . . . one's own performance by comparison with others'.
11 His foot s . . . . . on the top step and he fell down the staircase.
12 The horse t . . . . . around the field.

R5 Match appropriate features with each of the following words:

1 generate 2 plight 3 infer 4 conceit 5 wig 6 date
7 task 8 grimy 9 rate 10 self-esteem 11 bump into

[+justified] [+covering of hair] [+meet] [+appointment]
[+energy, force] [+usu assigned] [+count up the worth of]
[+bad situation] [+dirt covering surface] [+by imaginative
deduction from given information] [+good opinion] [+of oneself
or what one has done] [+piece of work] [+form an opinion about]
[+by placing or as if by placing on a numerical scale]
[+exaggerated] [+artificial] [+accidentally] [+with a member of
the opposite sex]

R6 Match words from list a with as many words/ expressions from list b as possible. Words from list a may be used more than once.

a 1 forestall 2 assess 3 grimy 4 value 5 pretty 6 generate
7 handsome 8 grubby 9 ghastly 10 overt 11 lucrative
12 injure 13 harm 14 damage 15 hurt

b 1 lecture 2 money 3 face 4 view 5 present 6 flower
7 hatred 8 dinner party 9 house 10 clothes 11 man
12 electricity 13 proposal 14 occupation 15 the importance
of sth 16 sb's ability 17 sb as a leader 18 sb's action
19 sb's reputation 20 an attempt 21 sb's feelings

R7 Choose the word that best fits the context. Modify its form where necessary.

1 She turned out to be a most . . . . . secretary. (effective, efficacious, efficient)
2 They were . . . . . cousins on her mother's side of the family. (distant, remote, far away)
3 He put forward such . . . . . arguments that we had to agree with him. (right, relevant, valid)
4 She provided me with the . . . . . details, and I duly made out my report. (valid, relevant, right)
5 His grocer's shop is . . . . . nicely now that the supermarket has closed down. (flourishing, blooming)

6 We tried to . . . . . the level of petrol in the tank. (evaluate, assess, gauge)

7 We based our survey on a . . . . . selection of people. (unplanned, random, unsystematic)

8 She . . . . . with wonder for what seemed like minutes at the view before her. (glimpse, glance, gaze)

9 We all have . . . . . instincts within us. (devastating, damaging, destructive)

10 A man was . . . . . to death by the crowds of people fleeing from the burning department store. (trample, tread, walk)

11 Her behaviour began well, but . . . . . as her visit grew longer. (decline, deteriorate, worsen)

12 The effect of the earthquake was . . . . ., not a single house remained standing. (destructive, devastating, damaging)

R8 Find words to fit the following definitions/descriptions:

1 sand, mud, etc carried by moving water and left, eg at the mouth of a river

2 self-satisfaction; not seeing need for action

3 the act of splitting or breaking apart the nucleus of a radioactive atom leading to the release of energy

4 responsibility for a possible or actual loss, damage, etc

5 be present in large numbers, esp so as to render unpleasant or unsafe

6 opposed in character; unable to exist in harmony

7 look closely, as if unable to see well

8 rapid multiplication, reproduction

9 existing as a natural and permanent part or quality of

10 unreal sense of well-being

11 chemical substance that removes dirt

12 sit on the heels with the knees bent

R9 Complete the story with appropriate words from the list below, modifying their form where necessary. Notice that not all of the words mentioned are relevant.

shoddy, arid, plaintive, distant, remote, sad, pernicious, harmful, achieve, gain, accomplish, reach, attain, sever, squat, cut, ruffle, retaliate, munch, chew, look at, glance, glimpse, peer, decline, turn down, reject, spurn, shake, tremble, quake, shiver, shudder, examine, scan, check, scrutinize, antics

Desperately tired, he nevertheless managed to 1 . . . . . the river and after regaining his breath, slid into the water. Swimming weakly, he at last 2 . . . . . the opposite bank. Looking back at the outline of the 3 . . . . . town, he told himself he had at least 4 . . . . . the first part of his plan.

To 5 . . . . . what he had in mind meant, he knew, 6 . . . . . a peak of personal endurance he had never yet experienced. He breathed deeply, doing his utmost to expel the last traces of that 7 . . . . ., no, 8 . . . . . gas that had killed all except himself. His 9 . . . . . clothes looked even worse after the swim and he realised he'd have to dry them as quickly as possible. Looking round, he found the perfect hide-out behind some bushes, and here he undressed and laid his clothes out till they were dry. He 10 . . . . . on his heels for some

moments, then lay down on the warm soil. He 11 . . . . . his hair
which had matted somewhat from the swim. High above him he
heard the 12 . . . . . call of the seagulls which reminded him of the
cries he had heard the previous night in the town. He 13 . . . . . at
the thought of what had happened there, and a 14 . . . . . went up
and down his spine. The day must come for them to 15 . . . . ., to
16 . . . . . these quasi-diplomatic relations that had previously
existed. They would 17 . . . . . the enemy, as a dog 18 . . . . . a rat,
and he, the enemy would 19 . . . . . in his boots. . . .

He 20 . . . . . short-sightedly into the distance and all he saw was a
distant windmill; he let his gaze cover the flat land between, but all
was silent. He 21 . . . . . a rabbit, and had to laugh at its 22 . . . . .
as it disappeared chasing another rabbit. He 23 . . . . . his last carrot
before getting ready to go. Finally he stood up, 24 . . . . . the
thought of new dangers ahead of him, and 25 . . . . . the immediate
vicinity. Then he began walking towards the distant windmill,
26 . . . . . every bush that he passed. His military training had taught
him to 27 . . . . . and 28 . . . . . again, every move he took. To
29 . . . . . the advice they had pumped into him before he had begun
this mission would have been folly of the highest order. Oddly, he
could not remember ever having 30 . . . . . sound advice in his life.

Unit 5   **All in the family**

Family: New breed v. the old

In *The Greening of America*, Charles Reich offered the **giddy**[1] prediction that the values of the 1960s **counter-culture**[2] would remake America. Although his thesis was vastly **over-stated**[3], those values are indeed becoming widespread.

Last week the results of a poll by Daniel Yankelovich indicated that this **shift**[4] in values 'seems to be reshaping the nature of the American family and its child-**rearing**[5] practices'.

The study, *The American Family Report: Raising Children in a Changing Society*, was based on a probability sampling of 1,230 households with one or more children under 13. It found that 43% of the parents belong to the 'New **Breed**'[6]. They stress freedom over authority, self-fulfillment over material success, and duty to self over duty to others – including their own children. The study found that New Breed parents are loving but self-oriented, and they take a **laissez-faire**[7] attitude to their own child rearing. Says Yankelovich: 'It's not the **permissiveness**[8] of the '50s, which was child-centered and concerned with the **fragility**[9] of the child. Today, the parent says in effect, "I want to be free, so why shouldn't my children be free?"'

Yankelovich sees 'the gradual evolution of a new implied contract between parents and their children'. In his view, Traditionalists – the 57% of parents committed to stricter child rearing and older American values – implicitly say

"It is so important for our children to grow up without complexes."

FAMILY: NEW BREED vs. THE OLD

1 dizzy, having the feeling that everything is turning around
2 culture opposed to traditional, prevailing culture
3 exaggerated
4 change
5 raising, bringing up young
6 race
7 *French* the policy of interfering as little as possible or not at all
8 the state of allowing freedom
9 the quality of being easily harmed or damaged

to their children, 'We will sacrifice for you and be repaid by your success and sense of obligation'. The New Breed message: 'We will not sacrifice for you, because we have our own lives to lead. But when you are grown, you owe us nothing.'

HEAVY STRAIN.[10] Yet the New Breed feel the **tug**[11] of old values and Traditionalists feel the pull of the new. The study reports that Traditionalists are less willing to make sacrifices for their children than their parents were. Moreover, Traditionalists generally agree with New Breeders (though by a smaller majority) that unhappy parents should not remain married simply for the sake of the children.

One significant finding is that New Breed parents are so uncertain about their new values that they **set aside**[12] their own beliefs when teaching their children. For example, only 13% of all parents firmly believe that 'people in authority know best', but 69% want to teach the principle to their young. Reports the study: 'The children of the New Breed are being taught patriotism, the importance of saving, the need for hard work, respect for authority and that having sex outside marriage is morally wrong, all of which their parents no longer believe themselves.' Some other findings:

• Single parents (11% of the total) are more insecure about child rearing. Their children seem more unhappy: they get along less well with other boys and girls, and complain more about their parents than other children do.
• Belief in traditional sex roles is **eroding**[13] but a **slim**[14] majority (52%) still feel that boys and girls should be raised differently.
• Most parents (82%) believe that mothers of small children should not work outside the home unless necessary for economic reasons, but three-quarters of their children (aged 6 to 12) see nothing wrong with mothers taking jobs.
• A majority of parents are dubious about the care in **day-care centers**[15], and **esteem**[16] for **elementary schools**[17] is low. Four out of ten parents do not believe that schools can be counted on to teach reading and writing.

Though nine out of ten parents in the survey say they would choose to have children if they had it to do again, Yankelovich reports that they are generally **plagued**[18] with doubts and under heavy strain because of changing attitudes. Says he: 'It's clear that the new values and the old have not yet found a synthesis.'

Time

10 nervous tiredness, emotional pressure
11 influence, *lit* pull
12 put aside, forget about
13 wearing out, diminishing, become less
14 small, thin
15 nurseries which look after children during day while parents work
16 high regard, favourable opinion
17 *Br* primary schools
18 worried, annoyed, troubled

Family

A mother (or father) says: 'I wanted to give my children what I didn't have myself as a child.' The **upshot**[1] is that she exhausts herself in the effort, becomes envious of her own child, and ends up **withdrawing**[2] and giving her child even less than her parents had given her.

The moral: consider yourself lucky if you take as good care of your children as your parents have of you. You might even do a little better, provided you don't aim too high.

Childhood

In the United States today there is a **pervasive**[1] tendency to treat children like adults, and adults like children. We speak of infantilizing adults, and call their childish behavior infantilism. We should recognize the counterpart of this pattern: causing children to behave in an adult-like fashion, which results in 'adulticism'. The options of children are steadily expanded, while those of adults are progressively **constricted**[2].

In short, we treat fewer and fewer people as they really are. By **allegedly**[3] protecting children from the **evils**[4] of authoritarianism, and adults from the evils of competition, we define and maintain control over them, while claiming that we are helping them.

Thomas Szasz, *The Second Sin*

FAMILY

1 result, outcome
2 pull or draw back

CHILDHOOD

1 widespread, and with a tendency to increase
2 limited, restrained
3 supposedly, claiming that one is
4 bad aspects, drawbacks, sins

Spare the rod but don't spoil the child's life if you truly care

Growing up is easier when there are guidelines to follow.

SPARE THE ROD

1 put under pressure to do something, *lit* to extract money from somebody by threatening to make public damaging information
2 *coll* children
3 ask in a humble way
4 persuaded usu by flattery
5 children
6 *informal* people
7 the level of awareness of life attained by adults
8 *coll* regular
9 deal with, manage, understand
10 complained in a sullen, bad-tempered way
11 polite, well-behaved
12 ability to keep material things neat and in order
13 politeness
14 *coll* avoid by using tricks or by cunning
15 disagreeable routine jobs in the house
16 purchase by instalments, (a number of sums of money to be paid at intervals)
17 traps, unexpected dangers
18 not by instalments, at once, right away
19 calmness of mind
20 a long, straight, thin piece of wood or metal, a stick used for punishment

When you read about crowds of teen-agers waiting all night at an airport to welcome pop-stars home, or about the increasing numbers of all-night parties frequented by young folk, don't you wonder why parents allow this behaviour?

Many of these boys and girls **blackmail**[1] by declaring: 'I'll run away if I can't go', or 'All the other parents let their **kids**[2] go.' Others **beg**[3]: 'Let me go this once, Mother,' so you're tempted to abandon your principles temporarily. Next time, you're **cajoled**[4]: 'You allowed me to go last week' – so you weaken again.

'I can always tell which youngsters have no discipline at home,' said a schoolmaster. 'These children don't want to obey our rules either, so are frequently in trouble.'

Many parents expect to be regarded as friends and contemporaries by their **offspring**[5], but young **folk**[6] prefer authoritative parents. One 15-year-old girl said: 'I don't know what's right; often I wish my people would tell me what time to come in at night, instead of simply moaning when I'm late.'

School-children now comparatively few years of carefree happiness. Forced to **adult-awareness**[7] before their time, by continual sex-propaganda from television, films, records and magazines, they are anxious to find a '**steady**'[8] boy or girl-friend.

Numbers of girls are marrying at 16 or 17, sacrificing the wonderful early years by accepting the heavy responsibilities of grown-ups too soon. One girl told me: 'I was too young to know my own mind . . .'

The youngsters are often not sufficiently mature or experienced **to cope with**[9] personal relationships, while financial problems can destroy young love rapidly.

Parents should encourage their children to entertain their friends at home sometimes, but they should also be taught to respect the neighbours and other members of their own family.

A friend **grumbled**[10] recently: 'My children will never come for meals when they're called' – but this was her fault. Had she taught them to be **well-mannered**[11] during their early childhood?

Parents must insist on punctuality, **tidiness**[12], and **courtesy**[13] from their children; for if they are not polite at home, why should they act differently outside?

Should we grant permission lightly for our young daughters to holiday alone with their boyfriend? Why are we afraid to say 'No'? Are we wise to permit our children to '**dodge**'[14] all the **household chores**[15]? They gain experience by tackling jobs in the home.

If a teenager suggests: 'I'm going to buy a stereogram on **hire-purchase**,'[16] why doesn't his father act firmly and refuse to sign the agreement? Far better to explain the **pitfalls**[17] of the system, then advise the youngster to wait and save up his money to buy the article **outright**[18].

With diminishing parental control, many of our youngsters are reaching maturity without learning the hard lessons of life. And having had their own way too often, they are unable and unwilling to accept with **equanimity**[19] the inevitable reverses in later life.

Though we spare the **rod**[20] nowadays, don't let us spoil the child.

The Universe

Is your child a bully?

Tom Crabtree tells you how to cope with the problem

IS YOUR CHILD A BULLY?

1 one who uses his strength to frighten or hurt those who are not so strong
2 annoyed, teased, bullied
3 insist on his rights, put himself forward and try to be important
4 cunning, artful (as crafty as a fox)
5 card with easily recognisable word, symbol, or letter on it, often used to teach word recognition
6 colour filled pen with soft tip
7 preference, liking

Tony was eight, and a **bully**[1]. He **picked on**[2] other children in the playground, spoilt their games and, sometimes, hit them. He was a big boy, and the other children were afraid of him. His mother wouldn't believe me when I told her about Tony's behaviour at school. 'He's such a good boy at home,' she said.

What made Tony into the playground menace? There were two reasons for his behaviour: one to do with school, and the other concerning his home.

At school, Tony could hardly read; his reading age was at the six year level. He felt ashamed and very frustrated about his lack of reading skills – particularly since most of the children he knew were better readers than he was. Tony was compensating for his own inadequacy by using physical strength to **assert himself**[3], this was to make him look big when, inside himself, he felt small.

Tony was frustrated at home, as well as at school. He had an older brother, Patrick, who teased him by taking away his comics and toys and generally making his life a misery. When I asked their mother what she did about Patrick's behaviour she said: 'It annoys me so much, I just lose my temper and hit him.'

By using physical punishment to stop Patrick's victimisation of Tony, she was really sending out a message, loud and clear, to both boys: it's all right to be a bully, but make sure you're bigger than anyone else.

Tony was in a perfect learning situation to become poor, quiet Tony at home (where he was the little innocent) and Tony the

menace in school where his real feelings of desperation expressed themselves. He had become two different personalities.

So how was Tony helped? First, he was given extra reading lessons and extra attention in school. He was made responsible for ringing the bell at break time, and for looking after the Nature Table in the classroom. The headmistress, **crafty**[4] soul, made him a 'playground monitor' with the duties of seeing that none of the smaller children were knocked about at playtime. 'I'm relying on you,' she told him. He was given responsibility.

He was also chosen to act the part of Goliath in the school play. The script was altered so that Goliath came over as very strong, but very kind. 'You are a soldier, but you're very gentle,' the headmistress told Tony. Tony was very good in the play, and he began to get the new message: it's possible to be strong without being a bully.

Tony soon learned to read. I made a book for him about giants, and Father Christmas, and a schoolboy hero called – you've guessed – Tony. He made up some of the story himself and I taught him to recognise and build up the words as he went along, using large **flashcards**[5] and **felt-tip pens**[6].

Tony never bullied again. I suspect that his mother was too indulgent towards both boys, and that to be given some responsibility and some self respect was all that was needed to cure Tony's **predilection**[7] for hitting smaller children.

Family Circle

A new approach

I am an adopted child and I welcome the new law that permits children to trace their natural parents. But, after years of wondering about my own, I have decided not to trace them. I thought of how my natural mother would feel if a 32-year-old bad memory **turned up**[1] on her **doorstep**[2]. I have nothing but thanks for her giving me life, I just pray that she's forgiven herself for what must have been, in 1944, a social disgrace. Would it be an idea for leading adoption societies to publish a newsletter listing details of children and parents who wish to find each other?
– Mrs W T, Dorset.

Woman

A NEW APPROACH
1 showed up, appeared
2 step up to the door of a building

Trouble in the family
BY THE **DOC**[1]

I bumped into young Fiona the other day – not her usual cheerful self, by any means.

'Just walked down the road with my dad,' she said **ruefully**[2]. 'And, as usual, we fought all the way.'

Well, I've news for Fiona, and her dad.

Nothing is more natural.

Indeed, I'd go so far as to say if there are NO tensions in a family, something is wrong!

It's a sign they either don't care enough, or they're building up pressure that will eventually explode.

Oh, I know there's nothing more **exasperating**[3] for a mother than to see her teenage boy **at loggerheads with**[4] Dad.

It's as bad for Dad to see a teenage girl seemingly unable **to hit it off with**[5] her mother.

It may comfort them to know teenage rebellion is a sign of normality, not a sign they've failed as parents.

Changing standards always lead to family tension, too.

I honestly don't think we can expect youngsters **to stick to the rules**[6] our parents set for us.

TROUBLE IN THE FAMILY

1   *coll abbr* doctor
2   regretfully
3   irritating, producing ill-feeling
4   *coll* disagreeing or quarrelling with
5   *coll* get on well
6   *coll* respect the rules
7   to stop retreating, to stop giving in
8   to give in, to make concessions
9   shutting violently, banging
10 outside school
11 all the fixed forms connected with an activity or ceremony
12 people
13 suppose, think
14 end
15 cure, medicine
16 lessening, removing
17 quarrel, fight
18 advantage
19 quarrelling about unimportant things

Oh, yes, up to about the age of 12, you can impose your standards.

After that, wise parents know when **to make a stand**[7], and when **to give way**[8].

But nothing is more likely to send a teenager **slamming**[9] out of the door than a parent who says, 'In my young days . . .'

Mind you, modern life has its part to play in family tensions.

Families don't talk nearly so much as they used to. If someone tries, the rest say, 'Sssshhh – we can't hear the TV!'

Oddly enough, all these **extramural**[10] activities at school, &c., tend to rob family life of some of its togetherness.

Visits to concerts, swimming baths, and so on, were once family things. Now, more and more, our leisure is organised for us.

The Sunday afternoon walk used to be **a ritual**[11] with many a family.

That hour, when a family had time to take their time, to talk over their problems, to meet other **folk**[12] who were also out as families.

I **reckon**[13] it did more than we'll ever realise to **dissolve**[14] tensions.

D'you know one of the best **remedies**[15] for coping with family tension?

Two words. 'I'm sorry.'

It's amazing how hard some folk find them to say. They think it implies weakness or defeat.

Nothing of the kind. Exactly the opposite, in fact.

Another good way of **relieving**[16] tension is a **row**[17]!

The sea's ever so much calmer after a storm.

But a row has another **bonus**[18]. When tempers are raised, unspoken truths usually come out.

They may hurt a bit, especially at the time. Yet, at the end, you know each other a bit better – and that can't be bad.

But beware of insults simply said to hurt. That only makes matters worse.

Lastly, most of the tensions and **bickering**[19] between children are natural.

Even when they seem to be constant, wise parents don't worry overmuch about it.

P.S. – Surprisingly, money is not nearly as often at the root of family tensions as you'd imagine.

Emotional need is a far greater source of trouble than financial need.

The Sunday Post

Discussion

1 In retrospect do you think your parents brought you up well?
For which things are you particularly grateful to them? Which
things do you wish they had done differently? Are you going to
bring up your children in the same way?

2 Did your parents 'sacrifice' to bring you up? Do you feel you
owe them something? If so, how do you 'pay' the debt you
have?

3 Why do couples choose to have children? Or perhaps they don't
choose, it just happens without their thinking too much about it?
If you haven't got children, would you like to have some, and if
you have, are you glad you have them? Why?

4 What is the importance of the family unit in society? Do you see
its existence as positive or negative (a) for you personally and
(b) for other people?

5 Argue for or against the following statements:
a Parents should not want to be regarded by their children as
their friends or equals.
b Children are being 'pushed' into adulthood too early.
c Small children should be spanked when naughty or
disobedient. This is the only form of punishment they
understand. It goes without saying that the rod should not be
spared.
d Youngsters have no respect for soft and lenient teachers.
e People who are knowledgeable in educational theory are often
the worst educators themselves. One educates by what one *is*,
not by what one knows and says.

Word Study

A Semantic Fields

1 Making Grow

rear	bring up	breed	grow

Notice that **rear** and **bring up** apply to [+animate] objects only;
rear is usually for animals and **bring up** for children. **Breed**
includes the feature [+reproduce] or [+cause to reproduce, esp by
selection of parents]; it is often used figuratively in the sense of
[+be cause of]. This sense can be illustrated by:
EXAMPLES
Dirt **breeds** disease.
Ignorance **breeds** prejudice.
Familiarity **breeds** contempt.
War **breeds** misery.
Slums are the **breeding-ground** of crime.

	a family	children	cattle	chickens	horses	germs	bacteria	vegetables	fruit	flowers	crops	a beard	one's hair
rear	+	(+)	+	+									
bring up	+	+											
breed			+	+	+	+	+						
grow								+	+	+	+	+	+

2 Keeping within limits

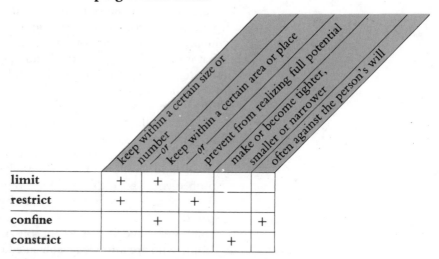

	keep within a certain size or number	keep within a certain area or place	prevent from realizing full potential	make or become tighter, smaller or narrower,	often against the person's will
limit	+	+			
restrict	+		+		
confine		+			+
constrict				+	

All these verbs are transitive and **constrict** is also intransitive. All, except **constrict**, occur in the construction **to . . . . . sb/sth to . . . . ..**

EXAMPLES

limit   We have **limited** our research to problems of vocabulary acquisition.

The number of books one may borrow has been **limited** to three at any one time.

restrict   I have so much reading to do that I have to **restrict** myself to two hours of language practice a day.

As a result of the boy's bad behaviour, his father **restricted** the number of occasions on which he was allowed to go out.

confine   I am **confined** to my bed until my temperature goes down.

Please **confine** your remarks to those which are immediately relevant to the matter in hand.

constrict   If you take this drug, your veins may **constrict**.

Given his temperament, he found that army life had a very **constricting** effect on him.

The sense of **limit** and **restrict** may alternatively be rendered by nominal expressions:

	limit	restriction(s)	
They decided to set a	+		of a maximum of 3 cars per person.
They placed a	+	+	on electricity consumption.
They have put a	+	+	on the amount of time you can talk on the telephone.
They placed		+	on the import of foreign wines.
A		+	has been placed on the import of foreign wines.

3 Complaining

	express discontent									
	non-verbally			verbally						
	by low-pitched wailing sounds	by high-pitched sounds	usu long-drawn out	usu without good reason	without being definite about subject	by continually repeating the complaint	about trivial things	usu in a high voice	expecting the person to whom one complains to do sth about the complaint	usu without any positive attempt to change the situation
complain									+	
bellyache				+		+				
grouse					+	+				
grumble						+				+
moan	+		+	+		+				
whine		+	+			+	+	+		

All the words, except **complain**, are colloquial or informal and express irritation with the complainer. That is why **bellyache**, **grouse**, **grumble**, **moan** and **whine** are usually said of others and not of oneself.

The following scale shows how formal and informal they are:

formal		informal	colloquial		slang

←───

complain	**complain**	**grumble**	**grouse**	**moan**	**bellyache**
		whine			

The verbs can all appear in the construction **to . . . . .** (**to sb**) **about sth.**

EXAMPLES

complain   I **complained** to the airline about the loss of my luggage but they couldn't help me.

bellyache   Don't **bellyache** to me because there's no food left – you are an hour late for supper.

She is always **bellyaching** about the house being untidy but she never does anything about it.

grouse   He is always **grousing** to everyone about how he is overworked and underpaid.

grumble   Don't **grumble** to me about the people next door – go and complain to them.

moan   Everybody is always **moaning** about the rising cost of living.

You are strict with the children, then they come **moaning** to me about it.

whine   'What's that noise?' 'The dogs are **whining** to come in.'

She came **whining** to me this afternoon that no-one sympathized with her and that she felt she did not fit in with the rest of the group.

4 Disturbing

	give sb no peace of mind	give oneself no peace of mind	cause anxiety	disturb physically	interrupt sb	provoke a reaction	by irritating actions	by making fun of	by making demands and requests	torment, as with continual attacks, persecutions, anxieties or misfortune	tire	by or as if by chasing	suggests persistence
worry	+	+	+	+									
bother	+	+			+								
tease						+	+	+					
get on at	+								+				
nag	+								+				+
pester			+	+					+				+
plague	+								+	+			+
harass										+	+		+
harry										+		+	+

All the verbs are transitive, and **worry**, **bother** and **nag** are also intransitive. **Bother**, **tease** and **nag** occur in the construction **to . . . . . sb about sth**; **worry** and **bother** may also be immediately followed by **about**. **Bother**, **pester**, **plague** and

harass can take the preposition **with**. **Get on at**, **nag** and **plague** are colloquial.

The verbs can be placed along the following scale:

slightly disturbing   very disturbing

←——————————————————————————————→

tease	**pester**	**nag**	**worry**	**plague**	**harass**
bother		**get on at**			**harry**

	worry(ied)	bother(ed)	tease(d)	get/got/getting on at	nag(ged)(ging)	pester(ed)(ing)	plague(d)	harass(ed)	harry(ied)(ing)	
The girl's mother	+									about her staying out late in the evening.
I am	+									about my weight.
Dogs which	+									sheep have to be shot.
Our boss has		+		+	+					us three times this afternoon about the same problem.
I thought I would go mad if she	+					+	+			me again with such stupid questions.
The landlord	+						+	+		his tenants continually until they were forced to move out.
The children	+		+	+	+	+				their father until he agreed to take them to the sea.
The Director has been				+	+	+		+		me for my progress report.
The refugees were								+		from one country to another.
My classmates			+							me about my new hairstyle.
When I first came to England, everybody			+							me about my accent.
My wife has been				+	+					me to buy her a new washing machine.
The class						+	+			me with questions about the forthcoming exam.
Since moving to this house we have been							+			by worries and problems.

5 Quarrelling

quarrel		
bicker	squabble	wrangle

	bicker	squabble	wrangle
over unimportant matters	+	+	
unreasonably and childishly		+	
angrily, noisily and heatedly			+

All the verbs can be used transitively and intransitively, and all occur in the construction **to . . . . . (with sb) about/over sth**. They are not used in formal style.

EXAMPLES

bicker   There is nothing worse than a couple who are really bored with each other and are constantly **bickering**.

squabble   The children are **squabbling** again about which television programme to watch.

They have **squabbled** with their next-door neighbours about who should trim the hedge between their two gardens.

wrangle   I do not see why we have to **wrangle** over every detail of the children's education.

6 Being quick-witted

	having or showing sound judgement	having or showing cleverness	having or showing secretive nature	suggests skill in deceiving	often suggests caution and/or subtlety
shrewd	+				
sly		+	+		
cunning		+	+		
crafty		+	+	+	

Notice that **crafty** is colloquial.

	judge of character	assessment of the situation	politician	diplomat	move	person	way of going about things	smile	nature	plot	trick
shrewd	+	+	+	+	+	+					
sly					+	+	+	+			
cunning				+	+	+	+	+	+		
crafty			+	+	+	+	+				+

7 Manifesting order

	manifesting order	(or) manifesting careful execution	(or) manifesting proper behaviour	order habitually maintained	pleasing to the eye	only of material objects	implies previous disorder
tidy	+				+		
neat	+	+		+	+		
orderly	+		+				
shipshape	+					+	+

	village	little house	garden	kitchen	room	study	office	clothes	worker	person	household	appearance	habits	work	mind	handwriting	queue of people	demonstration of the facts	presentation of the facts
tidy	+	+	+	+	+	+	+	+	+	+	+	+	+	+					
neat		+	+	+	+			+	+	+	+	+	+			+			
orderly								+	+	+	+	+	+	(+)			+	+	+

Shipshape is never used attributively, neither is it used in formal contexts.

EXAMPLES

shipshape   We must get the kitchen **shipshape** before we go out. The square was transformed into a magic garden by the fair, but the next day everything was **shipshape** and back to normal.

B   Synonymous Pairs

1   **to attend**   [+ be present at]
    to frequent   [+ go to] [+ habitually] [+ usu of places of amusement]

	a conference	a meeting	lectures	pubs	clubs	bars	cinemas
attend	+	+	+				
frequent				+	+	+	+

2   **to keep up**   { [+ cause to stay at the same level or standard]
    to maintain   or [+ continue] }

	one's French	one's typing	a rapid expansion of the business	one's contacts with sb	a good relationship with sb	a walking speed of 4 miles per hour	order	control over sth	prices
keep up	+	+	+	+	+	+			
maintain			+	+	+	+	+	+	+

3 **to deal with**
   to cope with [+suggests difficulties to be overcome]

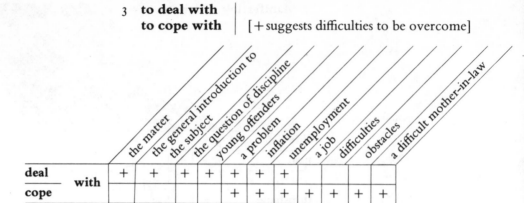

	the matter	the general introduction to	the subject	the question of discipline	young offenders	a problem	inflation	unemployment	a job	difficulties	obstacles	a difficult mother-in-law
deal with	+	+	+	+	+	+	+				
cope					+	+	+	+	+	+	+

4 **to change**
   to shift [+slightly] [+only position, direction or time]

The verb **shift**, unlike the noun **shift**, is not used in formal contexts.

	change(d)	shift(ed)	
I always	+		my clothes when I get home from work.
She has	+		her mind three times about what she wants to eat.
The weather has	+		for the worse.
You haven't	+		much since I last saw you.
The government's economy measures have not	+		people's attitude to the purchase of consumer goods.
The new director has	+	+	the emphasis of the study.
Would it be possible to	+	+	your course from Monday to Thursday?
I have to		+	all these boxes out of the way.
The wind has		+	a few points to the West.

5 **to change**
   to alter [+often suggests slightly]

The verbs differ mainly in their collocations, but where either **alter** or **change** is acceptable, **alter** would be more formal.

	one's name	one's mind	one's point of view	sb's attitude	one's attitude	one's plans	a time-table	course (of a ship)	a dress
change	+	+	+	+	+	+	(+)		
alter				+	+	+	+	+

Both verbs can occur with the following sequence of prepositions: **from** sth **to** sth; **change** can also occur with **into**.

EXAMPLES

The student wants to **change from** psychology **to** linguistics.

I **changed from** full-time **to** part-time teaching.

The witch **changed** the prince **into** a pig.

Ugly little girls often **change into** beautiful women.

The country **altered from** being democratic **to** being totalitarian in six months.

The relationship between the two sides has **altered from** close co-operation **to** open hostility.

6 **lenient** | [+not imposing severe punishments]
permissive | [+allowing too much freedom]

	laws	judge	parents	teachers	society	legislation	sexual behaviour	morals
lenient	+	+	+	+				
permissive				+	+	+	+	+

7 **even** | [+ of unchanging quality] or [+ showing natural calmness]
steady | [+ lack of variation, interruption or change] or [+ firm or dependable]

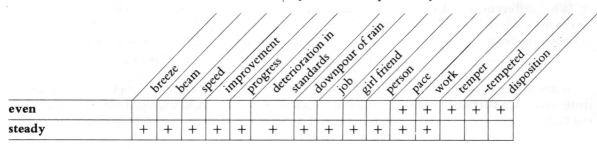

	breeze	beam	speed	improvement	progress	deterioration in standards	downpour of rain	job	girl friend	person	pace	work	temper	-tempered	disposition
even										+	+	+	+	+	
steady	+	+	+	+	+	+	+	+	+	+	+	+			

8 **doubtful** { [+lack of certainty or conviction] }
dubious { [+sometimes arousing suspicion or mistrust]

Dubious is not usually used predicatively.

EXAMPLES

Matthew still seems **doubtful** about whether he wants to go to University or not.

In spite of the applicant's good references, I am very **doubtful** of his ability to do the job.

He enjoys the **dubious** distinction of being the only student to have failed every paper in the examination.

I've heard he earned his fortune by rather **dubious** means.

Exercises

1 Explain the meaning of the following in your own words:

1 adult-awareness   2 infantilism vs adulticism   3 a steady boy-friend   4 single parents   5 hire-purchase   6 hit it off with sb
7 A 32-year old bad memory turned up on her doorstep. (See *A New Approach*)   8 They stress self-fulfillment over material success. (See *Family: New Breed v. the Old*)   9 a giddy prediction
10 Don't spare the rod.

2 Who or what could you . . .?

1 spoil   2 belong to   3 report   4 impose   5 slam   6 dissolve
7 breed   8 be plagued with   9 withdraw   10 aim at
11 blackmail   12 obey   13 squabble about   14 tackle   15 claim
16 maintain   17 frequent   18 alter

3 Provide synonyms of the following words:

1 children   2 threat   3 result   4 grown-up   5 change (eg in values)   6 keep up (eg a good relationship with sb)   7 get angry
8 give up (eg one's principles)   9 moan about sth   10 give (eg permission)   11 persuade (eg by using flattery)   12 neat (eg room)

4 Fill in the missing prepositions or adverbs.

1 to be plagued . . . sth   2 to count . . . sb   3 to set (sth) . . .
4 to stick . . . sth   5 to restrict oneself . . . sth   6 to moan . . . sth
7 to bicker . . . sth   8 to bicker . . . sb   9 to get on . . . sb
10 to insist . . . sth

5 What differences and/or similarities are there between the following?

1 to state/to overstate   2 to get along with/to like   3 to dodge/to avoid   4 to trace back/to search   5 to hit/to kick   6 to arrive/to show up   7 slim/skinny   8 polite/courteous   9 crafty/intelligent   10 a newspaper/a newsletter/a magazine

6 What differences and/or similarities are there between the following?

1 sly/shrewd   2 tidy/orderly   3 dubious/doubtful   4 lenient/permissive   5 chore/job   6 to bicker/to squabble   7 to rear/to bring up   8 to attend/to frequent   9 to bellyache/to grumble
10 to get on at/to nag

7 Fill in the missing prepositions.

1 to withdraw sb/sth . . . sth   2 to cope . . . sth/sb   3 to save . . .
(money)   4 to protect sb/sth . . . sth   5 to wonder . . . sth
6 to place a limit . . . sth   7 to complain . . . sb . . . sth
8 to pester sb . . . sth   9 to limit sth . . . sth   10 to harry sb . . . sth

8 Match words from the adjective list with words from the noun list. Notice that some of the adjectives can modify several nouns.

1 cunning   2 orderly   3 lenient   4 tidy   5 shrewd   6 neat
7 sly   8 permissive   9 steady   10 crafty   11 even

pace, disposition, judge, laws, progress, smile, morals, person, boyfriend, society, judge of character, queue of people, trick, politician, garden, clothes, handwriting

9 In what styles (formal, informal, colloquial, slang) are the following words used?

1 shift (noun)   2 folk   3 alter   4 grouse   5 shift (verb)
6 complain   7 nag   8 crafty   9 get on at   10 plague
11 shipshape   12 grumble

10 Guess the right word.

1 She promised to g . . . . . her hair long.
2 The g . . . . . voice of welcome won the Prince's heart!
3 Pornographic books and sex films are some of the signs of our p . . . . . society.
4 As she was the first to apply, she had first o . . . . . on the house.
5 The detective's f . . . . . s in the case proved interesting but hardly constructive.
6 He decided to s . . . . . his own ambitions, so that his wife could go to University.
7 The man pr . . . . . his child from the rain under his raincoat.
8 They br . . . . . horses.
9 The man cl . . . . . he had stolen the money because he had eaten nothing all day.
10 By a process of research and correspondence David tr . . . . . his ancestors back to the 11th century.

11 Choose the word that best fits the context. Modify its form where necessary.

1 We decided to . . . . . roses in the front garden. (breed, rear, grow)
2 Motorists are . . . . . to speeds of less than 70 mph on the motorway. (constrict, limit, restrict)
3 She was . . . . . to the tiniest of prison cells. (restrict, confine, constrict)
4 Agatha was a strict teacher but for once she showed she could be . . . . . . (lenient, gentle, permissive)
5 He had a . . . . . look in his eyes, which meant that he had thought up a good plan. (crafty, tricky, shrewd)
6 A psychoanalyst has to be . . . . ., capable of knowing how far she can 'push' her patient. (crafty, clever, shrewd)
7 During their holiday, they had to . . . . . a leaking tent and hurricane winds. (manage, deal with, cope with)
8 He . . . . . under his breath at the injustice of the world. (grumble, complain, moan)
9 The poor thing has had a tooth out, so she can't talk but does manage to . . . . . to attract attention. (complain, moan, grumble)
10 There is nothing shocking in this film for a(n) . . . . . audience. (grown up, mature, adult)

12 Summarize, orally or in writing the article on 'Family: New Breed v. the Old', using the following words:

value, shift, authority, duty, permissiveness, respect, principles, day-care centers, self-oriented, strict, insecure, morally wrong, rear, stress, commit oneself to, sacrifice for sb, esteem

Revision Exercises

R1 Explain the meaning of the following in your own words:

1 in single file 2 for minutes on end 3 make for the woods 4 a council house 5 have a sneaking suspicion 6 genetic mutation 7 catch sb's eye 8 side effects 9 carbon monoxide 10 work without respite 11 on all fours 12 a lag in food production 13 be at loggerheads with

R2 Group the given words into fields and arrange them along scales.

EXAMPLE

formal	informal	colloquial	slang

←——————————————————————————————————————→

**complain   complain   grumble   grouse   moan   bellyache
whine**

vanity, tease, astound, grubby, nag, pride, amaze, plague, harry, self-esteem, bother, filthy, worry, dirty, flabbergast, conceit, grimy, surprise, harass, astonish, get on at

R3 List at least four compounds/set expressions formed with '-ware' and 'goods'.

R4 Which of the given semantic features are relevant to these words?

1 retaliate   2 antics   3 squat   4 bluff   5 scrutinize
6 contaminate   7 reckless   8 arid   9 spurn   10 shudder
11 attain

[+make impure or poisonous] [+often because of fear] [+reach] [+look at/over] [+usu of sth above the average] [+by contact with harmful matter] [+not worrying about possible bad consequences] [+movements] [+return] [+dry] [+on the heels, with the knees bent] [+mislead] [+refuse] [+momentarily] [+negative] [+grotesque] [+having the power to bring about good results] [+the same sort of ill treatment] [+usu closely, carefully] [+shake] [+sit] [+in order to detect errors] [+often without life] [+contemptuously] [+by presenting false information]

R5 The following nouns appear in compound/set phrases. List as many of these phrases as possible.

EXAMPLE: hand → *hand-bag*, eye → *eye-glassses*
1 bottle   2 eye   3 household   4 leather   5 consumer   6 flash
7 court   8 lip   9 pit   10 paper and pencil   11 side   12 weather
13 brain   14 insurance   15 stock   16 crutch   17 application
18 city   19 nail   20 life   21 skin   22 door

R6 The texts contain a number of compounds with 'self-' (eg 'self-esteem', 'self-centred'). List as many of them as you can.

R7 Guess the right word.

1 She is in the stable g . . . . . ing the horses.
2 She affectionately r . . . . . his hair.
3 The house literally q . . . . . every time there was a strong wind.
4 The fieldmouse is common p . . . . . for the night owl.
5 In the army he would be given a good r . . . . . straight away.
6 She was feeling anx . . . . . because they had not returned when they said they would.
7 We sc . . . . . the horizon from east to west, looking for them.
8 Sherlock Holmes sc . . . . . the fingerprints through his magnifying glass.

9 He was fa . . . . . about washing the new car every week.

10 For someone of her age, her mind was surprisingly a . . . . .

R8 Supply the words that best fit the following definitions/descriptions:

1 the highest order of animals, including man, apes and monkeys
2 supports to help a lame person to walk
3 beasts of prey which kill and eat others
4 a shady place in the garden, in a wood or forest
5 anything made by human work or art
6 the overhanging edges of a roof
7 light comfortable shoes worn indoors
8 groups of people or animals, often when moving together
9 an act showing great ability
10 break by twisting or bursting
11 run with short, quick steps as if in a hurry
12 unite for the purpose of producing young
13 clean and tidy; or fashionable; or formally dressed

R9 Fill in the collocational grids.

1

		a journey	spring	winter	cancer	hostilities
onset	of					
beginning						

2

	meal	diet	evidence	bikini	life style
scanty					
frugal					

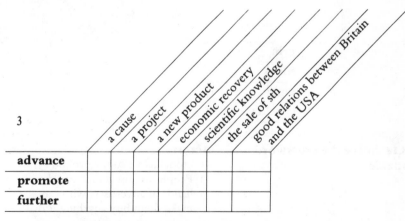

3

	a cause	a project	a new product	economic recovery	scientific knowledge	the sale of sth	good relations between Britain and the USA
advance							
promote							
further							

R10 Choose the word that best fits the context. Modify its form where necessary.

1 The snowy roads in Scotland can be quite . . . . . for the uninitiated. (perilous, risky, hazardous)
2 How were we to . . . . . that they wouldn't be coming back with us? (forecast, predict, foresee)
3 Fitted with a . . . . . motor, the boat soon overtook the yacht. (sturdy, strong, powerful)

4 Using that washing powder, clothes seem to . . . . . quicker. (decline, deteriorate, worsen)

5 Although he was on a diet, the food . . . . . him enormously. (lure, tempt, attract)

6 She had to . . . . . her dress because she had lost weight. (shift, change, alter)

7 He . . . . . over his shoulder to make sure he wasn't being followed. (glimpse, gaze, glance)

8 Personality is often . . . . . in terms of sociability. (gauge, evaluate, assess)

9 In hot countries, you can still see flowers . . . . . in winter. (flourish, bloom)

10 Having received John's boot on his head, Sam . . . . . by punching John in the face. (return, pay back, retaliate)

11 He . . . . . them of the dangers of swimming after a meal. (threaten, warn)

12 It's not . . . . . victory that counts, it's the trials along the way. (gain, reach, attain)

R11 Which nouns can be derived from the following?

1 believe 2 behave 3 aware 4 courteous 5 strong
6 victimize 7 authority 8 gigantic 9 heroic
10 environmental 11 proud 12 vain

R12 Give the British equivalents of the following words/expressions:

1 elementary school 2 apartment building 3 telephone booth
4 drugstore 5 billboard 6 garbage 7 diaper 8 gas(oline)
9 mad 10 to mail

R13 Fill in the componential grid.

	smile	laugh	broadly	in an affected or conceited manner	often at sb else's misfortune	nervously	— or in a silly way	with a low-pitched sound	as if to oneself	of short duration
grin										
smirk										
giggle										
chuckle										

R14 Solve the crossword puzzle.

Across

1 crouch close to the ground (5)

3 People are just p . . . . . in the hands of advertisers who can make them buy anything. (7)

7 agree to do sth (6)

9 the day before Christmas (3)

10 The government has imposed a b . . . . . on large cars which use a lot of petrol. (3)

11 a quick turning of the eyes towards sth (6)

15 joined together for mutual gain (6)

16 The s . . . . . in the football match was 3-0 (three nil) to England. (5)

19 amazing and impressive, of an achievement (10)

21 sth all powerful, which knows everything (11)

23 a short sleep, during the day (3)

24 draw out or cause a response from sb (6)

27 four-legged furry domestic animal (3)

28 thick cord used to secure, eg a boat (4)

29 Birds build . . . . . in which to lay their eggs. (5)

30 tying 28 results in one of these! (4)

31 sweet cake containing fruit (4)

Down

2 move slightly from fear, excitement or anger (6)

3 cleans and arranges feathers (5)

4 domestic animal, kept for pleasure (3)

5 area of land owned by one person (6)

6 above our heads! (3)

8 The mother's s . . . . . care of her children impressed everyone. (10)

12 what we see with (4)

13 Can you s . . . . . any light on this difficult problem? (4)

14 something which does not have any success at all (*coll*) (4)

17 having the appearance of being very expensive (7)

18 cleaned an animal's fur (7)

20 opposite of *guilty* (8)

22 thinly covering the ground, not numerous (6)

25 He c . . . . . loving glances towards his bride. (4)

26 move by means of the feet, faster than walking, slower than running (4)

Unit 6 · Get down to work!

Parkinson's Law

WORK expands so as to fill the time available for its completion.

... **Omitting**[1] **technicalities**[2] (which are numerous) we may distinguish at the **outset**[3] two **motive forces**[4]. They can be represented for the present purpose by two almost axiomatic statements, thus: (1) 'An official wants to multiply **subordinates**[5], not rivals' and (2) 'Officials make work for each other'.

To comprehend Factor 1, we must picture a civil servant, called A, who finds himself **overworked**[6]. Whether this overwork is real or imaginary is immaterial, but we should observe, in passing, that A's sensation (or illusion) might easily result from his own **decreasing**[7] energy: a normal symptom of middle age. For this real or imagined overwork there are, broadly speaking, three possible remedies. He may **resign**[8]; he may ask to halve the work with a colleague called B; he may demand the assistance of two subordinates, to be called C and D. There is probably no instance in history, however, of A choosing any but the third alternative. By resignation he would lose his pension rights. By having B appointed, on his own level in the hierarchy, he would merely bring in a rival for promotion to W's **vacancy**[9] when W (at long last) retires. So A would rather have C and D, junior men, below him. They will add to his **consequence**[10] and, by dividing the work into two categories, as between C and D, he will have the merit of being the only man who comprehends them both. It is essential to realize at this point that C and D are, as it were, inseparable. To appoint C alone would have been impossible. Why? Because C, if by himself, would divide the work with A and so assume almost the equal status that has been refused in the first instance to B; a status the more **emphasized**[11] if C is A's only possible successor. Subordinates must thus number two or more, each being thus kept in order by fear of the other's promotion. When C complains in turn of being overworked (as he certainly will) A will, with the **concurrence**[12] of C, advise the appointment of two assistants to help C. But he can then **avert**[13] internal friction only by advising the appointment of two more assistants to help D, whose position is much the same. With this recruitment of E, F, G, and H the promotion of A is now practically certain.

Seven officials are now doing what one did before. This is where Factor 2 comes into operation. For these seven make so much work for each other that all are fully occupied and A is actually working harder than ever. An incoming document may well come before each of them in turn. Official E decides that it falls within the province of F, who places a **draft reply**[14] before C, who **amends**[15] it drastically before consulting D, who asks G to deal with it. But G goes on leave at this point, handing **the file**[16] over to H, who drafts a **minute**[17] that is signed by D and returned to C, who revises his draft accordingly and lays the new version before A.

What does A do?

A might be tempted to sign C's draft and have done with it. But A is a conscientious man. **Beset**[18] as he is with problems created by his colleagues for themselves and for him – created by the mere fact of these officials' existence – he is not the man to **shirk**[19] his duty. He reads through the draft with care, **deletes**[20] the **fussy**[21] paragraphs added by C and H, and restores the thing back to the form preferred in the first instance by the able (if **quarrelsome**[22]) F. He corrects the English – none of these young men can write grammatically – and finally produces the same reply he would have written if officials C to H had never been born. Far more people have taken far longer to produce the same result. No one has been **idle**[23]. All have done their best. And it is late in the evening before A finally **quits**[24] his office and begins the return journey to Ealing. The last of the office lights are being turned off in the gathering **dusk**[25] that marks the end of another day's administrative **toil**[26]. Among the last to leave, A reflects with **bowed shoulders**[27] and a **wry**[28] smile that late hours, like gray hairs, are among the **penalties**[29] of success.

C Northcote Parkinson, *Parkinson's Law*

New Ways to Work

Six-month long vacations? Factories and offices designed by the employees themselves? Labor and management meetings in the nude? These are just a few of the innovations now being tried by business firms in Europe and the United States to combat the increasing dissatisfaction of employees at every level with the quality of their working lives; despite higher salaries, more attractive **fringe benefits**[1], and improvements in on-the-job-safety and comfort. In addition to the widely reported boredom of the assembly line, a growing number of white-collar workers see themselves as **conscripted**[2] into a slave army of paper pushers. Such long-sought benefits as the five-day, forty-hour week, the fixed **vacation**[3], and the standard length of service **pay raise**[4] are no longer enough to compensate many industrial and office workers for the **drabness**[5], lack of recognition, impersonality, and apparent pointlessness of their jobs.

The Ten Worst Jobs

Roy Walters, a private **consultant**[6] in the fast growing field of **job enrichment**[7] lists the following as the 'Ten Worst Jobs in America':

- Assembly-line worker
- Highway toll collector
- Car-watcher in a tunnel
- **Pool typist**[8]
- Bank guard
- Copy-machine operator
- **Bogus**[9] **typesetter**[10] (those who set type not to be used)
- Computer tape librarian (which means 'tape-spool roller')[11]
- Housewife (not to be confused with 'mother')
- **Automatic-elevator operator**[12]

While readers may disagree with some of these choices, they were not made lightly. For instance, Walters did not put housewife on the list just to be provocative, but because he is firmly convinced that that job is 'one of the worst, most boring, unrewarding and unrewarded' that has ever been created.

What makes these jobs the worst in Walters' opinion is that they are **stripped**[13] of almost every opportunity for meaningful self-development, and most opportunities for meaningful interaction with other human beings. In short, the jobs frustrate the worker's need to maintain his self-respect and win the respect of others.

The cost of worker dissatisfaction can be measured in dollars of lost profit, delays in production, careless damages, and even sabotage, let alone the cost to individuals in hostility, depression, and nervous tension, and to the stability of family life and social institutions.

There are hard-headed economic reasons as well as humanitarian motives behind current efforts to make work more meaningful and personally satisfying for the worker.

In the United States, most efforts to improve the work experience are identified as 'job enrichment'. But in Europe, particularly in Scandinavian countries, similar programs are described as experiments in 'industrial democracy'.

One technique that has succeeded on both sides of the Atlantic is to redesign the workplace itself.

Office workers at the Federal Aviation Agency's new **facility**[14] in Seattle, Washington, took an active role in planning both the appearance and the **layout**[15] of the building, opened in 1973.

In Sweden, industrial workers at SAAB and Volvo have helped to design new factories and even special low-noise tools. The Swedish workers have also redesigned their jobs in ways that provide variety and opportunity for continually learning more about their present jobs and acquiring skills that will prepare them for taking on greater responsibilities later.

Naked Negotiators

Another example of 'industrial democracy' is a company in Finland whose labor and management representatives meet regularly in a sauna to discuss matters of company policy and conditions in the factory.

An officer of the Finnish company explained the reasoning behind this policy:

'First, it makes the meetings more relaxed and, second, when you're sitting in a sauna, you're not reminded who is a manager and who is a worker – because nobody has any clothes on.'

Innovations are also being made in the area of **work scheduling**[16]. **As of**[17] summer 1974, more than 2,000 companies in the United States had switched all or part of their employees to a work-week of four ten-hour days.

A less spectacular but increasingly popular form of re-arranging the work schedule has developed in Germany. Many German firms now allow their employees to arrive at work anytime within a two-hour period in the morning and leave at an unspecified time within a similar **time-frame**[18] in the afternoon. While the employees must still **accumulate**[19] the total standard German work-week of 40 hours, they have greater freedom now to **accommodate**[20] **leisure time**[21] activities and family responsibilities more easily.

Sabbatical[22] for Workers?

There is good reason to predict therefore, that the future of work is likely to be based on increasing flexibility, more **scope**[23] for personal decision-making, and continuous learning on the job and off. One recommendation of the US Department of Health, Education and Welfare's 1972 study, *Work in America*, was that every employee be offered the opportunity to take a six-month 'sabbatical leave' with pay so that he can return to school for more education. Sabbaticals have long been traditional among college professors; and in some places, local laws already require certain professionals (**notably**[24] physicians) to return periodically to school to familiarize themselves with the latest advances in their **field**[25]

The Futurist

14 *Br* building
15 plan or general arrangement
16 setting up of a time-table for people's hours at work
17 *Br* would prefer 'By the summer of 1974 . . .'
18 period of time
19 gather together, acquire
20 fit in, make time for
21 time when one is free from work or duties
22 sabbatical leave, a period of paid free time for rest and special study given to a university teacher in Britain and the US after a certain length of service
23 freedom of action, opportunity
24 more specifically, for example
25 province or department of study or activity

REED EXECUTIVE SECRETARIES

1 administrative
2 personal assistant
3 no shorthand
4 more than 3000 pounds
5 fringe benefits
6 West 2, postal district in London
7 opportunity, freedom of action
8 the state of being involved, mixed up with, part of
9 secretary
10 executive,
11 circa, about
12 East–Central 2, postal district in London
13 diverse, quite different, entirely unlike in character
14 smart, of good appearance
15 here, answer; usu listen to, to gain information
16 routes, plans for journeys

AUDIO SECRETARY

1 secretary who types letters from tape recordings
2 personal assistant
3 British solicitors work in groups in which the chief members are known as partners
4 firm of lawyers
5 per annum, per year
6 luncheon vouchers, tickets provided by the firm to pay for a meal at a restaurant

CLASSIFIED ADS

1 room where goods are stocked or stored
2 person who takes care of a house or building, who keeps it clean
3 firm that rents cars
4 full time
5 part time

THE GOSPEL OF WORK

1 philosophy of life which says that the pursuit of pleasure is the only true goal of life
2 difference between the total value of goods imported, and the total value of goods exported from a country, in any given period
3 objects used by social groups in primitive societies as symbols of their relationship to a god, or to nature
4 artificially fixed equality of purchasing power between money of different countries
5 amount of money coming in as a result of sales
6 using strong verbal encouragement

REED EXECUTIVE SECRETARIES

The Selection Consultants for Top Secretaries   Admin.[1] P.A.[2] (no sh.)[3]   £3,000 plus[4] leads to £4,000 & perks[5] W.2.[6]

Enter the exciting, informal world of advertising research working with our small successful client company. They need an intelligent, attractive and lively person (20's) who can drive, and is looking for **scope[7]** and **involvement[8]** in a 'non routine' environment. U.K. and overseas travel.
(*ref.* X.10)

Sec.[9] to the Chief Exec.[10] c.[11] £3,800 E.C.2.[12]

This international firm with **diversified[13]** interests, particularly in oil exploration, requires an elegant, highly skilled, **personable[14]** secretary (35–40). Besides secretarial duties you will **monitor[15]** all his telephone calls, greet his many visitors and arrange travel **itineraries[16]**. Own office.
(*ref.* Y.11)

The Times

Audio Secretary[1]/ PA[2]

required for **partners[3]** by West End **solicitors[4]**. Legal experience essential. Salary to £3,200 **p.a.[5]** + **L.Vs[6]**. Electric typewriter.
Tel. 737-8640 (Ref P.B.)

CLASSIFIED ADS

CAPABLE **stockroom[1]** assistant required immediately for Kensington toyshop. Excellent wages 5-day week.
Tel 876-7034
CARETAKER[2] non-resident, required for flats in W1 area. £45 p.w. Box F297
CARWASHER/DRIVER for busy West London **Car Rental** office[3]. Phone manager. Tel 337-6111
CASHIER F/T[4] or P/T[5] reqd. for Times Centa Cinema. Telephone 01-842-7922

Evening Standard

The Gospel of Work

'What has replaced Christianity is not **hedonism[1]**, but its opposite; the gospel of work, accompanied by its theological abstractions, such as the **Balance of Payments[2]**, its **totems[3]** in the shape of **parities[4]** and the monthly trade **returns[5]**, its deadly sins like "higher productivity", and its **exhortatory[6]** slogans bidding "earn our way in the world".'

New Statesman

BRITISH COUNCIL

1 *Br* higher than level of first degree (known as 'graduate' in US), *Am* higher than second university degree
2 related
3 qualification obtained after first studies at university, usually 3 or 4 years in length
4 finding texts and designing exercises for second language teaching
5 amounts of money allowed or given for certain purposes
6 amount of money paid for going to and returning from a destination

The British Council

invites applications for the following post:

Specialist in Language Teaching Methodology (Specialized Uses of Language) (Singapore)

Southeast Asian Ministers of Education Organization Regional English Language Centre

Postgraduate[1] qualification in applied linguistics, second/foreign language teaching or an **allied**[2] field and teaching experience at school and university levels essential. **First degree**[3] in literature and experience of research in **materials development**[4] desirable.
Preferred age range 35–50.
Salary: £6,638–£8,350.
Benefits: free accommodation; overseas and children's **allowances**[5]; other benefits. Two-year contract.
Return fares[6] are paid. Local contract is guaranteed by the British Council.
Please write, briefly stating qualifications and length of appropriate experience: quoting relevant reference number and title of post for further details and an application form to **The British Council (Appointments), 65 Davies Street, London W1Y 2AA.**

Times Educational Supplement

LUDICROUS

1 an enclosure where ships are built or repaired
2 period of work where day (and sometimes night) is divided into several periods covered by different workmen
3 a man who is in charge of a group of workmen
4 *coll* to begin, or speed up in completing, a job or a journey

Ludicrous

A new executive in charge of the building of a ship at a large **shipyard**[1] looked out of his office window half-an-hour before the **shift**[2] ended and saw several men sitting talking instead of working. He telephoned the **foreman**[3] in charge of them and told him to **get the men cracking**[4].

The next day at the same time the executive looked out again and saw that there were no men sitting talking, but there were no men working either. He telephoned the foreman again. "Oh" the foreman said, "now the men know you can see them from your office, they are sitting talking round the corner where you can't see them". It isn't surprising that our shipbuilding industry has problems, is it!

The Evening Clarion

A youthful frivolity[1]

A YOUTHFUL FRIVOLITY

1 an action performed exclusively for one's amusement
2 act or speak falsely
3 from fiction, ie not real, invented for a book
4 enthusiastic supporter
5 date exactly one hundred years after another date
6 set free from mistaken belief
7 *coll* puzzled, at a loss
8 *coll* began, caused
9 examine thoroughly so as to completely understand
10 sent away from a university and not allowed to study there any more

Have you ever wished you could **pretend**[2], just for a while, to have a different job, and yet still go on leading your own everyday life as well? This is just what Humphrey Berkeley succeeded in doing, while he was a student at Cambridge in the late 1940s. He invented a public school called Selhurst, and appointed himself headmaster, under the name H Rochester Sneath.

The **fictitious**[3] Mr Sneath then began a series of correspondences with various important persons around England. He wrote to George Bernard Shaw (of whom Berkeley was a **fan**[4] in real life) inviting him to attend the school's **centenary**[5] celebrations; to a well-known architect inviting him to submit plans for a new school house, and to the Headmaster of Harrow, to tell him that some of his pupils had been involved in a scandal in a nightclub in London. From the quite serious (but, of course, to young Berkeley and his friends, highly amusing) replies he received, it appears that most of his correspondents had no reason to doubt that Selhurst School was real. Berkeley did not **disillusion**[6] them, but continued writing. He was not even **stumped**[7] when he received an enquiry from a lady wishing to send her son to Selhurst, but replied that the school had few, if any, vacancies.

Finally, he became too confident and Rochester Sneath's letter to the *Daily Worker* about the difficulty of obtaining textbooks for the teaching of Russian, **sparked off**[8] a storm of queries. A magazine called *News Review* decided to **get to the bottom**[9] of the mystery and sent a reporter to 'Rochester Sneath's' Cambridge address. So the whole story came out, and *News Review* subsequently carried a story entitled 'Death of Rochester Sneath'.

In case you fancy copying Berkeley's idea, perhaps I should tell you that he was **sent down**[10] from Cambridge in disgrace and not allowed to continue his studies for two years afterwards.

You can read the letters in *The Life and Death of Rochester Sneath* by Humphrey Berkeley, published 1974 by Davis–Poynter, London

LIFE'S LIKE THAT

1 advertisements which describe job without giving exact information on name of firm, location, etc
2 appreciate and keep by one
3 originally French, list of one's personal details, qualifications, and job experience, *Br curriculum vitae*

Life's like that

Last autumn, my husband decided he wanted to change jobs. He placed **'blind' ads**[1] in several business publications, describing his present job and the sort of position he was hoping to find. He received a number of responses, but the one we **cherish**[2] most was a note from a fellow job-seeker who enclosed one of his own **resumes**[3].

The note read: 'Sir, Please give my résumé to your present employer when you find another position. I've been looking for a job like yours for the last two years.'

Reader's Digest

SOME CAREER TIPS FOR
STUDENTS

1 *Am* leaving school in possession of the final diploma, no *Br* equivalent
2 *Br* secondary school
3 specialists giving advice as to the job or profession somebody could choose
4 belonging to the present time
5 a place of higher education, beyond secondary school
6 give a right to
7 the best people in a group or society
8 large business
9 having to do with the management of the company
10 that which is supplied, available
11 is greater than
12 of or relating to a manager, a person who manages, controls or directs a business or a department of a business
13 lacking glamour, mysterious attractiveness
14 *Br* localities, neighbourhoods, districts
15 one who calculates risks to make insurance-policies more accurate
16 cautious, looking out for possible danger or trouble
17 interest for reasons of personal advancement or security
18 postponing, putting off
19 school giving training for a specialised trade, closest *Br* equivalent would be technical college
20 coming out, coming into view
21 tendencies
22 skills or abilities connected with the work of a clerk (copying, writing, filing, accounting)
23 complete and well-finished

Some career tips for students

The following list of suggestions for a young person **graduating**[1] from **high school**[2] is based on the thinking of educators and **vocational counselors**[3] and **current**[4] job market statistics:

1. Expect to change jobs at least six or seven times. **College**[5] ideally should prepare you for many jobs – not just your first one – and should prepare you for life in general. An increasing number of college graduates are being forced to take jobs outside their major field of interest.

2. Remember that college education does not **entitle**[6] *you to an* **elite**[7] *job.* Many current **corporation**[8] **executives**[9] started at the bottom and worked their way up. Because the **supply**[10] of college graduates far **exceeds**[11] the number of available professional and **managerial**[12] positions, many recent college graduates are taking jobs as salesmen, clerical workers, and waitresses.

3. Consider **non-glamorous**[13] *jobs and non-glamorous* **locales**[14]. It's easier to become a small-town **insurance adjuster**[15] than a Hollywood star.

4. Be **wary**[16] *of people who assure you that a degree will be profitable.* Academic people have a **vested interest**[17] in attracting more students; parents often view their children's degrees as status symbols.

5. Consider **delaying**[18] *going to college until you have had experience working at one or more jobs*, so that you will know more about what you want to do and how much education you will

need to do it. At 18, you may not have enough information or experience to make a decision on a lifelong career. And remember that there are alternatives to college. Your parents may be willing to send you to a **vocational school**[19], help you to start your own business, or subsidize you while you work as a volunteer or in a low-income situation.

6. Be aware of the tremendous variety of jobs that exist. Vocational experts estimate that there are around 30,000 occupations.

7. Keep an eye on **emerging**[20] **trends**[21] *in the job market.* Jobs related to space, the oceans, and energy research may increase considerably in coming years.

8. Learn things that can be useful in many situations. No matter what your major field turns out to be, you will generally be able to use typing and **clerical skills**[22]. Taking a few business and statistics courses can improve your job prospects, too.

9. Develop your communication skills. Many employers complain that few job applicants can write and speak really well.

10. Learn how to use libraries. Knowing how to locate information is an important component of a **well-rounded**[23] education.

11. Give some thought to going into the family business. With good jobs in such short supply, the family enterprise may turn out to be your best alternative.

12. In weighing the possible benefits of a college education, keep in mind that there is absolutely no job guarantee attached to a degree.

The Futurist

Discussion

1 Why do people have to work? Isn't part of the reason for work dissatisfaction the fact we are conditioned to believe that we have to do it?
2 Look at the list of the 10 'worst jobs'. Suggest some reasons why each one is so bad. Do you disagree with any of the choices? Would you add any jobs to the list, and why?
3 Are there any jobs which give opportunity for 'meaningful self-development'? What are they?

4 Have you had any experience of the working of Parkinson's Law? Is this example exaggerated or realistic? How might knowledge of Parkinson's Law change our attitude to our jobs and those of others?

5 If you could have any job, anywhere in the world, what would you choose and why?

6 Are the studies you are now undertaking a direct preparation for a job? If not, how do you justify doing them?

7 'All work and no play makes Jack a dull boy,' but is the reverse also true? Does it in fact do us good to work? Or would you like never to have to work? How would you spend your time?

Word Study

A   Semantic Fields

1 Work

work			
drudgery	grind	labour	toil

	non-creative	tedious	routine	long	often physical	tiring
drudgery	+	+				
grind		+	+	+		
labour					+	
toil				+		+

Work, **drudgery** and **toil** are uncountable. **Labour** may be used in the plural, in which case it means 'a great deal of hard work' but not necessarily of a physical kind. In the singular, it rarely appears without the adjectives **manual** or **physical**. **Grind** can be preceded by the indefinite article but is not used in the plural. **Grind** is colloquial. **Toil** is more common as a verb.

EXAMPLES

drudgery   The **drudgery** of working on a factory production line can hardly be imagined.

Looking after four young children and a large house by oneself is sheer **drudgery**.

grind   At the beginning I enjoyed this job, but now it has become a real **grind**.

After three weeks holiday I can't believe I am back to the Monday-morning **grind**.

labour   My **labours** in the spring were well rewarded by a beautiful crop of cabbages.

toil Her **toil** was not in vain, since she passed all her exams.
I don't think it is good for her to be **toiling** away till so late every night in the laboratory.

2 Lawyers

lawyer	
solicitor	barrister

Note: Although **lawyer** is the cover term for these two words, in speaking of a British lawyer British speakers hardly ever use it, preferring to specify if the person is a solicitor or a barrister.

Everyone in the British legal profession is either a **solicitor** or a **barrister**. Both require several years of study and many difficult examinations, which are administered by their respective professional bodies, *The Law Society* (solicitors) *The Bar Council* (barrister). When they qualify, barristers are **called to the Bar**. Solicitors must serve a period of training (known as **articles**) before qualifying. During this time they are known as **articled clerks**.

solicitor
1 gives legal advice
2 prepares legal documents, eg wills, contracts for the sale of property
3 helps a person accused of a crime to arrange his defence
4 represents his client in magistrates' courts, ie courts dealing with non-serious offences

barrister
1 represents either the prosecution, ie the accusing side or the defence, ie the person being accused, in court
2 may not be directly approached by a member of the public without the help of a solicitor

3 Ways of avoiding

avoid	an approaching object	by a quick movement	by a quick downward movement	or	sth one is supposed to do	by deception	usu work or duty because of laziness	or cowardice	or	a question or point in discussion
dodge	+	+			+	+				
duck	+		+		+					+
evade					+	+				+
shirk					+		+	+		

	a blow	a falling branch	a speeding motorcyclist	the police	military service	taxes	the issue	one's head	out of doing sth	a question	work	one's duty	one's responsibility
dodge	+	+	+	+	+	+	+			+			
duck							+	+	+				
evade				+	+	+				+	+		
shirk											+	+	+

In their literal sense, **dodge**, and especially **duck**, may be used intransitively.

EXAMPLES

dodge   He **dodged** behind a wall to avoid being hit.

duck   They **ducked** down behind the hedge so as not to be seen by the guards.

In their figurative sense, **dodge** and **duck** are colloquial.

4 Uncovering or taking away

	take off or take away surface covering	furnishings or decorations	usu by pulling, tearing or scraping off	usu suggests complete removal	emphasises making object completely bare *or*	take away	distinction *or*	mark of special privilege or treatment
strip	+	+	+	+	+		+	+	+
denude	+	+			+				
divest	+	+					+	+	+

All these verbs are commonly used with the preposition **of**.

In certain constructions, **strip** also collocates with **off**.

COMPARE   We **stripped off** our clothes.

   We **stripped** the bark **off** the tree.

   but

   We **stripped** the tree **of** its bark.

When used intransitively, **strip** means 'take off one's clothes'.

EXAMPLE

He **stripped** and plunged into the water.

	a house of its contents	the room of furniture	the beds	sb of his titles	sb of all privileges	the walls of decoration	land of every living thing	a hill of vegetation	sb of his clothes	oneself of one's coat	sb of his power
strip	+	+	+	+	+	+	+	+			
denude						+	+	+			
divest									+	+	+

5 Acting against

fight	
combat	struggle

All these verbs are transitive. **Fight**, and occasionally **struggle**, may be intransitive. **Fight** is the most general term and refers to any kind of aggression between animals or people. **Struggle** denotes hand-to-hand fighting between two or more individuals or one individual and a physical object. In another sense, **struggle** suggests aggression towards a majority by a minority group. **Combat** is not much used to denote actual fighting but rather activities directed against something abstract.

	over sth	with an enemy	the enemy	disease	boredom	depression	inflation	poverty	against poverty	against prejudice	for independence	for freedom	to preserve freedom	to get free	with oneself	with an attacker	to get out of a trap
fight	+	+	+	+	+	+	+	+	+	+	+	+	+	+	+		
combat			+	+	+	+	+										
struggle									+	+	+	+	+	+	+	+	+

6 Not being real or true

	not real or true	made in close imitation of sth else	always intended to deceive	usu of money and documents	implies negative value judgement	made in obvious and naive imitation of sth good	arousing suspicion	intended as a substitute for the real thing
false	+							
spurious	+							
counterfeit		+	+	+				
fake		+	+					
bogus		+			+			
phony	+		+		+		+	
sham					+	+		
mock		+						+
artificial	+							+

	modesty	pride	grief	teeth	hair	eye-lashes	argument	theory	information	statement	passport	certificate of medical competence	money	letters	alarm	fire place	impression	leg	Gothic style	prehistoric finds	picture	jewellery	pearls	diamonds	address	business deal	gun	robbery	cream	sympathy	smile	fertilizers	sweeteners	flowers
false	+	+	+	+	+	+	+	+	+	+	+	+			+	+	+	+							+					+	+			
spurious							+	+	+	+																								
counterfeit											+	+	+	+																				
fake											+	(+)	+			+			+	+	+	+	+	+										
bogus												(+)					+	+			+	+												
phony								+	+	+		(+)														(+)	+							
sham																+	+				+													
mock																+	+												+	+	+			
artificial																	+	+					+	+						+	+	+	+	+

Phony and **sham** are not used in formal contexts. **Fake, sham** and **mock** cannot be used predicatively.

B Synonymous Pairs

1. **occupation** { [+ what one does to } or [+ anything one does]
   profession { earn one's living] { [+ requiring higher education or special training]

EXAMPLES

His main **occupation** appears to be sitting in cafés and watching people go by.

Being a truck driver is not an **occupation** for someone who likes staying at home.

In many countries the most lucrative **professions** are medicine and the law.

The acting **profession** is one of the hardest in which to make a steady living.

	hazards	disease	skills	touch	ability	job	way of doing things	status	assistance	advice	writer	musician	politician	football
occupational	+	+												
professional			+	+	+	+	+	+	+	+	+	+	+	+

Note that when **profession** becomes an adjective it takes on the sense of 'opposite of amateur', whereas **occupational** simply means 'connected with an occupation'.

2 **salary** | [+paid monthly] [+usu by cheque]
wages | [+paid weekly] [+in cash] [+usu for manual or clerical work]

Pay replaces **salary** and **wages** in the armed forces and can also be used generally to denote the money one earns.

EXAMPLES

Teachers are constantly complaining about their **salaries**, which they feel are low considering the amount of training necessary to become a teacher.

Very high **wages** are offered for working on oil rigs, or diving, because they are considered dangerous occupations.

The miners are on strike for more **pay** and better working conditions.

3 **officer**
official

Officer Functionary appointed to a specific position of responsibility in the Police or in certain Government services. Also used for those having rank above others; eg in the Armed Services – Lieutenant, Major, Colonel; in the Civil Service – executive officer; in unions or clubs – Chairman/woman, President, Secretary; in non-naval ships – First Officer, Purser.

Official General term for person acting in a properly authorized capacity in Government services or in an organization such as a Trade Union. Also used for person who supervises sports, races and competitions, eg time-keeper, referee.

Only police officers may be addressed as 'officer'.

4 **to revive** ⎱
⎰ [+to bring back] ⎱ [+ to life] ⇒ [+ cause to exist or take place again]
to restore ⎰ ⎱ [+to a former condition] or [+into use]

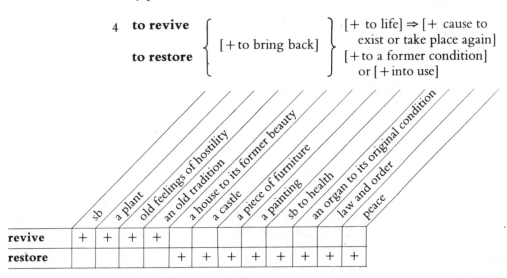

	sb	a plant	old feelings of hostility	an old tradition	a house to its former beauty	a castle	a piece of furniture	a painting	sb to health	an organ to its original condition	law and order	peace
revive	+	+	+	+								
restore					+	+	+	+	+	+	+	+

Revive can also be intransitive.

EXAMPLE

I'm sure this withered plant will **revive** if I look after it.

5   **to ward off**   [+ keep at a distance or away]   ⎱ [+ of undesirable
    to avert   [+ prevent from happening]   ⎰ things]

	wild animals	a blow	evil	the effects of the cold winter	an attack	an accident	a crash	disaster	open warfare	any serious consequences	suspicion	one's eyes	one's gaze
ward off	+	+	+	+	+								
avert					+	+	+	+	+	+	+	+	+

Note the expressions **avert one's eyes** and **avert one's gaze** which mean 'look away, often from something one does not want to look at'.

6   **to change**   ⎱
    to amend   ⎰ [+ of sth written or drawn] [+ often to improve]

	one's mind	one's plans	one's attitude	one's method	one's style	the decorations	the relationship between the two countries	a bill	a law	a statement	the records	chapter one	a programme	a diagram	a constitution	a dictionary
change	+	+	+	+	+	+	+	+	+	+	+	+	+	+		
amend								+	+	+	+	+	+	+	+	+

7   **to get**   ⎱
    to acquire   ⎰ [+ often by long-term effort]

Get is not used in formal writing.

	a job	an idea	good qualifications	a degree	a PhD	a boyfriend	some sleep	some practice	a sun tan	a lot of prestige	a reputation as an excellent lecturer	a good knowledge of English	a taste for sea food	fluency in five languages	useful contacts	wealth	new skills
get	+	+	+	+	+	+	+	+	+	+	+	+	+				
acquire									+	+	+	+	+	+	+	+	+

8 **dull** $\left.\begin{array}{c} \\ [+\text{dark in colour}] \end{array}\right\}$ $\begin{array}{l} \text{or } [+\text{monotonous}] \\ [+\text{uninteresting}] \end{array}$

drab $\left.\begin{array}{c} \\ \end{array}\right\}$ $\Rightarrow [+\text{unattractive}][+\text{cheerless}]$

	person	lecturer	film	book	day	sky	weather	job	dinner party	dress	existence	neighbourhood	room	building	old curtains
dull	+	+	+	+	+	+	+	+	+	+	+	+	+		
drab											+	+	+	+	+

9 **fastidious** | [+imposing near perfection]
  fussy | [+giving too much importance to minor details]
  | [+negative]

Fussy is used in colloquial style.

EXAMPLES

His report was written with **fastidious** attention to detail.

Lucy always makes me feel untidy because she is so **fastidious** about her appearance.

My boss is so **fussy** that if I leave a comma out of a letter, I have to retype it.

I've never met a dog before that was so **fussy** about where it slept!

Exercises

1 Explain the meaning of the following in your own words:

1 graduate student   2 colleague   3 foreman   4 expert   5 applicant   6 caretaker   7 insurance adjuster   8 pension   9 appointment   10 shipyard   11 sabotage   12 sabbatical

2 What adjectives can be derived from the following?

1 manager   2 provoke   3 continue   4 attract   5 live   6 glamour   7 vocation   8 skill   9 form   10 diversify   11 person   12 quarrel   13 clerk   14 profit   15 occupation   16 axiom   17 imagine   18 death   19 spectacle   20 fiction

3 In each case provide one or two nouns that can collocate with the following:

1 (an) appropriate . . .   2 (an) informal . . .   3 (a) secretarial . . .   4 (a) skilled . . .   5 (a) major . . .   6 (a) magic . . .   7 (an) emerging . . .   8 (a) profitable . . .   9 (a) glamorous . . .   10 (a) vested . . .   11 (an) exciting . . .   12 (a) spectacular . . .

4 Fill in the blanks with appropriate prepositions.

1 to be stumped . . . sth   2 to hand sth . . . . . . sb,   3 to be wary . . . sth   4 to be based . . . sth   5 to switch . . . sth   6 to pick . . . sb   7 to be entitled . . . sth   8 to lose touch . . . sb   9 to turn . . . to be   10 to divest sb . . . sth   11 to struggle . . . sb   12 to struggle . . . sth

5 Give synonyms of the following words:

1 answer   2 component   3 drabness   4 rationale   5 time-table
6 subordinates   7 punishment   8 leave out   9 measure
10 get acquainted with   11 be in the nude   12 give up
13 postpone   14 quit   15 remember

6 What differences and/or similarities are there between the following?

1 grind/labour   2 fan/friend   3 query/question   4 solicitor/
barrister   5 drudgery/toil   6 alive/lively   7 mock/sham
8 unrewarding/unrewarded   9 false/bogus   10 strip/divest
11 remember/remind   12 be at a loss/be stumped for
13 evade/shirk

7 What is the meaning of the following?

1 overseas job   2 balance of payments   3 slogan   4 mock cream
5 pool typist   6 counterfeit certificate of medical competence
7 fringe benefits   8 occupational disease   9 luncheon vouchers
10 vested interest   11 clerical skills   12 professional football
13 return fares   14 spectacular   15 avert one's gaze   16 totem

8 Fill in the collocational grids.

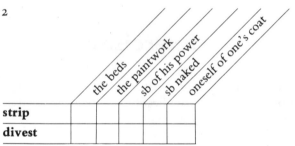

1

	a falling brick	the police	taxes	military service	one's head	the issue	a question	work	one's duty	a blow
dodge										
duck										
evade										
shirk										

2

	the beds	the paintwork	sb of his power	sb naked	oneself of one's coat
strip					
divest					

9 Fill in the appropriate word.

1 He doesn't want to . . . . . additional responsibilities.
2 He wanted to place an . . . . . in the newspaper.
3 Prices are regulated by supply and . . . . ..
4 Pupils and students in their last year of school or university are
   encouraged to visit a . . . . . counsellor to help them make up
   their minds about their future career.
5 She was . . . . . for an answer to such a difficult question.
6 What is your major . . . . . of interest?
7 Vegetables will be in short . . . . . because of the drought.
8 Could you . . . . . an eye . . . . . the baby?

10 What differences and/or similarities are there between the following pairs?

1 wages/salary   2 profession/occupation   3 dull/drab
4 fastidious/fussy   5 counterfeit/phony   6 change/amend
7 revive/restore   8 ward off/avert

11 Fill in the grid.

	modesty	cream	pride	impression	passport	money	Gothic style	jewellery	diamonds	teeth	prehistoric finds	gun
false												
fake												
sham												
mock												

12 Choose the word that best fits the context. Modify its form where necessary.

1 He . . . . . himself by going to night school. (amend, improve, change)
2 . . . . . of criminals in recent years has been less severe. (penalty, punishment)
3 He made a . . . . . face on seeing the very present he did not want. (forced, disappointed, wry)
4 He wore a . . . . . moustache and beard for the fancy-dress ball. (bogus, false, counterfeit)
5 The cargo in the hold of the ship . . . . . many times in the storm. (shift, switch, change)
6 The cobra has a . . . . . bite. (deadly, destructive)
7 She was a . . . . . old lady, insisting on everything remaining in its proper place. (fastidious, fussy)
8 It was during the time I lived in India that I . . . . . a taste for very hot curry. (get, acquire, gain)
9 The . . . . . of the work lay in the exactness of its detail. (worth, quality, merit)
10 Her sole . . . . . in the hotel kitchen was slicing up onions. (job, occupation, profession)

13 Write the following:

You are an employer seeking four people to fill vacant posts in your firm. Write out the advertisements, briefly describing the jobs and specifying the qualifications and experience you expect prospective applicants for the jobs to possess.

Revision Exercises

R1 Explain the meaning of each of the following. Your explanation may include mime, descriptions, enumeration of uses or examples.

1 disposable diapers   2 commercials   3 labels   4 wrapping paper
5 top-quality   6 bargain price   7 punch line   8 be immune to sth   9 mark a product down   10 fall back on   11 fly in the face of   12 in single file   13 hit it off with sb   14 by the same token   15 disperse all doubts   16 shed light on sth

R2 What may cause one to:

1 grumble?   2 wrangle with sb?   3 tease sb?   4 dodge military service?   5 blackmail sb?   6 hit sb?   7 be anxious?   8 pick on sb?   9 nag?   10 be baffled?   11 smirk?   12 crouch down?   13 be flabbergasted?   14 shudder?   15 scrutinize sth?   16 mutter?   17 moan?

R3 What prepositions do these verbs collocate with?

1 grin . . . sb   2 be surprised . . . sb   3 slip . . . sth   4 scamper . . . 5 be immune . . . sth   6 respond . . . sth   7 range . . . sth . . . sth   8 judge . . . sth   9 be obsessed . . . sth   10 suffer . . . sth

R4 What verbs can be derived from the following nouns?

1 argument   2 theory   3 description   4 maintenance   5 threat   6 entailment   7 obligation   8 burial   9 abundance   10 consumption   11 perception   12 response   13 suspicion   14 proliferation

R5 Guess the right word.

1 She t . . . . . her dress while climbing over the fence.
2 If they were able to a . . . . . their goal before nightfall, they would be saved.
3 His one a . . . . . in life was to become a pilot.
4 Telephone kiosks are easy p . . . . . for vandals.
5 Seeing the police approach, the man d . . . . . back behind the tree.
6 He am . . . . . the rules to benefit everyone.
7 The cathedral was showing signs of age and it was decided to r . . . . . it to its original state.
8 She c . . . . . of a stomach-ache, which later turned out to be appendicitis.
9 Farm work is comprised of much t . . . . . and sweat, but we enjoyed it!
10 He lost his t . . . . . and hit the boy.
11 Mountain climbing is a p . . . . . sport, which may involve loss of life.

R6 Find words to fit the following descriptions/ definitions:

1 a person or thing that can be relied on in time of stress or emergency   2 any kind of grain used for food   3 a board intended for the display of posters   4 tricks used in selling situations   5 religious men living in a monastery   6 sb who inherits or receives sth from another when he dies   7 giving material evidence of great riches   8 to smile broadly

R7 Add a few appropriate nouns to each of the following:

1 (a) widespread . . .   2 (a) gradual . . .   3 (an) insecure . . .
4 (a) heavy . . .   5 (a) childish . . .   6 (a) steady . . .   (a) crafty . . .
8 (a) care-free . . .

R8 Match appropriate features with each of the following words:

1 scan   2 accomplish   3 foretell   4 mar   5 overt   6 mutter   7 devastate   8 hazardous   9 lucrative   10 assess   11 cower   12 baffle

[+in a low voice] [+count up the worth of] [+indistinctly] [+tremble] [+lower oneself with the legs drawn up under the body] [+look at/over] [+usu of area of land, city village] [+have bad effect on] [+make extremely difficult to understand] [+tell of some future event] [+usu quickly, superficially] [+success in completing task] [+open] [+often searching for one specific thing] [+dangerous] [+make less than perfect] [+leave nothing that can be used] [+with abstract objects] [+confuse] [+chance] [+without a sound factual basis] [+bringing in a lot of money] [+of actions, attitudes] [+to be noticed] [+speak] [+implies precise analysis] [+in great fear]

R9 Choose the word which best fits the context. Modify its form where necessary.

1 'I can't . . . . .', she wailed as she clung to the cliff looking up at the lowered rope. (attain, achieve, reach)
2 She . . . . . her way through the interview. (deceive, bluff)
3 Her interviewer was not . . . . .. (deceive, bluff)
4 She was the innocent . . . . . of an accident that could have been prevented. (prey, victim)
5 We received daily . . . . . reports of their new life in Egypt. (warm, passionate, glowing)
6 The Trade Unions promised . . . . . action if government promises were not kept. (militant, aggressive)
7 That noise is . . . . . me, he said. (ruffle, disturb)
8 This big old house is difficult to . . . . .. (groom, keep clean, care for)
9 Having heard so much about Mr Brown, we were . . . . . to meet him. (anxious, eager, solicitous)
10 '. . . . . me once more with violence and I'll divorce you,' she said. (warn, menace, threaten)
11 She . . . . . to prepare the tea, her skirts swishing as she walked. (hurry, hurry off, bustle off)
12 . . . . . what's on your plate, otherwise you'll have no dessert. (munch, chew, eat)

R10 Find words to fit the following descriptions/ definitions:

1 starting signals for specific actions in a play   2 dust which leaves dirt behind   3 a dog of no special breed or of mixed breed   4 an object to be aimed at, eg in shooting   5 an outcome of an enquiry or research   6 well-balanced judgement of, and respect for, oneself   7 containing contradictory and opposing tendencies or features   8 take a living organism to pieces to examine how it works   9 meet accidentally or strike against or knock into   10 take the place of because better or more important

R11 Fill in the following collocational grids:

1

	London	land	one's hopes	a victory	a speed of 150 miles per hour	a great success	one's goals	one's ambitions
reach								
achieve								
accomplish								

2

	with cold	with anger	with fear	with rage	with horror	with laughter	with excitement	with disgust
shake								
tremble								
quake								
quiver								
shiver								
shudder								

3

	view of the tower	cousin of ours	future	past	possibility	little town
distant						
remote						

R12 What are the semantic differences and/or similarities between the following pairs?

1 confine/constrict   2 tackle/attack   3 tease/pester   4 grumble/grouse   5 breed/grow   6 claim/say   7 welcome/receive   8 beg/ask   9 moan/whine   10 plague/harass   11 run away/leave   12 have a child/adopt a child

R13 Give as many words as you can whose meaning includes the general terms listed.

EXAMPLE: dirty – grubby, filthy, grimy
1 to look   2 to laugh   3 to smile   4 to avoid   5 to quarrel   6 work

R14 Produce a logical and coherent story by filling in the blanks with appropriate words from the list below, modifying their form where necessary.

gimmick, nappy, consumer, puppet, outset, pursuit, aim, grocer, baker, trick, bargain, outburst, wares, frugal, scanty, ludicrous, affluent, austere, immune, costly, disposable, legitimate, drastic, opulent, to promote, to hunt, to panick, to astound, to flabbergast, to mark down, to admit, to surprise, to alarm, to amaze, to manipulate, to roam, to slice, to go, to make

'The number of shops that use 1 . . . . . to sell their goods is becoming quite 2 . . . . .. Even the 3 . . . . . offered during the sales are expensive, while the amount of money spent on advertisements is of course paid by the 4 . . . . . in the end. It is almost impossible to be 5 . . . . . in this 6 . . . . . society in which quantity reigns over quality and the commercial over the necessary. A 7 . . . . . for example will 8 . . . . . the price of his bananas, so that they are cheaper than those of his competitors. Once he has gained more customers, the price rises again. And it may 9 . . . . . you to know that he will even 10 . . . . . it! These 11 . . . . . are well known in the trade. You could argue that it's quite 12 . . . . . practise in a capitalist country, but it does 13 . . . . . me to think that everything is done in the name and 14 . . . . . of profit. Everything, right down to baby's 15 . . . . ., has become 16 . . . . ., to be thrown away, so that we can go on consuming. I know I'm rambling on a bit, but I feel very strongly about all this. It 17 . . . . . me that so few people react against our 18 . . . . . society. We are like 19 . . . . . being 20 . . . . . by some unseen hand, but the price we shall have to pay for our apathy will be 21 . . . . .. Unless there's a 22 . . . . . change in our way of life, the end of the 20th century will be also the end of the human race.'

We were strolling through Oxford's old buildings as he was pronouncing these words. I had often 23 . . . . . round the outside looking up at the 24 . . . . . walls, and imagining the 25 . . . . . interiors. But having lived here now for some years, I had grown 26 . . . . . to its beauty. At the 27 . . . . . of my walk with the Professor, we had talked a little about the country's economy, but this sudden 28 . . . . . against our society did not just 29 . . . . . me but left me quite 30 . . . . .. I 31 . . . . . in my mind for something non-committal to say. 'Is it really possible to 32 . . . . . our society down the middle like that?' I asked. 'I mean,' I said, 33 . . . . .   a little lest I had offended this eminent man, 'is it really as bad as all that? Shouldn't we be trying to 34 . . . . . understanding between

people, rather than setting them up against one another?'
I 35 . . . . . in my mind for a way of turning the conversation away
to less troubled waters.

R15 Solve the crossword puzzle.

Across

1 a shady place in a garden or wood (6)
4 the act of placing a dead body in the ground (6)
8 the age when one passes from childhood to adulthood (7)
10 You . . . . . clever! (3)
12 I'm going . . . . . learn English, however hard it is! (2)
13 smooth like silk (6)
16 large panel on which a pictorial advertisement is placed (8)
17 . . . . . and west (4)
19 dig or scratch with the paws (6)
21 spoil, make less than perfect (3)
23 past tense of *light* (3)
26 run quickly (of small animals) (7)
28 rejects advances or invitations (6)
29 an answer can be right . . . . .
wrong, but not both! (2)
30 type (of animal, bird) (7)
32 a search for sth not yet known about (5)
33 liquid found underground, which provides fuel for cars (3)
34 opposite of 'no' (3)
35 trying to succeed, wanting to do sth (4)

Down

2 brilliant, brightly coloured objects used for decoration (7)
3 opposite of *even* (6)
4 get by paying money (3)
5 walk around or travel with no special purpose in mind (4)
6 short question about sth which has just been said (5)
7 to do with dogs (6)
9 A man feels a very close b . . . . . with his dog. (4)
11 There is a strong connection between body image and self- . . . . . (6)
14 small yellow insect which stings (4)
15 the inhabitants of the world who will come after us (9)
16 control and make positive use of (7)
18 a loose-fitting lightweight shoe, worn indoors (7)
20 grain-based product eaten for breakfast in GB and USA (6)
22 I spent the day . . . . . home. (2)
24 result of a severe shortage of food (6)
25 opposite of *down* (2)
26 go quietly or furtively (*in, out,* etc)
27 money you have to pay to drive on certain roads (4)
31 This crossword puzzle is . . . . . easy, isn't it? (2)

Unit 7   Do you love me?

CHANGING PATTERNS OF
PREMARITAL SEXUAL
BEHAVIOUR

1 moved
2 the state of being married
3 complex effects
4 a thing or a quantity that is changeable
5 going away from generally accepted ways of behaving, usu used for sexual habits
6 *lit* group of stars fixed in relation to each other
7 the amount and kind of
8 antisocial conduct, often breaking the law

Changing patterns of premarital sexual behavior

Recently, the focus of concern about premarital sexual intercourse has **shifted**[1] from the college student down to the high school student. Since 40% of babies born out of **wedlock**[2] are born to teenage mothers, the **ramifications**[3] of this for the infant, the mother, and for society as a whole justify this concern. A recent study isolated these **variables**[4] which may enable us to predict which students will lose their virginity during high school years.

They tend to have higher values on and expectations for independence, to value and expect achievement less, to be more tolerant of **deviance**[5] and less religious, to have friends whose views agree with those of their parents and who influence them more than do their parents, to have parents who disapprove less of deviant behavior and friends, and who provide more models for deviant behavior, and finally to have engaged more in general deviance and less in conventional activity related to church and school.

There appears to be a **constellation**[6] of related behaviors for those who are irresponsible sexually. A study at the Institute for Juvenile Research in Chicago revealed a correlation between the use of drugs and alcohol and the **incidence**[7] of juvenile **delinquency**[8] and irresponsible sexual activity.

NOW...

MACHO

and THEN...

9 *Am* first year student in college
  (no *Br* equivalent)
10 *Am* final year student in college
  (no *Br* equivalent)
11 comes out
12 too much involvement, feeling too
  attached to another person or thing
13 the act of concealing or hiding
14 secretive, in a manner so as not to
  be noticed by others
15 carried along by circumstances

Another aspect of premarital sexual behavior which is occurring with increasing frequency, particularly with college students, is 'cohabitation' or 'living together under conditions which approximate those of the marriage situation'. Estimates now range from 20% to 40% of the student body, with numbers increasing from **freshman**[9] to **senior**[10] year.

From surveys carried out among cohabiting college students, a very varied pattern, summarised in the table below, **emerges**[11].

negative features	positive features
overinvolvement[12]	emotional security
lack of identity	mutual affection and loyalty
jealousy	deeper understanding of self
lack of privacy and space	clarification of what marriage is
guilt	about
concealment[13] from parents	more dignity and meaning than in
sexual problems	**furtive**[14] experimentation

Of students who had **drifted**[15] together gradually because they enjoyed being together or because it was more convenient, half had had an unsuccessful experience. The stage of the relationship at the time that cohabitation begins appears to be a strong determinant of success.

Of students who had entered the arrangement with strong affection, 70% expected cohabiting to continue indefinitely.

Condensed from *Intellect*

CHILDREN'S SAYINGS
 1 a piece of meat large enough to
  feed several people, cooked in fat in
  the oven
 2 variety of small pet animal

I know my mother and father love each other because my mother cooks him his favorite **roast**[1] every night

Theresa aged 8

True love is when something has died and you still remember it like my **hamster**[2]

Bobby aged 6

Sex is a part of love but not a very good part

Joanna aged 6

God Bless Love, A Collection of Children's Sayings Compiled by Nanette Newman

Why Love?

There is only one passion which satisfies man's need to unite himself with the world, and to acquire at the same time a sense of **integrity**[1] and individuality, and this is *love*. *Love is union* with somebody, or something, outside oneself, *under the condition of retaining the separateness and integrity of one's own self*. It is an experience of sharing, of communion, which permits the full **unfolding**[2] of one's own inner activity. The experience of love does away with the necessity of illusions. There is no need to **inflate**[3] the image of the other person, or of myself, since the reality of active sharing and loving permits me to **transcend**[4] my individualized existence, and at the same time to experience myself as the bearer of the active powers which constitute the act of loving. What matters is the particular *quality* of loving, not the object.

Love is one aspect of what I have called the productive orientation: the active and creative relatedness of man to his fellow man, to himself and to nature. In the **realm**[5] of *thought*, this productive orientation is expressed in the proper **grasp**[6] of the world by reason. In the realm of *action*, the productive orientation is expressed in productive work, the prototype of which is art and **craftsmanship**[7]. In the realm of *feeling*, the productive orientation is expressed in love, which is the experience of union with another person, with all men, and with nature, under the condition of retaining one's sense of integrity and independence. In the experience of love the paradox happens that two people become one, and remain two at the same time. Love in this sense is never restricted to one person. If I can love only one person, and nobody else, if my love for one person makes me more **alienated**[8] and distant from my fellow man, I may be attached to this person in any number of ways, yet I do not love. If I can say, 'I love you,' I say, 'I love in you all of humanity, all that is alive; I love in you also myself.' Self-love, in this sense, is the opposite of **selfishness**[9]. The latter is actually a **greedy**[10] concern with oneself which springs from and compensates for the lack of **genuine**[11] love for oneself. Love, paradoxically, makes me more independent because it makes me stronger and happier – yet it makes me one with the loved person to the extent that individuality seems to be **extinguished**[12] for the moment. In loving I experience 'I am you', you – the loved person, you – the stranger, you – everything alive. In the experience of love lies the only answer to being human, lies **sanity**[13].

Erich Fromm, *The Sane Society*

'Tis better to have loved and lost
Than never to have loved at all.

Alfred Lord Tennyson

Nancy Williams' PROBLEM PAGE

STILL SINGLE

*I am a single woman in my late 30s and nearly all of my friends are married. Although we **get on well**[1] somehow the conversation always **gets round to**[2] me and my single state and whether or not I'm ever going to do anything about it. They all think it isn't 'natural' for a woman to remain single. I've been engaged a couple of times and broken it off, perhaps selfishly, because I simply do not want to be tied. A couple of unmarried girlfriends do share my opinion, but we are certainly in the minority. I get terrible periods of doubt and wonder if I really am right in the way I feel, but all my instincts say I am. I have a marvellous job, plenty of friends and, **oddly**[3] enough, whenever my friends' marriages have run into trouble, it's always me they've come to for a shoulder to cry on.*

In fact, you're probably a nicer person for being single. Did you ever stop to think about that? Fascinating research done in America showed that single women adapted best to all the demands made of them in life – domestic, pro-

fessional, personal and social. Of course your friends come to you. You've had the courage to live life the way you wanted to. It isn't always **a bowl of cherries**[4] but there's a certain peace which comes from having made a decision, especially when it's so important. You probably have more time to give your friends and they're quick to reach out towards a caring person **undeflected**[5] by family demands.

He wants sex

We've been going out for two years but can't get married until my boyfriend is really secure in his job. He's becoming very dominating lately and is trying to make me go on the Pill so that he can have sex with me. I'm frightened of losing him if I don't. But I don't want sexual intercourse until we're married. What shall I do?

I won't **beat about the bush**[1]. If he truly understands your wishes about sex and still won't see your point of view I should take the risk of losing him. Quite honestly, it'll be no loss in the end.

Woman

STILL SINGLE

Not-so-tender trap

In 1770 a **Bill**[1] was introduced into Parliament 'denouncing women who seduce men into marriage by the use of **scents**[2], paints, cosmetic **washes**[3], artificial teeth, false hair, **iron stays**[4], **hoops**[5], high-heeled shoes and **bolstered**[6] **hips**[7]. If a woman were convicted of thus **ensnaring**[8] a husband, the marriage could be declared **null and void**[9].

The Bill never did become law, fortunately for the institution of matrimony – for there never can have been a wife who did not **resort to**[10] one or other of the 'crimes' listed!

The Daily Mirror, Old Codgers

LOST LEGEND

1 those who elope, run away secretly together in order to marry without the consent of their parents
2 need, worry about, be concerned about
3 jump

THE FUTURE MOTHER-IN-LAW

1 opposed in nature and character
2 clear and exact, not doubtful or uncertain

MY KIND OF MAN IS.....

1 which makes sb/sth appear different from other similar things/people
2 *coll* a marriage-partner, *lit* (of animals) animal of the opposite sex with which sexual coupling occurs
3 stay in (an emotional state) for lengthy periods, not trying to get out of it
4 nasty, disagreeable, very unpleasant
5 to be unable to go on, lose control of one's emotions

A GOOD OLD-FASHIONED KISS

1 instruction, teaching
2 *of* forming a romantic attachment to someone with a view to marriage

ANY OFFERS?

1 marry
2 *of* madhouse, mental hospital

MY DREAM GIRL

1 not loose, fully stretched
2 strange, surprising
3 *sl* clothes
4 *poetic* young woman
5 pretty, neat and delicate in appearance

Lost Legend

Marriages in the Border village of Gretna Green have dropped from around 500 to just over 70.
Why? Four years ago, English law was changed to allow youngsters to marry at 18, without parents' consent, instead of 21.
So the **elopers**[1] don't **bother**[2] coming to Scotland.
So much so, even the Lovers **Leap**[3] Hotel has changed its name – to Gretna Motor Inn!

The Sunday Post

My kind of man is . . .

Women often say that they are looking for a man who is gentle and loving. However, I believe that **distinctive**[1] characteristics such as strength, ability to succeed, and physical attractiveness, are really more important to a woman when she is choosing a **mate**[2].
Stephen B, Sidcup.

My kind of man is strong, yet also able to express his feelings when necessary. I think it's true that men who keep all their disappointments and problems to themselves often **wallow**[3] in self-pity and become **obnoxious**[4] to the people they love. A man who can **break down**[5] and cry when things get bad is one I really respect.
Miss P S, South London.

ANY OFFERS?

Did you know that one of the very first matrimonial advertisements appeared in 1695 and read: 'A Gentleman about 30 years of age, that says he has a very Good Estate, would willingly **match himself to**[1] some young Gentlewoman that has a fortune of £3,000'. A woman who tried this method of finding a partner (in the Manchester Weekly Journal in 1727) was sent to a **lunatic asylum**![2]
– Edward P, London.

Woman

The future mother-in-law

Marriage isn't so much losing a mother as gaining a mother-in-law. It may be that you are just **incompatible**[1], in which case it is probably best to make your position clear to all concerned. But, on the whole, it tends to be better to achieve as good a working relationship as possible. Most men's mothers are somewhat suspicious of the women that enter their son's life and they have a very **definite**[2] sense of their own unforgettable place in it. If you misunderstand how the average man's mother reacts you will make all sorts of mistakes. Payment on these can be very long term. Remember she will think of herself as losing a son and she is obviously concerned about it, so don't be oversensitive.

Penny Vincenzi

Honey

My Dream Girl

These days all the girls I see are so unfeminine, wearing **tight**[1] *jeans and* **odd**[2] **clobber**[3] *and covered in heavy make up. Does anyone know whether, somewhere deep in the country, in a remote village, the old-fashioned* **damsel**[4] *can still be found?*

By damsel, I mean a homely girl who never wears make up. She has neat **dainty**[5] *clothes and a natural, easy, hair style. Perhaps after all she doesn't exist and will always be only the girl of my dreams.*
Brian, *London SE23*

A good old-fashioned kiss
Every time I pick up a paper there seems to be something in it about sex manuals.
I don't know why people need this sort of **tuition**[1]? Why don't they just have a good old-fashioned kiss and see what happens next? That's how we did our **courting**[2] during the war.
Mrs E C, Sunderland.

Weekend

The singles scene: poetic Germans, bargain-hunting Americans

Personals – classified **ads**[1] written by men and women looking for temporary or permanent mates – appear in newspapers around the world. Recent studies in the US and Germany interpreted the ads differently in the two countries.

Ulrich Schulz-Buschhaus, an Austrian professor of romantic literature, found the German **personals**[2] poetic. He quotes this metaphorical sample:

'**Birch**[3], 5' 7'', 30 rings, **shimmering**[4] leaves and standing free in its own **glade**[5], rough **bark**[6], seeks experienced gardener who will transplant it into his own garden. Rooting in new home guaranteed if watered and given proper care.'

The professor quoted another innovative writer:

'Someone
To whom even the muses' gift
Can no longer give a spiritual lift,
Is filled with **longing**[7] for a man

Who will let her say "Yes, I can".'

American psychologists Catherine Camerson, Stuart Oskamp, and William Sparks were less kind. They saw the writers of American personals as bargain hunters who presented very detailed, very positive pictures of themselves to attract the best possible **catch**[8]. For example:

'Gentlemen prefer blondes and here I am looking for just one gentleman 45–55, tall, sharp, good-natured. I am 41, petite, 5' 3'', attractive, and have one dependent. Need someone to share a meaningful relationship with possibility of marriage.'

The newspaper used in this study, the *Singles News Register*, asked its writers to state their age, height, and weight. This could be one reason that American ads contained more statistics. Many German writers **belittled**[9] the use of statistics. One student **led off with**[10]: 'I think it's too silly to start with the standard **pap**[11] . . . Here's a little about me: . . .'

The American study pointed out that women find it easier to praise their physical attributes, while men prefer to talk about their careers and schooling. Women advertisers mentioned their beauty almost twice as often as men mentioned their handsomeness. Men, on the other hand, described their professions and education twice as often as women did. Both sexes were interested in the man's financial status. To these lonely hearts, the man's bankbook is still more important than the female's.

Maybe women with beauty, brains, and money don't need this lonely hearts service. Or maybe women find it easier to exaggerate physical attributes, while men find it easier to **boast**[12] about their careers. – Nanelle Napp

Psychology Today

THE SINGLES SCENE

1 *coll* abbreviation for advertisements
2 *Am* classified advertisements
3 variety of tree
4 shining in a wavering way, glistening
5 clear, open space in a forest
6 skin on the trunk of a tree
7 strong desire
8 that which is caught
9 presented as less important
10 started with
11 *coll* soft food, any soft stuff of a pulpy nature (*lit & fig*)
12 praise oneself excessively

Discussion

1 Compare the attitudes to sexual relations and marriage described here with those prevalent in your country. Would you like to see any changes in the laws or social norms concerning sexual behaviour?
2 'Love is admiration or awe; compassion or pity. One might thus speak of the human tragedy of the improbability of love between equals.' (Thomas Szasz, *The Second Sin*) Does this seem to you to be true?
3 What do you think of Erich Fromm's definition of love? Is it what people usually mean when they speak of love?
4 What are the reasons for the recent vast increase in sexual freedom? Have all its effects been beneficial?
5 What factors prevent single young people having sexual relations? Which are the more important, social, religious or practical reasons?
6 Why do you think people have difficulty finding partners and have to advertise or go to agencies? Would you consider doing this?

Word Study

A   Semantic Fields

1 Identifying with the problems of others

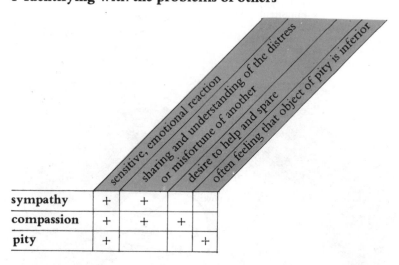

	sensitive, emotional reaction	sharing and understanding of the distress or misfortune of another	desire to help and spare	often feeling that object of pity is inferior
sympathy	+	+		
compassion	+	+	+	
pity	+			+

All three words may follow the preposition **out of**. They are all used in the constructions **feel . . . . . for sb** and **have . . . . . for sb**. **Pity** and **compassion** also occur in the constructions **have . . . . . on** and **take . . . . . on**.

EXAMPLES

sympathy   I feel a lot of **sympathy** for her because I have been through the same kind of unhappiness myself.

We helped the poor immigrants not out of pity but out of **sympathy** for their plight.

compassion   His superiors showed a lot of **compassion** in allowing him time off with pay to visit his wife when she was seriously ill.

Despite the tide of public opinion, the Court had no **compassion** for the man who murdered his wife's lover.

He shot the injured dog out of **compassion**.

pity   I thought I loved him but I realise all I felt was **pity**.

We took **pity** on a lonely walker in the rain and gave him a lift to the nearest town.

2 Liking and loving

	find to one's taste, agreeable	feel strong ties with / or	feel tenderness for / or	feel great passion	feel inferiority to object of adoration	result of prolonged contact usu sexually motivated	to the point of unreasonableness and illogicality	often temporary
like	+							
be attached to		+			+			
be fond of		+	+		+			
love		+	+	+				
be in love with		+	+			+		
feel / have an affection for			+		+			
be infatuated				+			+	+
adore				+	+			

Be infatuated may be followed by the preposition **with** or **by**.

The words can be arranged along a scale according to the strength of the feeling.

— intense   + intense

←——→

like   feel affection for   be attached to   be fond of   love   be in love with   be infatuated   adore

The use of most of these words is often extended to situations where their real meaning would be too strong.

EXAMPLES

I am very **fond of** roast beef.
I **love** big cars.
'Would you **like** a cup of tea?' 'I'd **love** one.'
I **am in love with** your beautiful country.
He **is infatuated** with his new television and can't stop watching it.
I **adore** dogs.

3 Praising oneself

| | praise oneself or something produced by, belonging to or related to oneself | | |
	showing too much pride and satisfaction	showing triumph, esp over a weaker or defeated opponent	so as to be noticed	often about sth which is not true
boast	+			
crow		+	+	
brag	+		+	+

Brag and **crow** are informal. As the feature analysis shows, **crow** is the most contemptuous of the words. It is also less common. All three words collocate with the prepositions **to** and **about**. **Crow** often occurs with **over**, and **boast** may also (but less frequently) occur with **of**. **Boast** and **brag** can be followed by a **that**-clause.

EXAMPLES

boast   She is **boasting** to the whole class that her work has been personally praised by the professor.
The author was **boasting** of the success of his latest novel.
crow   She was **crowing** to me how her daughter has married into such a good family.
The opposition party is **crowing** over its latest election success.
brag   He is always **bragging** about how well he speaks French, but I never hear him saying much.
Robin was **bragging** that he could easily swim 30 lengths of the pool, so we made him do it, and of course, he couldn't!

Note the idiomatic use of **boast** in:
Our town now **boasts** no less than four cinemas.
The University **boasts** one of the largest libraries in the world.

4 Sending out light
a Sending out a continuous light

	sending out or reflecting light						
	light	dull light	ray of light through a dark background,	from a smooth, reflective surface	not very bright, as from a wet surface	of varying intensity	often from a large expanse of water
shine	+			+			
glow		+					
gleam		+	+				
glisten					+		
shimmer				+		+	+

All five verbs are intransitive and **shine** may also be transitive.
They all collocate with the preposition **with**.
Shine and **glow** are often used figuratively.

EXAMPLES

shine   Her face **shone** with excitement as she announced the news of her trip to the States to her parents.

glow   His face **glowed** with pride as he watched his son go up and collect his prize.

b   Sending out an intermittent light

	sending out or reflecting	suddenly and briefly	a very bright light	a medium-intensity light	a soft light	once	or repeatedly	as if several lights simultaneously	usu through darkness
glimmer	+				+		+		+
twinkle	+	+			+		+	+	+
flash	+	+	+	+		+	+		
glitter		+		+			+	+	
sparkle		+		+			+	+	

All these verbs are intransitive and **flash** is also transitive. They can all be followed by **with**. **Flash, glitter** and **sparkle** are often used figuratively, especially as participles.

EXAMPLES

flash   He **flashed** her a look of sympathy.

glitter   The guests at the dinner were a **glittering** galaxy of stars from the theatre and the cinema.

sparkle   I have never seen her as **sparkling** as she was that evening.

The words may be arranged along a scale indicating the intensity of light produced or reflected:

very dull ←——————————————————————————→ very intense

glimmer	gleam	glow twinkle	glisten	shine shimmer	sparkle	flash glitter

	shine (shone)	glow(ed) (ing)	gleam(ed) (ing)	glisten(ed) (ing)	flash(ed) (ing)	glimmer(ed) (ing)	sparkle(d) (ing)	glitter(s) (ed) (ing)	shimmer(ed) (ing)	twinkle(d)	
She polished the old table until it	+										
He	+										the lantern towards us so that we could see where to put our feet on the treacherous path.
Her long hair	+		+								in the bright sun.
The light of a lamp	+	+	+		+	+					at the other end of the tunnel.
The lights of the village	+	+	+			+			+		in the distance.
The surface of the lake	+					+		+			in the brilliant sunshine.
The wet stones uncovered by the falling tide	+		+	+		+					in the morning sun.
Right at the bottom of the hole something		+	+	+		+	+				.
The first star			+			+			+		in the darkening sky.
Her eyes				+							with tears.
He					+						his torch around the cave.
Her eyes					+						with indignation.
When the signal lights are					+						you must reduce speed.
A large diamond							+				on her finger.
Her eyes							+				with pleasure.
All that								+			is not gold.
The bright lights made the mirror-lined hall								+			like a fairy-tale palace.
The hot air									+		in the intense desert heat.

5 Being true to fact or reality

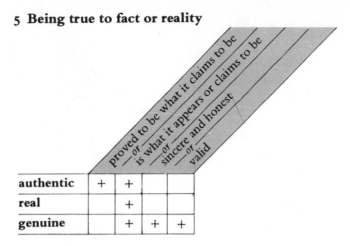

	proved to be what it claims to be	is what it appears or claims to be	sincere and honest	valid
authentic	+	+		
real		+		
genuine		+	+	+

Authentic is more formal than the other two words.

	report	signature	sculpture by Moore	stone-age skeleton	French porcelain	pearls	silk	thing (coll)	reason	love for one's country	interest in helping others	grief	antique	sympathy	person	article (coll)
authentic	+	+	+	+	+											
real					+	+	+	+	+	+	+					
genuine					+			+	+	+	+	+	+	+	+	

6 Being simple

	not rich, ornamental or patterned	straightforward	unattractive (of people)	with nothing added	uncomplicated	without sophistication or education	not having much brains	not difficult	comfortably informal / warm and friendly
plain	+	+	+	+					
simple	+				+	+	+	+	
homely								+	+

	water	grey walls	speaking	language	words	facts	cooking	dress	village girl	woman	man	style	explanation	calculation	recipe	device	mechanism	surroundings	meal	little hotel	atmosphere
plain	+	+	+	+	+	+	+	+	+	+											
simple				+	+	+	+	+	+	+	+	+	+	+	+	+	+	+	+		
homely				+					+									+	+	+	+

7 Hiding

	known to no-one or	known to a deliberately restricted number of people	usu of activities contrary to usage or authority	not telling anybody what one is doing or thinking	careful not to be seen or	careful not to be recognized or caught	deceitful(ly)	not open or straightforward
secret	+	+						
clandestine		+	+					
secretive				+				
furtive					+			
stealthy					+	+		
underhand							+	+
underhanded							+	+

Clandestine is more formal than the other words.

	marriage	methods	activities	meetings	door	passage	society	agent	character	person	manner	behaviour	glance	way	movements	footsteps	deal
clandestine	+	+	+	+							+						
secret			+	+	+	+	+										
secretive								+	+	+	+	+	+				
furtive								+	+	+	+	+		+			
stealthy										+		+			+		
underhand		+						+	+	+	+		+				+
underhanded											+						

B Synonymous Pairs

1 **to keep** $\left\{\begin{array}{l}[+\text{to continue}\\ \quad\text{to have}]\end{array}\right\}$ or [+continue to be or do]

to retain [+stresses the possibility of losing]

	one's sanity	one's integrity	a clear idea of what happened	one's self-control	control over the situation	one's balance	one's assistant for another year	old newspapers	old love letters	calm	smiling	in touch with sb	sb in mind
keep			+	+	+	+	+	+	+	+	+	+	+
retain	+	+	+	+	+								

2 **to hide**
  to conceal | more literary, sometimes suggests the feature [+deliberate], always transitive

	a fact	one's money	one's true identity	one's feelings	sth from sb	oneself	sb's shoes	from one's pursuers	in the woods
hide	+	+	+	+	+	+	+	+	+
conceal	+	+	+	+	+				

3 **to support**
  to bolster | [+strengthen] [+of sth weak or weakening], in contemporary usage almost always figurative

EXAMPLES

The captain did his best to **bolster** the failing morale of his team, now 3 goals behind their opponents.

Knowing that I had won the scholarship to America certainly **bolstered** my confidence for the final exams at University.

The local amateur operatic society, **bolstered up** by professional soloists hired for the occasion, gave a very creditable performance of 'The Marriage of Figaro'.

4 **to wallow** | [+roll about] [+usu in mud or some liquid] ⇒ [+take excessive pleasure in]
  to flounder | [+stumble or struggle] [+helplessly or without progress] [+as in deep mud or snow] ⇒ [+be confused and make no progress]

EXAMPLES

It was so hot we did nothing but **wallow** in the swimming pool all the afternoon.

After six months of living alone, he's just **wallowing** in the luxury of someone else preparing his meals for him.

The child **floundered** helplessly in the deep mud going neither forwards nor back.

He is a good student in everything except economics where he is really **floundering** because of lack of background.

5 **unpleasant**
  obnoxious | [+to the senses] ⇒ [+very rude, nasty]

	remark	behaviour	way of saying things	letter	person	idea	smell	colour	journey	custom	job	interview	meeting
unpleasant	+	+	+	+	+	+	+	+	+	+	+	+	+
obnoxious	+	+	+	+	+	+	+	+					

Exercises

1 Explain the following in your own words:

1 a glade   2 a metaphor   3 a dependant (person)   4 an eloper
5 a teenager   6 tuition   7 homely   8 alienated   9 a pattern of
behaviour   10 juvenile delinquency   11 bedside reading
12 to beat about the bush   13 to get on well with sb   14 to
bolster sth up   15 to share sb's opinion   16 to be one with
oneself   17 to break down (of people)   18 to be infatuated with
sb

2 Name the things you can:

1 reach out (for, towards)   2 water   3 guarantee   4 resort to
5 inflate   6 secure   7 predict   8 isolate   9 carry out   10 belittle
11 hunt   12 interpret   13 issue   14 share

3 Fill in the missing word.

1 to . . . . . a survey   2 null and . . . . .   3 to . . . . . round sb
4 to run . . . . . trouble   5 to be born out of . . . . .   6 to . . . . . a
bill into Parliament   7 to . . . . . risks   8 to . . . . . sb a lift
9 to be convicted . . . . . sth   10 to be tolerant . . . . . sth

4 What differences and/or similarities are there between the following?

1 pity/sympathy   2 reason/brains   3 bark/talk   4 leave/go out
5 cook/boil   6 isolate/insulate   7 wallow/flounder   8 gleam/
glisten   9 be fond of/be in love with   10 be greedy/desire
11 be frightened/be afraid   12 be engaged/be married

5 Add appropriate nouns to the following adjectives:

1 (a) confidential . . .   2 (an) innovative . . .   3 (a) positive . . .
4 (an) unspoiled . . .   5 (a) clandestine . . .   6 (an) average . . .
7 (a) tight . . .   8 (a) remote . . .   9 (an) odd . . .
10 (a) secretive . . .   11 (a) deviant . . .   12 (an) irresponsible . . .
13 my favourite . . .   14 (a) stealthy . . .   15 (a) genuine . . .
16 (a) plain . . .

6 List synonyms of the following words:

1 odd   2 sincere   3 stupid   4 furtive   5 reciprocal   6 sane
7 plain   8 wonderful   9 for ever   10 a leap   11 (a) concern
12 wedlock   13 to keep   14 to occur   15 to weep
16 to limit oneself

7 Give the main features of the following words:

1 awe   2 a bargain   3 a grasp   4 guilt   5 compassion
6 a trap   7 obnoxious   8 dainty   9 greedy   10 homely
11 genuine   12 underhand   13 stealthy   14 handsome
15 to brag   16 to crow   17 to flash   18 to shimmer

8 Which verbs correspond to the following nouns?

1 satisfaction   2 unity   3 retention   4 permission
5 application   6 ability   7 loss   8 disapproval   9 entrance
10 achievement

9 What differences and/or similarities are there between the following?

1 a bowl/a cup   2 a thought/an illusion   3 a stranger/a foreigner
4 a bill/a law   5 plain/homely   6 secret/clandestine
7 handsome/pretty   8 to keep/to retain   9 to roast/to toast
10 to boast/to exaggerate   11 to drift/to move   12 to reveal/to
tell

10 Fill in the following collocational grid:

	water	grey walls	speaking	language	words	facts	cooking	dress	village girl	woman	man	style	explanation	calculation	recipe	device	mechanism	surroundings	meal	little hotel	atmosphere
plain																					
simple																					
homely																					

11 Find appropriate adjectives to fill in the blanks.

1 a(n) . . . . . stranger 2 a(n) . . . . . feeling 3 a(n) . . . . . grasp
4 a(n) . . . . . offer 5 a(n) . . . . . height 6 a(n) . . . . . bargain
7 a(n) . . . . . achievement 8 a(n) . . . . . career 9 a(n) . . . . . kiss
10 a(n) . . . . . friendship 11 a(n) . . . . . choice

12 Which nouns can be related to the following?

1 sane 2 vary 3 frequent 4 relate 5 clear 6 gentle
7 lose 8 give 9 high 10 weigh 11 choose 12 find
13 tend 14 question

13 Choose the word that best fits the context. Modify its form where necessary.

1 The . . . . . guest was rude about everything, from the food to the sheets on his bed! (distasteful, obnoxious, unpleasant)
2 What he had to say was . . . . ., so they retired to another room where they could be alone. (secret, confidential)
3 You may . . . . . the change. (keep, retain)
4 They have been faithful to me, so I will . . . . . their services for another year. (keep, retain)
5 How far can you . . . . .? (jump, leap)
6 He . . . . . the fact that he had to leave until the evening of his departure. (hide, conceal)
7 The dog . . . . . his bone in the garden so that the cat couldn't have it. (hide, conceal)
8 Anyone would lose their . . . . . living with that madman. (health, sanity)
9 There was . . . . . in the doctor's tone, as he spoke of his patient's recovery. (anxiety, fear, uncertainty)
10 Her . . . . . mounted as she heard the footsteps of her pursuers coming closer and closer. (anxiety, fear, uncertainty)
11 His . . . . . at her continued absence was mounting every minute. (anxiety, fear, uncertainty)
12 He . . . . . up her flagging confidence by assuring her she was well-liked. (support, bolster)

14 Write a description.

Describe yourself and the person you are seeking for a 'lonely hearts' column. The accuracy of the descriptions are to be assessed in turn by the rest of the class!

Revision Exercises

R1 In each case, give other words which belong to the same semantic field as the one mentioned.

1 to quiver   2 to cower   3 to mar   4 to prevent   5 to refuse
6 to glisten   7 to look   8 to quarrel   9 to attain   10 dirty

R2 Fill in the right preposition.

1 to result . . . sth   2 to head . . . sth   3 to bustle . . . somewhere
4 to apply . . . sth   5 to apply . . . sb . . . sth   6 to benefit . . . sth
7 to bump . . . sb/sth   8 to trigger . . . sth   9 to lie . . . sb
10 to compensate (sb) . . . sth

R3 Give the compounds/set phrases in which these nouns can be used.

1 telephone   2 fringe   3 return   4 felt   5 five-day   6 family
7 middle   8 assembly   9 work   10 head   11 reference
12 job   13 status   14 ship   15 day-care

R4 What are the British English equivalents of the following words/expressions?

1 pay raise   2 vacation   3 elevator   4 high school
5 elementary school   6 gasoline   7 garbage   8 telephone booth
9 apartment building   10 to mail

R5 Which of these words/ suffixes will pair with 'life', which with 'self'? What do the resulting compounds mean?

1 long   2 less   3 ish   4 cycle   5 time   6 insurance
7 centered   8 expectancy   9 confidence   10 guard
11 oriented   12 control   13 span   14 respect   15 possessed
16 fulfilment   17 jacket   18 esteem   19 conscious   20 belt
21 pity   22 like

R6 Fill in the following componential grids:

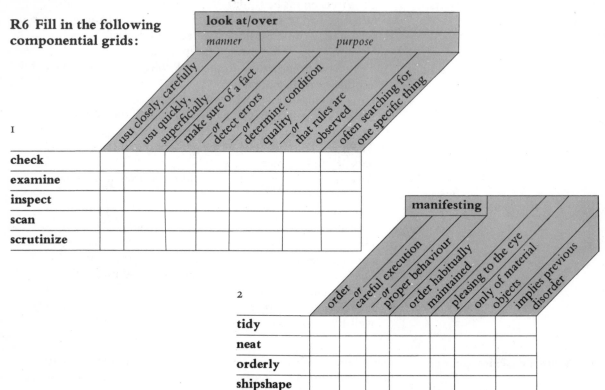

R7 Give the opposite of the following:

1 inflate   2 tight   3 insincere   4 smooth (surface)   5 fertile
6 simple   7 rising (sun)   8 plump   9 top   10 obey
11 get in touch with   12 major

R8 What differences and/or similarities are there between the following?

1 limit/restrict   2 complain/bellyache   3 rear/breed
4 promote/further   5 astonish/amaze   6 squabble/wrangle
7 get on at/harry   8 wares/commodities   9 chain-store/general stores   10 crafty/sly

R9 When would you refer to somebody as an 'officer' and when as an 'official'?

R10 Divide the following words into two groups:

words with a negative connotation
words with a positive or neutral connotation

1 homely   2 phony   3 lucrative   4 ludicrous   5 clerical
6 fastidious   7 prodigious   8 touching   9 fussy   10 scruffy
11 genetic   12 infantile   13 sly   14 selfish   15 hard-headed
16 skilled   17 well-rounded   18 greedy   19 hostile
20 confident   21 rewarding   22 juvenile   23 filthy
24 tremendous   25 shrewd   26 conceited   27 genuine
28 underhanded   29 efficacious   30 drab

R11 Test your collocational competence. It took a native speaker $1\frac{1}{4}$ minutes to mark the collocations in this table.

	over sth	with an enemy	disease	boredom	poverty	against poverty	against prejudice	for freedom	to get free	with oneself
fight										
combat										
struggle										

R12 Choose the word that best fits the given context, modifying its form where necessary.

1 He got the . . . . . at the standard rate of £1.50 an hour. (occupation, job, profession)
2 He was a psychiatrist by . . . . . . (occupation, job, profession)
3 If you . . . . . the house, put the key under the mat. (abandon, leave)
4 To . . . . . is surely the supreme faculty of the soul. (cherish, adore, be in love, love)
5 The notes in the bag were all . . . . . US dollars. (false, counterfeit, phony, mock)
6 She . . . . . into warmer clothing and then went out. (shift, switch, change)
7 Judging by the . . . . . this pupil has put into the essay, she should do well. (labour, work, toil)
8 Each sailor was allotted a daily . . . . . by the captain. (work, grind, task)
9 'When I'm . . . . . I shall eat sweets all day,' said the little boy. (adult, grown-up, mature)

10 '. . . . . you,' she said enviously as I packed my suitcase.
(happy, lucky, fortunate)

11 The news of Kennedy's assassination . . . . . people all over the
world. (surprise, amaze, astound)

12 In the river-beds of Wales it is possible to see . . . . . pieces of
gold dust. (sparkling, glistening, gleaming, glittering)

**R13 Group the given words
into semantic fields. Discuss
the differences and
similarities between the
members of each field.**

1 squabble   2 smash   3 smart   4 squat   5 shatter   6 bicker
7 crack   8 cower   9 lovely   10 strong   11 well-groomed
12 powerful   13 chip   14 attractive   15 snap   16 charming
17 potent   18 burst   19 crouch   20 snap   21 wrangle
22 good-looking   23 crush   24 elegant   25 handsome
26 pretty

**R14 Solve the crossword
puzzle.**

Across

1 break a stick in two pieces (4)
4 I haven't got time to read the paper, but I'll just s . . . . . the headlines. (4)
6 means of transport (3)
8 long hole dug in the ground (6)
12 dry (region) (4)
13 carved decorated pole having magical significance (5)
14 I try to do my work but I am b . . . . . by problems. (5)
16 You must pay a . . . . . to take your car across the bridge. (4)
17 deal with, manage, understand (4)
20 If you drop an egg, it will c . . . . . . (5)
21 to trouble and bother continually (5)
22 obviously artificial and intended to deceive (4)
24 sth which threatens, which may become dangerous (6)
25 Autumn is beautiful, but it signals the o . . . . . of winter. (5)
29 The director shook . . . . . hand and smiled at me. (2)
31 The students will m . . . . . if they get any more work to do! (4)
32 Nuclear . . . . . is an important source of energy. (7)
35 spare time, when you don't have to work (7)
36 part of the body, on the foot (3)
37 I'm staying . . . . . London. (2)
38 used for boiling water (6)
40 dirty, with dirt rubbed into it (6)
42 privileged group of people in a society (5)
43 make fun of, laugh at sb (5)
46 changed in order to improve (7)
47 If I take this job, I will c . . . . . myself to a 45-hour week of drudgery, with very little reward. (6)

Down

1 just sufficient (5)
2 dull coloured and sad-looking (4)
3 Switch . . . . . the light, please! (2)
5 shape a piece of wood with a knife to make a decoration (5)
7 what you need to find to solve a problem, or difficult situation (6)
9 person who works in an office (5)
10 persuade by flattery or promises (6)
11 straight rigid stick (3)
15 I tried to ask him about that, but he managed to e . . . . . all my questions. (5)
18 keep and look after because one likes (7)
19 of a smile, expressing discontent (3)
22 examining a quantity of sth, as an example of the whole (8)
23 listen to, to get information (7)
26 only (4)
27 work which is long and hard (4)
28 laugh quietly to oneself (7)
30 Every day that I was abroad, I y . . . . to come home again (7)
32 . . . . . -tip pen (4)
33 open structure from which things are sold in a market (5)
34 complain unnecessarily, for too long, and in an annoying way (3)
39 close a door quickly, so that it bangs (4)
41 tell sb that they should do sth (3)
44 I wish all students worked . . . . . hard . . . . . you do! (2)
45 If they did, teachers would have much less work . . . . . do. (2)

Unit 8   **There is more to it than meets the eye**

The Search for Psychic Power

Psychic Energy

THE SEARCH FOR PSYCHIC POWER

1 relating to the mind or spirit, especially in connection with spiritualism
2 consciousness
3 express in concepts, abstract notions or ideas
4 latent power, unrealised possibilities
5 psychic persons, mediums
6 consisting of two poles, two opposite points
7 acting and reacting
8 deviated from its original path
9 giving out light
10 the sending out of energy, heat, etc in rays
11 transmitted, carried along
12 a fine, soft natural fabric
13 prevent the passage of
14 protected, guarded, insulated
15 small box, usually metal
16 *lit* the silky covering which a caterpillar makes for itself before it changes into a moth or a butterfly
17 really, in fact
18 a person who can pick up information about persons or events (past, present and future) from an inanimate object
19 recovered, got back
20 Extra Sensory Perception. The term has traditionally covered three phenomena
   a telepathy; awareness of thoughts, impressions, and mental states of another person
   b clairvoyance; awareness of an object or an objective event not 'obtained through the use of the other senses
   c precognition; foreseeing and foretelling an event that has not yet come to pass
21 psychic
22 guide, conduct, direct
23 extend, be circulated and scattered
24 all over
25 at last, in the end
26 *Br* would prefer 'telephoned'

Psychic[1] energy is not new in terms of intuitive human **awareness**[2]. Since the earliest history of civilization, philosophers and scientists have **conceptualized**[3] its structure and **potential**[4] according to their cultural conditioning and personal belief systems. It is new only in the sense that scientists have recently established its existence and are learning how to measure it in the laboratory.

Such modern **psychics**[5] as Robert Pavlita have discovered that psychic energy is **bipolar**[6] and capable of **interacting**[7] with other bodies. It can be **refracted**[8], polarized, and combined with other energies. It can create effects similar to magnetism, electricity, heat, and **luminous**[9] **radiation**[10], but in and of itself it is none of these. It can be **conducted**[11] by paper, wood, glass, **silk**[12], and many substances that **insulate**[13] electricity. It can pass through water and any known metal.

Pat Price, a psychic being studied at Stanford Research Institute (SRI), is capable of receiving and transmitting psychic energy from within a **shielded**[14] room designed to prevent the entrance, or exit, of any previously known waves. Ingo Swann, another psychic working with SRI, can use it to affect an underground instrument locked inside a similarly shielded **canister**[15].

Russian scientists working with Ninel Kulagina and Alla Vinogradova have developed machines that register psychic energy at a distance.

This energy seems to envelop the human body like a **cocoon**[16], penetrating it and emanating from it. Certain psychics can **actually**[17] see it.

Peter Hurkos, the famous **psychometrist**[18], has shown that it surrounds inanimate objects and can be **retrieved**[19] to learn about people and events surrounding those objects.

Harold Sherman, the **ESP**[20] expert and himself a **sensitive**[21], believes that man's psychic sense can **channel**[22] psychic energy for any number of mind-controlled purposes, including telepathy, mind over matter, and clairvoyance.

Peter Hurkos

Hurkos is probably best known to the public as a psychic detective – a career that began in Holland when he was asked to help locate a little girl who was missing. After finding the body and helping solve the case, his reputation **spread**[23] **throughout**[24] Europe.

His next case concerned the coronation stone, which had been stolen from Westminster Abbey. Scotland Yard, which had heard of his work with the police in Holland, called him in as a consultant, and the stone was **eventually**[25] found. Since, he has been involved in a number of widely publicized cases. He describes two of them:

'Once when I was in Palm Springs the chief of police **called**[26] about a friend, a pilot who was missing on a flight. I told him I

27 possessions
28 sent to San Diego
29 felt, was aware of by intuition
30 no longer on the correct route
31 something that helps to solve a
   problem or mystery
32 the marks made by the fingers
33 find, show, discover
34 determined the exact position of
35 vehicle drawn by another vehicle,
   habitation which can move on
   wheels, *Br* caravan
36 covered with stains, marks, patches
37 habitable part of a building wholly
   or partly below ground level
38 arrested
39 go aboard, go on
40 has become black or dark
41 refilling with fuel, eg petrol, oil, etc
42 *Br* lawyer
43 *coll* to arrive safely
44 evidence

would need some personal object from his friend's **belongings**[27], like clothing. The chief called the air force base outside San Diego, and they **sent up**[28] clothing from one of the pilots.

When I got the clothing I asked for a map of the general area they were flying in and began getting information about what happened. I **sensed**[29] the plane was **off course**[30], and I saw an explosion. I saw only two people in the plane and one out of the plane – all dead. Nine hours later they found the plane where I said they would – I was a mile off in an area of 600 square miles.

Then there was the time the Citizens Committee in Detroit invited me to help on the Ann Arbor case, where six girls were murdered. There were no **clues**[31] or **fingerprints**[32]. When I arrived, they met me, and we later drove out to where one of the girls was killed about a year and a half previously. It was a test to see what I could **come up with**[33]. I **located**[34] the place where the body had been found and determined in what position they'd found her.

Later, I went on TV in Detroit, describing the murderer, who I felt had a **trailer**[35] and a motorbike, and giving what I thought was his name. About two days later I received a threatening telephone call to get out of town.

The case was solved when the murderer's uncle found one of the victim's blood-**stained**[36] pieces of clothing in his **basement**[37]. His nephew had been staying there while he was gone. The uncle called the police, who **picked up**[38] the young man. He did have a trailer, too, which was found in California.

Ironically, Hurkos' abilities cannot be self-applied; not only is he incapable of telling his own past, present, and future, but he is sometimes incapable of finding his own shoes. There are times, though, when he can sense danger. He describes his experience:

I never **board**[39] a plane unless I touch someone who's also boarding. I can pick up the danger this way, if there is any. Also, when I see a person boarding a plane who no longer has color – who **is blacked out**[40] – I won't go on that plane.

Once I was at the airport in Bangkok waiting to pass customs, and a plane landed for rest and **refueling**[41]. I got talking with one of the passengers, a German **attorney**[42]. When I looked out at the plane later, it was completely black – no color. Since this means danger to me, I said to the attorney, 'Why don't you wait for another plane? I don't think that one's going **to make it**.'[43]. But he said he had to board, and he did.

The next morning we read in the paper that the plane had crashed in the mountains. I've tried to warn many people when I sense dangers on occasions like this, but they usually don't believe me; they won't listen. You see, everyone needs **proof**[44], and sometimes when proof comes, it's too late. But I do what I can at the time.'

David Hammond, *The Search for Psychic Power*

Shock from a gipsy on the doorstep

I'm **parted from**[1] my husband and have two small children. The other day an old **gipsy**[2] woman came to the door, saying she knew me when I was a baby, and she'd been a good friend of my **gran's**[3]. It's possible. My granny was a gipsy. This woman said my gran had saved **sovereigns**[4]. She claimed she'd been asked to keep them for me until I was in need of them. She passed over 200 sovereigns to me. How valuable are they? Can I sell them? – **M.**

They may have considerable value, depending on year and condition, Mrs M. Some may be worth up to £25 each.

The Sunday Post

Life after Death?

The experience is a familiar one to many an **emergency-room**[1]. A patient who has been pronounced dead and unexpectedly **recovers**[2] later describes what happened to him during those moments – sometimes hours – when his body **exhibited**[3] no signs of life. According to one repeated **account**[4], the patient feels himself rushing through a long, dark tunnel while noise **rings**[5] in his ears. Suddenly, he finds himself outside his own body, looking down with curious **detachment**[6] at a medical team's efforts to **resuscitate**[7] him. He hears what is said, notes what is happening but cannot communicate with anyone. Soon, his attention is **drawn**[8] to other presences in the room – spirits of dead relatives or friends – who communicate with him nonverbally. Gradually, he is drawn to a vague 'being of light'. This being invites him to evaluate his life and shows him **highlights**[9] of his past in **panoramic**[10] vision. The patient **longs**[11] to stay with the being of light but is **reluctantly**[12] drawn back into his physical body and recovers.

Clues: Once dismissed as nothing more than **hallucinations**[13], these 'near death' experiences are now being seriously examined by several psychiatrists and psychologists for possible clues to what happens at the moment of death. One such researcher, Dr Elisabeth Kubler-Ross, an internationally respected expert on the psychiatric dimensions of dying, now claims that she has proof that 'there is life after death' on the basis of hundreds of such stories. Although other psychologists believe that Dr Kubler-Ross **lends too much credence to**[14] **tales**[15] told by the dying, her outspoken views have recently **heightened**[16] scholarly interest in near-death phenomena.

What most impresses Kubler-Ross about the cases she has assembled over the last eight years is the evidence of out-of-body consciousness – that is, the apparent ability of people who exhibit no respiration, heartbeat or **brain-wave**[17] activity to describe events taking place around them. 'If you have a woman who has been declared dead in a hospital and she can tell you exactly how many people walked into the room and worked on her, this cannot be hallucination,' she

---

SHOCK FROM A GIPSY

1 live apart from, estranged from
2 belonging to Asiatic race found in most countries of Europe, usually living in caravan in which they move from place to place and reputed to possess mystical powers, especially for foreseeing the future
3 *coll* grandmother's
4 old British gold coins

LIFE AFTER DEATH

1 room in a hospital where emergency cases are treated
2 gets back to a former state of health
3 displayed, showed
4 story, description, explanation
5 sounds
6 (of the mind) state of being separate from and uninfluenced by surroundings
7 revive, bring back to life

8 pulled, attracted
9 the best or most memorable parts
10 extensive
11 wishes for very much
12 unwillingly
13 imagined sights or sounds which a person believes to be real
14 believes too easily
15 stories
16 increased
17 waves produced by the brain

18 differ, are not similar
19 tending to fill or pass through every part
20 integrity
21 arms and legs
22 dead
23 felt injured about
24 find
25 listed
26 good, not harmful, kind and gentle
27 ghosts
28 damaged
29 wide-awake, watchful
30 mad
31 uncertainty, doubt

argues. Although details of near-death accounts **vary**[18] somewhat, Kubler-Ross says that all her subjects report certain common experiences: a **pervasive**[19] sense of calm well-being, a feeling of personal **wholeness**[20] – even among accident victims who have lost **limbs**[21] – and the experience of being greeted by previously **deceased**[22] loved ones. As a result of such experiences, she says, 'many of them **resented**[23] our desperate attempts to bring them back to life. Death is the feeling of peace and hope. Not one of them has ever been afraid to die again.'

As part of yet another effort to **track down**[24] clues 'that would suggest an after-life,' psychologist Karlis Osis of the American Society for Psychical Research in New York City has **tabulated**[25] by computer interviews with 877 physicians who have reported deathbed visions by their patients. Most of them involve dying patients who see **benign**[26] **apparitions**[27] coming for their souls. Osis has determined, at least to his own satisfaction, that patients whose brains were **impaired**[28] by high fever or disease reported fewer visions than those who were fully **alert**[29] at death. Moreover, he asserts, powerful drugs such as morphine and Demerol actually decrease the coherence of such visions. 'The sick-brain hypotheses we considered do not explain the visions,' Osis concludes, 'and so far it looks as if patterns are emerging consistent with survival after death.'

Even if Kubler-Ross has not proved her point, she has presented phenomena that modern science has not yet adequately explained. 'I don't at all agree with Elisabeth when she says that the experiences she and I have both had working with the dying absolutely guarantee life after death,' says Dr Charles Garfield of the Cancer Research Institute of the University of California. 'I also don't take the extreme scientific-materialist position that these are the utterances of **deranged**[30] persons. I don't really know what is happening, and I am willing to tolerate the **ambiguity**[31].'
– Kenneth L Woodward
with bureau reports

Newsweek

SPOT CHEQUE

1 a small flying beetle, reddish-brown with dark spots
2 *poetic* announce
3 small marks
4 lost cattle
5 duration of life
6 the action of gathering in a crop, eg corn or apples

SPOT CHEQUE.

According to the folklore of many countries, **ladybirds**[1] are lucky. In Germany their appearance is said to **herald**[2] the arrival of a child. Farmers in America think the finder of a ladybird will receive as many dollars as the **spots**[3] on its back. In Canada they believe it means a new pair of gloves. Other folk believe ladybirds tell the time of day, where **stray cattle**[4] can be found, forecast **life spans**[5] and predict the value of the **harvest**[6].   *Weekend*

Elke Sommer claims . . .
I USED TO BE A MAN

ELKE SOMMER

1 *of* soldier
2 mediaeval Christian military expeditions to save the Holy Land (ie Palestine, where Jesus Christ lived) from Turkish invaders who were not Christians
3 having a likeness or attraction to
4 strange, mysterious
5 a rebirth in a new body
6 far off
7 a fraction of a second
8 a person who studies astrology, the pseudo-science of telling what will happen in the future by studying the position of the stars
9 raised platform in the theatre

QUESTION

1 of the spine or backbone
2 inflammation of the soft, thin, skin-like coverings (membranes) enclosing the brain or spinal cord
3 a section of a hospital
4 flat movable pieces of furniture, used to separate one part of a room from another
5 happens to meet
6 bringing down one's feet with force

Actress Elke Sommer could not look less like a man. Yet that's exactly what she believes she once was. She is convinced she was a tough, fearless **warrior**[1] who fought in the **Crusades**[2].

She says: 'I have a great **affinity**[3] with the Crusades era. It's more than a passing interest. I don't really know what it is — it's just an **uncanny**[4] feeling I get about it.

. . .'**Reincarnation**[5]? Yes, I do believe in it. I think it is possible for people to recognise a strange place because they actually have been there before — in some previous live.'

Peter McKellar, psychologist at Sheffield University, says seven out of 10 people experience that I-have-been-here-before feeling. 'We're still **a long way off**[6] understanding this phenomenon,' he says.

Some think it happens when one half of the brain is working **a split second**[7] faster than the other. Others say it can be explained by a dream or some experience that makes them think it has all happened before. Members of Britain's National Spiritualist Union have another explanation for that been-here-before feeling. They say we have two bodies. When we are conscious, they coincide. When we sleep, the spiritual body goes where it pleases.

Dr. McKellar has experienced the feeling. He says: 'Some people are worried by these sensations, but they have nothing to do with mental illness, that much is certain.'

Another actress, Faye Dunaway, is also sure she was once a man. 'I was a writer in 17th-century England,' she says. 'I'm convinced of this after having talks with an **astrologer**[8].'

As a child she was always writing stories but she wrote in an old-fashioned style of English. And she used to hear strange voices at night, like actors on some far-off **stage**[9] reciting ancient poetry. 'The astrologer caused me to remember things I knew darkly as a child,' says Faye. 'Suddenly it all came back to me.'

Weekend

Have you ever seen a ghost?

Tommy Steele, entertainer: Yes. When I was 16 I was in hospital with **spinal**[1] **meningitis**[2] diagnosed and not expected to survive the night. I was put in a **ward**[3] full of old men. During the night I heard a child running about and laughing. Then a ball came over the **screens**[4] and landed on my bed. Weakly, I threw it back. This went on until I was standing on the bed throwing the ball over the screen for all I was worth. In the morning I was completely cured. Months later I was telling my mum and she started to cry – when I was four I had given my young brother a similar ball. He died aged three. At the time my aunt saw him playing in the garden with a ball. I believe he came to fetch me that night or to make me well.

Duke of Wellington: I am not conscious of any psychic experience at all, but that doesn't mean such things aren't possible. One **comes across**[5] people who have told one of experiences and one has no reason to disbelieve them.

Charlotte Bingham, novelist: Yes. We stayed in an old house in Scotland and every night our bed was shaken and we heard two children's voices, low and urgent. One night we heard **stamping**[6] outside the door and we went out and saw someone aged about 13 crossing from the window.

Observer Magazine

LORD LUCK

1 during the whole
2 gather together
3 keep up with, follow
4 lean heavily on, press
5 go forward
6 carefulness
7 upset, cause to fall (*lit & fig*)
8 difficult, inconvenient
9 exciting
10 opening
11 look after, see to, take care of
12 influenced
13 away, separate from

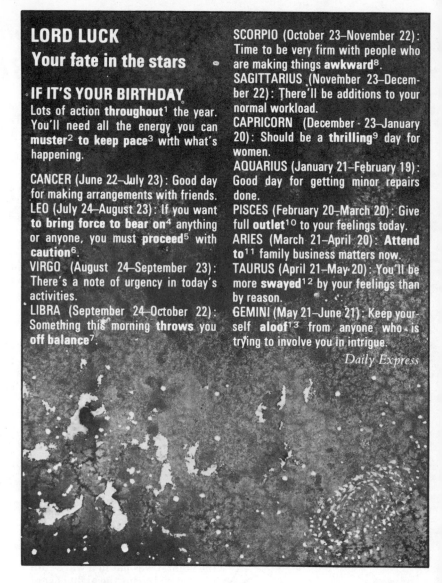

LORD LUCK
Your fate in the stars

IF IT'S YOUR BIRTHDAY
Lots of action **throughout**[1] the year. You'll need all the energy you can **muster**[2] **to keep pace**[3] with what's happening.

CANCER (June 22–July 23): Good day for making arrangements with friends.
LEO (July 24–August 23): If you want **to bring force to bear on**[4] anything or anyone, you must **proceed**[5] with **caution**[6].
VIRGO (August 24–September 23): There's a note of urgency in today's activities.
LIBRA (September 24–October 22): Something this morning **throws** you **off balance**[7].

SCORPIO (October 23–November 22): Time to be very firm with people who are making things **awkward**[8].
SAGITTARIUS (November 23–December 22): There'll be additions to your normal workload.
CAPRICORN (December 23–January 20): Should be a **thrilling**[9] day for women.
AQUARIUS (January 21–February 19): Good day for getting minor repairs done.
PISCES (February 20–March 20): Give full **outlet**[10] to your feelings today.
ARIES (March 21–April 20): **Attend to**[11] family business matters now.
TAURUS (April 21–May 20): You'll be more **swayed**[12] by your feelings than by reason.
GEMINI (May 21–June 21): Keep yourself **aloof**[13] from anyone who is trying to involve you in intrigue.

Daily Express

Discussion

1 Are psychic powers latent in many more of us than we suppose? Describe any experience you have had of extrasensory perception or contact with ghosts.
2 How could development of psychic powers be useful to mankind? What might be the dangers?
3 What difference would absolute proof of some kind of life after death make to your attitude to life and death? Compare the attitudes of any religious creeds you know with each other.
4 Have you ever tried to find out what lies ahead for you by eg astrology, palmistry, a fortune teller or any other means? Why do you think people want to know about their future?

Word Study

A Semantic Fields

1 Having an effect on

	produce: an effect strong enough to cause a reaction	a change in action, attitude or nature	a deep or lasting effect	an effect which makes one turn from a given course	source of effect is always good
affect	+				
influence		+			
impress			+		+
sway				+	

All these verbs are transitive. When **impress** implies a [+deliberate] act on the part of the subject, it requires a prepositional adjunct with **on**.

	affect(ed)	influence(d)	impress(ed)	sway(ed)	
Nuclear tests have	+				the kind of weather we are having.
Her sight has been permanently	+				by her illness.
The student has been greatly	+	+	+		by the ideas of his teacher.
You must not let yourself be	+	+		+	by what other people say.
His impassioned speeches	+			+	the opinions of a lot of people.
Most people are far more easily		+		+	by advertising than they think.
They all tried to		+			him to change his mind.
The mother			+		on the child that he must not play in the road.
The doctor has			+		on us the importance of a balanced diet.
I was very			+		by the level of the students' vocabulary knowledge.

2 Making visible

	give evidence of (eg quality) or be visible	or make visible	spread out objects so that they can be easily seen	often to attract public attention or inspection	lay open, uncover or take away protection	in an ostentatious and boastful manner
show		+	+			
display	+	+	+	+		
exhibit	+	+		+		
expose		+			+	
flaunt		+				+

The verbs are all transitive, and **show** is also intransitive. All, except **flaunt**, are used in the construction **to . . . . . sth to sb**. **Flaunt** takes a direct object and **at**. **Show** may be immediately followed by an indirect object without **to**.

	sb a new dress	some books to sb	one's wares for sale	a wide knowledge of vocabulary	qualities of endurance	one's best flowers (at a show)	oneself before everyone	an illegal property deal	one's skin to the sun	the foundations of a 14th century castle	a large diamond at one's former boyfriend	one's newly acquired riches
show	+	+		+	+	+						
display			+	+								
exhibit				+	+	+						
expose							+	+	+	+		
flaunt							+				+	+

3 Stating openly

make known

	by stating explicitly	usu news	sometimes in the face of opposition	always by speaking	formally, solemnly and officially
announce	+	+			
declare	+		+		
pronounce	+			+	
proclaim	+				+

All these verbs are transitive and all can be followed by a **that** clause. **Pronounce** and **proclaim** are usually used only in the context of official declarations, or in fixed expressions.

	one's engagement	one's intention to become a dancer	that the price of coffee will rise	war	sb to be the winner	one's opposition to the project	oneself to be in agreement with the proposals	oneself quite recovered	sb dead	them man and wife	independence	peace	a day of national celebration	sb king
announce	+	+	+											
declare				+	+	+	+	+	+	+				
pronounce								+	+	+				
proclaim											+	+	+	+

4 Protecting

	keep safe from damage or injury by setting up a barrier	actively repel what threatens or attacks	speak or write in support of	keep safe from potential danger or threat	by watching over	by taking the necessary measures
protect	+					
shield	+	+				
defend		+	+			
guard				+	+	+
safeguard				+		+

The verbs are all transitive. They can all occur in the construction

$$\text{to} \ldots \text{sb/sth} \begin{Bmatrix} \text{from} \\ \text{against} \end{Bmatrix} \text{sb/sth}.$$

The sense of **protect** and **shield** is often extended to situations where there is no actual physical barrier.

	oneself against losses	a child from bad influences	the plants from the wind	one's eyes with one's hand	sb by not telling the truth	sb against accusations of ...	sb's point of view	a thesis	one's country against/from an invader	against losses	against disease	a prison	one's rights	sb from danger	one's health
protect	+	+	+	+										+	+
shield		+	+	+	+										
defend						+	+	+	+	+	+				
guard										+	+	+			
safeguard										+			+	+	+

5 Trying to find

	try to find	examine or go through/into	in order to find sb or sth	usu with difficulty	by feeling about	where one cannot see what one is doing	carefully	emphasises thoroughness	go into every part
look for	+								
seek	+								
grope	+			+	+	+			
search		+	+				+		
comb		+	+				+	+	
scour		+	+					+	+

The verbs occur in the following patterns:

**to look for sb/sth   to seek sb/sth   to grope (about) for sth
to comb sth**

$$\textbf{to search} \begin{cases} \textbf{sb/sth} \\ \textbf{for sb/sth} \\ \textbf{sb/sth out} \end{cases} \qquad \textbf{to scour} \begin{cases} \textbf{about for sb/sth} \\ \textbf{sth for sb/sth} \end{cases}$$

Grope is only followed by a direct object in the expression **to grope one's way**.

Seek in the sense described here is not now common in colloquial speech. It is used in formal circumstances and in official documents. Compare, for example:

A man seeking employment (official)

A man looking for work (normal spoken)

It is quite common both in speech and writing in its sense of [+ try].

EXAMPLES

Those who **seek** to cure all our economic ills by revisions to the taxation system are surely mistaken.

Scour is not used in formal style. The use of **grope** may be extended to non-physical situations.

EXAMPLE

The Selection Panel asked such difficult questions that most candidates were really **groping** for answers to them.

	look(ed) (ing)	seek (sought) (ing)	grope(d) (ing)	search(ed) (ing)	comb(ed) (ing)	scour(ed) (ing)	
Elaine has been	+						for you all day.
I have	+		+				everywhere for my watch but I can't find it.
Many ships were lost while	+		+				for a passage round the North West of Canada.
Many ships were lost while		+					a passage round the North West of Canada.
I			+				my way along an ill-lit passage, feeling for obstacles with my feet and hands.
He			+	(+)			about in the muddy water but could not locate the missing ring.
Passengers (and their luggage) are always			+				at airports, before they can board a plane.
Police			+				three houses in London following an anonymous report of drug hoarding.
Four helicopters are			+				for the missing yacht.
Four helicopters are			+	+			the area of sea where the fishing boat disappeared.
Volunteers with dogs are				+			the moorland where the child disappeared.
We have			+		+		the school without seeing any sign of the boy.
I have						+	the town looking for black lace but there is none to be had at any price.

6 Bringing or getting together

	bring together or ___	come together or ___	look for and bring back	in a pile or heap, or as if in a pile	often arrange in an orderly way	for a common purpose
gather	+	+	+			
accumulate	+	+		+		
assemble	+	+				
collect	+	+			+	
muster	+					+

All the verbs, except **muster**, are both transitive and intransitive. **Muster** is only transitive, and often occurs with **up**. **Gather**, **collect** and **muster** may be used figuratively, **gather** and **collect**, in the expressions **to gather one's wits** and **to collect one's thoughts**, both meaning 'to organize one's thoughts, usu after an upsetting experience'. **Gather** may also be used colloquially to mean [+understand].

EXAMPLE

Do I **gather** from what you're saying that you didn't much enjoy the party?

	collect(ed)	gather(ed)	assemble(d)	muster(ed)	accumulate(d)	
Snow	+					against the hedges, making many roads impassable.
On his travels he has	+					many rare plants.
The researchers have already	+	+	+			enough material to write two books.
The children went to		+				mushrooms.
After the accident it took me a few moments to		+				my wits and realise what had happened.
All the students		+	+			in the square to wish him farewell.
Over the years the professor has					+	a large collection of stone-age remains.
The whole family		+				at 6.30 for the evening meal.
Sergeant! Try to			+	+		your men for a renewed attack.
As many men as could be			+	+		at short notice set off to look for the missing child.
The boy				+		up all his strength to force open the heavy door.
During the 20 years we have lived here we have					+	a lot of useless things.
It took him a very short time to					+	his vast fortune.
Dirt					+	very fast if I don't clean the house each day.

7 Being strange and inexplicable

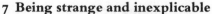

	very strange	possibly of supernatural origin	sometimes frightening	causing superstitious uneasiness or fear	not appearing to be of this world	unexplained, unknown or kept secret	difficult to understand or interpret	exciting curiosity	incapable of being understood or interpreted
weird	+	+	+						
eerie	+			+					
uncanny	+	+							
unearthly	+				+				
mysterious						+	+	+	
inscrutable									+
enigmatic							+		

	animal	story	feeling	experience	sight	sound	surroundings	disappearance of one's car	circumstances	person	smile	secret
weird	+	+	+	+	+	+	+		+	+		
eerie		+	+		+	+						
uncanny		+	+	+								
unearthly					+	+	+					
mysterious				+	+	+		+	+	+		
inscrutable										+	+	+
enigmatic									+	+	+	

B Synonymous Pairs

1 **to conduct** [+ carry along within itself]

   to transmit [+ cause to pass through the air or a medium]

      [+ energy supply] or [+ light]

EXAMPLES

Most metals **conduct** electricity.

Wooden houses are usually cool because wood does not **conduct** heat very well.

The programme was **transmitted** to all areas of the country.

2 **to flow**
   to emanate [+ of nonmaterial or intangible things]

Note that **emanate** requires the preposition **from**.

EXAMPLES

A most curious smell was **emanating** from the kitchen.

Judging by the noise **emanating** from next door, they are having a party.

3 **to receive** {when with non-material} **to pick up** {objects} [+often suggests accidentally or unexpectedly] ⇒ [+by the senses]

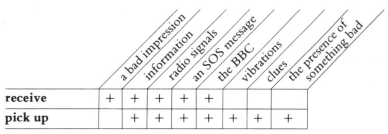

	a bad impression	information	radio signals	an SOS message	the BBC	vibrations	clues	the presence of something bad
receive	+	+	+	+	+			
pick up		+	+	+	+	+	+	+

4 **to have an accident** **to crash** [+only of motor-driven vehicles and planes] [+damage]

EXAMPLES

I lent my brother my car and he **crashed** it so seriously that I shall have to buy another.

The plane skidded and **crashed** into the end of the runway.

5 **strange** {[+out of the ordinary]} **odd** or [+irregular]

	sight	situation	occurrence	dream	habits	feeling	idea	food	man	person	jobs	times	moments
strange	+	+	+	+	+	+	+	+	+	+			
odd	+	+	+	+	+	+	+	+	+	+	+	+	+

6 **shiny** **luminous** [+able to glow in the dark]

	floor	leaves	hair	hands (of a watch)	road signs	safety clothing	paint
shiny	+	+	+				
luminous				+	+	+	+

7 **lost**
  stray   [+ which has gone away from the right place] or
              [+ having no place to go] ⇒ [+ occasional or
              infrequent]

EXAMPLES
Stray dogs are taken care of by the police.
It was very late, and nothing moved in the streets except a **stray**
taxi or two.

Exercises

1 Find words to fit the following descriptions/definitions:

1 awareness of the thoughts, impressions, and mental states of another person
2 a section of a hospital
3 habitable part of a building wholly or partly below ground level
4 something that helps to solve a problem or a mystery
5 feel, be aware of by intuition
6 a raised platform in the theatre
7 the action of gathering in a crop
8 inflammation of the membranes enclosing the brain and spinal cord
9 an electronic device which stores information on magnetic tape, analyses it, and produces selective information as required
10 a small flying beetle, reddish-brown with dark spots

2 Complete the expressions without looking back at the texts.

1 to . . . . . one's point
2 to draw somebody's . . . . . to something
3 to . . . . . a bell
4 to . . . . . somebody dead
5 to . . . . . customs
6 a split . . . . .
7 to . . . . . pace with progress
8 to throw . . . . . balance
9 to . . . . . credence to something

3 Add appropriate adjectives to the following words:

1 . . . . . power   2 . . . . . existence   3 . . . . . victim   4 . . . . .
flight   5 . . . . . experience   6 . . . . . road signs   7 . . . . . attempt
8 . . . . . workload   9 . . . . . pace   10 . . . . . safety clothing
11 . . . . . murderer   12 . . . . . phenomenon

4 What words are derivationally related to the following?

1 radiation   2 convince   3 victim   4 peace   5 fear   6 prove
7 coherence   8 ambiguity   9 urgency   10 caution   11 concept
12 diagnose

5 What differences and/or similarities are there between the following?

1 a gipsy/a nomad   2 a clue/a fingerprint   3 a canister/a box
4 a sound/a noise   5 a flight/a trip   6 to fall/to crash
7 to live/to survive   8 to cure/to recover   9 to hear/to listen
10 to help/to save

6 Match appropriate features with each of the following words:

1 stray 2 inscrutable 3 muster 4 flaunt 5 sway 6 assemble 7 shield 8 canister 9 proclaim 10 luminous 11 uncanny 12 expose 13 stamp

[+with force] [+small box] [+lay open, uncover, take away protection] [+put one's foot/feet down] [+usu of metal] [+make visible] [+produce an effect which makes one turn from a given course] [+possibly of supernatural origin] [+bring or come together] [+make known] [+by stating explicitly] [+in an ostentatious and boastful manner] [+which has gone away from the right place] [+able to glow in the dark] [+very strange] [+for a common purpose] [+actively repel what threatens or attacks] [+incapable of being understood or interpreted] [+formally, solemnly and officially]

7 In each case, provide two or three nouns that can collocate with the following:

1 (an) odd . . .   2 (an) urgent . . .   3 (an) awkward . . .
4 (an) enigmatic . . .   5 (an) outspoken . . .   6 (a) strange . . .
7 (a) firm . . .   8 (a) thrilling . . .   9 (a) blood-stained . . .
10 (a) benign . . .

8 Explain the meaning of the following:

1 doorstep 2 entertainer 3 cocoon 4   account
5 hallucination 6 apparition 7 astrologer 8 limbs
9 detachment (of the mind) 10 reincarnation 11 affinity
12 fate 13 pervasive 14 resuscitate 15 (to) herald
16 look down upon sb

9 Match words/phrases from the noun/noun phrase list with words from the verb list. Notice that some of the verbs can collocate with several nouns and vice versa.

1 to show 2 to protect 3 to declare 4 to collect 5 to safeguard 6 to pronounce 7 to flaunt 8 to shield 9 to proclaim 10 to defend 11 to expose 12 to announce 13 to display 14 to pick up 15 to gather

peace, a thesis, independence, flowers, war, mushrooms, one's health, one's thoughts, one's engagement, one's rights, one's skin to the sun, one's newly acquired riches, a wide knowledge of vocabulary, a child from bad influences, radio signals, them man and wife, one's eyes from the sun

10 Guess the right word.

1 In southern countries st . . . . . dogs roaming the streets are a common sight.
2 In the year 2000 heat will be c . . . . . in a completely revolutionary way.
3 She is e . . . . . this week at London's biggest art gallery.
4 The next moment the wild geese m . . . . . a kind of communal energy and took off into the morning sky.
5 The dec . . . . . left all her money to a stranger.
6 I r . . . . . the coat I'd left in the train by going to the Lost Property Office.
7 The lu . . . . . eyes of the owl stared unblinking into the night.
8 The car c . . . . . into the house, making a huge hole in the facade.
9 Often the first child will re . . . . . the intrusion of the newest

member to the family.

10 Judging by his peculiar behaviour, I'd say that the man is a bit de . . . . ..

11 The w . . . . . was bright and cheerful and filled with flowers at each bedside.

12 'It's not fair' she wailed, st . . . . . with impatience and frustration.

11 What differences and/or similarities are there between the following?

1 to affect/to influence   2 to penetrate/to enter   3 to hope/ to believe   4 to worry/to care for   5 to want/to long for   6 to stamp/to step   7 to impress/to sway   8 to display/to show   9 heat/warmth   10 an utterance/a sentence   11 a psychiatrist/ a psychologist   12 weird/eerie

12 The following expressions illustrate either the literal or the figurative sense of the given verbs. In each case, provide two or three collocations for the sense that has not been illustrated.

EXAMPLES

a   (literal) to wallow in mud
     (figurative) **to wallow in riches/in vice/in sensual pleasures**

b   (figurative) to shatter somebody's belief/one's nerves
     (literal) **to shatter windows/rocks/ice**

1 to cross a street   2 to spread rumours/knowledge   3 to channel ideas/thoughts   4 to gather flowers   5 to shake somebody's faith/courage   6 to muster all the soldiers/men   7 to dig out the truth/the facts

13 Choose from the words in brackets the one which is most appropriate in each case.

1 She . . . . . me the book, but it wasn't what I wanted. (exhibit, show, display)

2 The peacock does not always . . . . . its feathers to its admiring visitors. (exhibit, show, display)

3 The dog quickly . . . . . the dead pheasant for the huntsman. (find, get back, retrieve)

4 Did you . . . . . the address all right? (find, get back, retrieve)

5 At the sound of the alarm, everyone . . . . . in orderly fashion to receive their life-jacket. (gather, collect, assemble)

6 He . . . . . financial contributions from all the people present at the meeting. (gather, collect, assemble)

7 He refused to learn to shoot because he never wanted to . . . . . any animal. (murder, kill, slaughter)

8 If you saw how they . . . . . cattle, you would never eat meat again. (murder, kill, slaughter)

9 There was a dim light . . . . . from under the door. (flow, emanate)

10 There was nothing the politician could do or say to . . . . . the vote in his favour. (affect, influence, sway)

14 Summarize the article on life after death, using the following words:

to exhibit   to recover   to resuscitate   to impair   to vary   to resent   to track down   account   clues   heartbeat   brain-wave(s)   emergency-room   pervasive   benign   alert   deranged

Revision Exercises

R1 Explain the meaning of the following words and expressions:

1 bully 2 rebuff 3 flashcard 4 pitfall 5 euphoria
6 ability 7 plight 8 omniscience 9 leisure 10 merit
11 retaliate 12 supersede 13 pick on somebody 14 assert
oneself 15 hit it off with somebody 16 make a stand
17 keep an eye on somebody 18 gain in stature 19 on all fours
20 hire-purchase

R2 In each case provide two or three nouns that can collocate with the following adjectives:

1 clandestine 2 orderly 3 genuine 4 bogus 5 plain
6 underhand 7 obnoxious 8 sham 9 neat 10 furtive

R3 Find words to fit the following descriptions/ definitions:

1 culture opposed to traditional, prevailing culture
2 one who uses his strength to frighten or hurt those who are not so strong
3 a colour-filled pen with a soft tip
4 additional benefits apart from wages or salary
5 paying too much attention to little, unimportant details
6 the time just before it gets quite dark
7 a man who is in charge of a group of workmen
8 inferiors, people lower in rank
9 a collection of documents kept together for reference purposes
10 an enclosure where ships are built or repaired

R4 Fill in the collocational grids.

1

	fertilisers	sweeteners	flowers	leg	theory	information	argument	hair	grief	smile
false										
spurious										
artificial										

2

	a good knowledge of French	a job	an idea	a PhD	a lot of prestige	new skills	wealth	a taste for Havana cigars
get								
acquire								

3

	sb's car	a painting	the environment	one's health	sb's reputation	children	one's legs	sb's feelings	sb's pride	sb's speech	sb's enjoyment	sb's happiness
damage												
harm												
impair												
hurt												
injure												
mar												

R5 Guess the right word.

1 S . . . . . is an awareness of your own worth!
2 He has a l . . . . . smile.
3 The streets in the mining town were gr . . . . . .
4 Enjoying ourselves so much, we were r . . . . . to leave, but of course we did so in the end.
5 The recent earthquake in China must be one of the worst c . . . . . in history.
6 I wouldn't ha . . . . . an animal if you paid me.
7 Anyone with i . . . . . eyesight shouldn't be allowed to drive on the road.
8 The farmers could expect little from the da . . . . . crop after so much rain.
9 'Ouch! That h . . . . .!' she screamed as I pressed her wounded knee.
10 His lack of tact only i . . . . . his reputation further.
11 The tree was sufficiently stu . . . . . to resist the storm that followed.
12 The king had anticipated the coup and was therefore able to f . . . . . the revolutionaries.

R6 Match appropriate features with each of the following words:

1 drab 2 ward off 3 restore 4 phony 5 strip 6 wallow
7 drudgery 8 retain 9 stealthy 10 glimmer

[+usu in mud, dust or water] [+arousing suspicion] [+cheerless] [+to a former condition] [+work] [+continue to have] [+send out a soft light] [+roll about] [+keep at a distance] [+bring back] [+take excessive pleasure in] [+of undesirable things] [+always intended to deceive] [+take off/away covering or furnishing] [+tedious] [+stresses the possibility of losing] [+careful not to be recognized or caught] [+dark in colour]

R7 Place the given words on an appropriate scale.

1 adore 2 be attached to 3 be infatuated with 4 be fond of
5 love 6 like 7 be in love with 8 feel affection for

R8 What differences and/or similarities are there between the following pairs?

1 smart/well-groomed 2 scamper/scurry 3 crouch/squat
4 contaminate/pollute 5 unwilling/reluctant 6 be present/infest
7 responsibility/liability 8 respite/relief 9 profession/occupation

10 grind/toil   11 secret/secretive   12 duck/evade   13 revive/
restore   14 keep/retain

R9 Fill in the following componential grids:

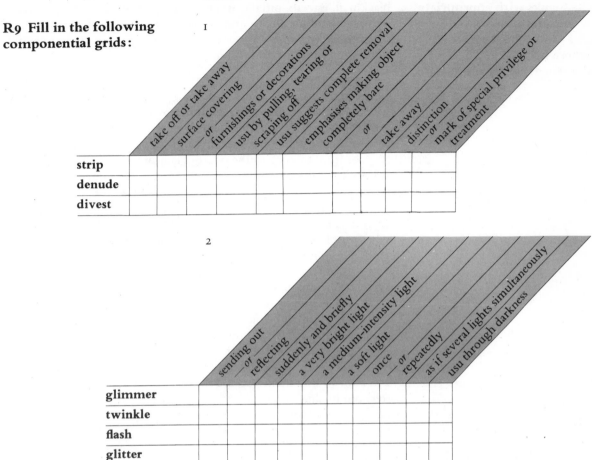

R10 Produce a logical and coherent story by filling in the blanks with appropriate words from the list below and modifying their form where necessary. Three of the words can be used twice.

giddy, dubious, shy, constricting, utmost, permissive, envious, mild, shrewd, lenient, gentle, indulgently, bully, sample, blackmail, esteem, pitfalls, strain, change, adolescence, to frequent, to be cajoled, to gaze, to grab, to grow, to be limited, to claim, to grumble, to tackle, to overstate, to breed, to cope with, to avoid, to bring up, to shift, to resume, to deal with

She stopped what she was doing and 1 . . . . . at us. My sister even expected me to 2 . . . . . her children, when she knew my time was so 3 . . . . .; what with 4 . . . . . all my own vegetables and trying to earn a living by 5 . . . . . these budgerigars. She pointed to the birds in question, which were watching us from their confined cage and 6 . . . . . from one leg to the other. Their only 7 . . . . . of position was to fly to the opposite perch and 8 . . . . . the same activity. She gave a 9 . . . . . laugh and her face 10 . . . . . its expression of 11 . . . . . surprise. 'Anyway,' she continued, 'as a parent I'm far too 12 . . . . .; my own children are bound to finish as members of what people like to call our 13 . . . . . society.' She smiled 14 . . . . . at the thought of them. 'But I do maintain that I've 15 . . . . . them 16 . . . . . as well as I could, and I think I can even 17 . . . . . some success.' She did not need to 18 . . . . . the point for we knew what she was referring to. Her children had 19 . . . . . up to be responsible human beings, able to 20 . . . . . difficulties when they arose, capable of 21 . . . . . even the most difficult of people. They did not avoid responsibility but rather enjoyed 22 . . . . . new problems, even if they did not always succeed. There was not a 23 . . . . . among them because they had been given the 24 . . . . . freedom in childhood and 25 . . . . .. They were neither frustrated nor, where others were concerned, 26 . . . . .. Visiting their house years ago we never heard them having 27 . . . . . into doing something in the house. They 28 . . . . . if they couldn't help their mother! This obviously took a lot of the 29 . . . . . off being a one-parent family, and indeed their mother had somehow avoided the 30 . . . . . most women fall into once a marriage is broken and they are left alone with children to bring up. Our 31 . . . . . for her knew no bounds, though obviously an outsider could be dubious about all this until he had seen for himself. Marriage for her had acted more as a 32 . . . . . influence than a liberating one. Her husband had always seemed to us rather a 33 . . . . . person, relying on emotional 34 . . . . . to get what he wanted from her. Fortunately she was 35 . . . . . enough to realize she could do just as well, if not better, without him. It was when he started to 36 . . . . . rather 37 . . . . . establishments that she gave him a 38 . . . . . of her independence by taking the children away with her to the country. It made us 39 . . . . . to think of all that she had had to go through alone . . .

Unit 9   Where shall we live?

The Explosive Growth of the World's Cities

Urbanization is one of the most pronounced trends of the twentieth century. Barbara Ward, in her recent book *The Home of Man*, describes how industrialization and world trade led to urbanization and to the development of big cities which she predicts will continue as shown in the tables below:

Percentage of population in cities		Cities with 1,000,000 people	
1900	15	1900	11
1960	33	1950	75
2000	50	1985	273

THE EXPLOSIVE GROWTH OF CITIES

1 a great and sudden change
2 doubtful, capable of two interpretations one of which is bad
3 a complex of towns, villages, and small cities closely associated with a central metropolis
4 sudden and complete failure
5 complete, absolute
6 *lit* a mass of snow, earth, stones, etc rushing down a mountain-side, *fig* a great mass
7 coming out of slowly and with great effort, arising from
8 1000 years
9 a great flood or rush of water, *fig* a large amount

'Even this vast multiplication does not fully measure the contemporary **upheaval**[1] in human settlements. The million-city begins to explode into the ten-million city. There were two of them in 1950 – New York and London. By 1970 there were four. But by 1985 there will be at least 17 of these gigantic agglomerations, ten of them in developing areas – with Mexico City at nearly 18 million, only a step behind New York. And at the head of the list, Tokyo will recover its earlier primacy with the **dubious**[2] distinction of bringing 25 million people together in a single **conurbation**[3].'

'We may, of course, question whether some of the more surrealistic predictions – for instance, Calcutta and Bombay with perhaps 100 million inhabitants – will ever be reached,' she writes. 'Various degrees of urban **collapse**[4] may well have intervened. But the projections are valuable as indicators of the **sheer**[5] **avalanche**[6]-like scale with which the world's people are increasing, **heaving themselves out of**[7] the **millennia**[8] framework of village and small town, and descending in **deluges**[9] of mixed hope and despair on the world's larger settlements.'

Condensed from *The Futurist*

CITY MONKEYS

1 living
2 a variety of small monkey with a tail, common throughout India
3 stealing little things or small quantities
4 make a raid or sudden attack on or into
5 stalls, places in public markets where things are sold
6 seize suddenly or rudely
7 hollow places or openings in a wall
8 sit on a branch or piece of wood to go to sleep, used of birds, chickens, monkeys, etc
9 limiting
10 searching for food
11 waging war with, fighting
12 set free
13 worked out in great detail
14 improve, increase
15 effect, influence

City Monkeys

A comparative study of the urban and forest-**dwelling**[1] rhesus **monkeys**[2] of India reveals profound differences between the two societies.

The former live by **pilfering**[3]: they **raid**[4] shops, kitchens and market **stands**[5]; they even **snatch**[6] food from people.

They tend to sleep in the same **niches**[7] each night, unlike their forest counterparts who generally **roost**[8] in a tree near where they have spent the day.

The urban monkey is far more aggressive, possibly due to his more **restrictive**[9] environment where **foraging**[10] is more difficult. He is always **warring**[11] with shopkeepers and is ready to attack strangers, be they monkeys or humans, of whom several are reported to have been bitten to death.

Despite his insecurity, he prefers the city to the wild; if seized and taken to the forest, he will always return home when **released**[12].

Contrary to expectations, **elaborate**[13] tests revealed that an urban environment does not significantly **promote**[14] intelligence. The reader is left to speculate on the implications for man and the **impact**[15] of urban life on his behaviour.

An abstract of 'Urban Monkeys' by Sheo Dan Singh from
Scientific American

The Problem of the Cities: It's an Old Refrain

Race **riots**[1], air pollution, filthy rivers, and inadequate **public transportation**[2] are not 20th-century inventions.

Charles Adrian and Ernest Griffith visited small towns, and **delved**[3] into historical-society records, local newspapers, and the memoirs of old community leaders to show that city governments faced the same problems 100 years ago as they do now. 'Pollution was a very important problem particularly with regard to the water supply in the 19th century', Adrian notes. City governments were 'handicapped because they didn't know how diseases were spread. . . . They knew some diseases were **communicable**[4], but it wasn't until the 1890s that the **germ**[5] theory was developed.'

Those of us who **decry**[6] the automobile's[7] **noxious**[8] **fumes**[9] tend to forget about the pollution that was caused by horses. According to Adrian, 'it took a long time to develop methods of controlling the pollution problem horses created — the horses wouldn't cooperate.'

Summer riots in **ghetto**[10] areas are an old story, too. They go way back, Adrian says, 'getting under way in the 1820s and reaching a climax in the 1860s.'

People tend to believe that we 'once had good public-transportation systems that were destroyed by the automobile.' Not so, says Adrian. Public transportation in the 19th century was minimal. 'The **horse-car**[11] of 1870 served the middle class. Working people walked.'

Public-planning agencies did not exist until the 20th century, and **land developers**[12] built town after town without leaving space for **greenery**[13]. Thomas Jefferson designed a couple of towns using a **checker-board**[14] approach with alternate squares of vacant and developed land. The models —

Jeffersonville, Indiana, and Jackson, Mississippi — 'never survived the **land pressure**[15], according to Adrian.

For those who **bemoan**[16] a lack of adequate police protection in our cities today, Adrian cites a letter published in a St Louis newspaper in 1821 in which a resident complained that 'the only night watch in the city was maintained by **prowlers**[17], **thugs**[18] and kidnappers.'

The persistence of these problems doesn't mean that we have learned nothing from the past. That's just the way the system works, says Adrian. 'Politics in a democracy is designed not to solve problems, but rather to find some way of **managing**[19] problems and to do this with minimal costs.'

— Jody Gaylin

Charles Adrian and Ernest S Griffith, A History of American City Government, 1775–1870, Praeger, 1976.

Psychology Today

THE PROBLEM OF THE CITIES

1 outbreaks of disorder, disturbances of the public peace
2 *Br* public transport
3 dug, went a long way into
4 that can be communicated, passed on
5 living organism, too small to be seen by the eye, which causes disease
6 condemn, complain about
7 *Br* car
8 harmful, poisonous
9 smoke, gas
10 poor urban quarter inhabited largely by minority racial groups
11 tramcar, car drawn by horses
12 people whose business is building new housing
13 grass and trees
14 a board for playing checkers, *Br* draughts
15 demand for land (for building houses)
16 complain about
17 people who roam the streets to find what they can
18 violent criminals
19 handling, controlling

GETTING
GENE LOGSDON

It was not so much the phrase 'getting **involved**[1]' that I had begun to distrust in the city, but the **tedious**[2] sort of people who used it too often. I found that for most of them, involvement meant discussing at lunch the latest injustice they had read about in the *New York Times*. So I was not surprised when I moved to a part of the country where the *Times* could not be bought locally at all, that they accused me of '**dropping out**[3]'.

Allow me to warn you, **prospective**[4] **homesteader**[5]: Buying a place in the country is no way at all to drop out of anything except perhaps the good graces of your banker.

My family and I have been living one full week now in a rented farmhouse from which the only permanent signs of human habitation we can see are the roofs of two **barns**[6] **nudging**[7] the horizon in the distance. Other than the cars on the road and the tractors in the unending fields, there is little else visible to remind us of the world of man. Yet we have had more visitors in a week than we had in two months in the suburbs of Philadelphia. Our farmhouse is a central command post for the farmers putting in the spring crops around us. They use the telephone to call in supplies and repairmen. Their families bring lunch and we all picnic in the grassy barnyard. Soon we are worrying farmer worries: Will it rain, but not too much? Why is oil **leaking**[8] out of that tractor? Are we planting corn too deep? What caused the **power take-off shaft**[9] to break? We become involved in the most basic, most important of human **endeavors**[10] – **raising**[11] food.

But such involvement is nothing compared to what happens when you actually buy some rural land of your own. Shortly after the ink is dry on your **deed**[12] – if not sooner – you will understand what involvement is all about. Here are some of our experiences which you may find helpful:

1. Phone rings. 'Mr Logsdon, I'm the **guy**[13] who has been farming that land you bought. You want me to farm it for you on-the-half?'

Farming 'on-the-half' means that landowner and land operator share equally the expenses of planting and harvesting the crops, and then share in the profits, if any. This type of renting is more complicated than just **leasing out**[14] the land for a **flat**[15] per-**acre**[16] **fee**[17].

At any rate, if you have only a few acres, you will probably want to farm them yourself. But if you are going to be very busy building or repairing your house or finding a job or business to

---

GETTING INVOLVED

1 mixed up with or in, caring about
2 dull, boring, uninteresting
3 *coll* stopping taking part in
4 relating to or expected to be in the future
5 *Am* owner of a homestead or farm
6 farm buildings for storing hay, straw, etc
7 just touching, *lit* touching with the elbow to attract attention
8 coming out accidentally

9 bar which turns by the power of the tractor engine, and drives the machine behind it
10 efforts, attempts
11 *Br* growing, producing
12 a written or printed agreement, esp made by a lawyer about ownership or rights
13 *Am coll* man
14 letting somebody else use, in return for payment (only for land and houses)

15 uniform, always the same, having no exceptions
16 4000 square meters
17 payment
18 *Br* boundary fence, a fence being a barrier put round a field, garden, etc especially one made of wood or/and wire
19 keeping away
20 fussy, difficult
21 planting and harvesting
22 *Br* look for, hunt for

NVOLVED

give you steady income, you might be wise to rent your land out even though you'd much rather farm it yourself.

2. Phone rings again. 'Hi, neighbour,' says an almost-too-cheerful voice. After small talk about the weather, he wants to know what we are going to do about the **line fence**[18] between us. Good fences make good neighbors – and if there is no fence between your crop field and your neighbor's he will be wondering how far to plow your way. He doesn't want to get onto your property, but he doesn't want to leave any land go to waste by **hanging off**[19] on his side too far either. If the two of you get along real well and aren't too **particular**[20], you may live in peace **cropping**[21] back and forth across the non-existent fence line. But you must have some understanding about it.

3. 'Can we go fishin' in your creek?'

4. 'Can we **hunt**[22] mushrooms in your woods?'

How you answer 3, 4 and similar requests is up to you, but a little friendliness will go a long way to keeping your community involvement pleasant.

Every activity of our homestead, no matter how minor, inevitably involves yet another member of the community. **Well-diggers**[23], foresters, **Soil Conservation agents**[24], rural mailmen, painters, **roofers**[25], **plumbers**[26], telephone linemen, electricians, **county engineers**[27], **surveyors**[28], **masons**[29], **plasterers**[30], **real estate brokers**[31], health officials, insurance agents, machinery **dealers**[32], **veterinarians**[33] and salesmen by the gross. Some will come when I call, some whether I call or not, and some even when I **pointedly**[34] say I'm not interested – like the **tax assessor**[35]. Suddenly I realize what a great number of people depend for their living on me, on the landowner and homeowner – and how much I depend on them. I learn all about the soil, everyday kind of involvement none of us can do without.

There is more time too, now, for another kind of involvement. Just today I became involved with a pale green luna **moth**[36] brought to me in a little girl's trembling hand . . . with a son's delight over the first **morel mushrooms**[37] he has ever found . . . with the aroma of bacon and eggs drifting from house to barn before breakfast. I look to the woods and I **bear witness**[38]: the **redbuds**[39] **bloom**[40] again as they have done every spring in the memory of man. I have become involved in the richness of existence.

Organic Gardening and Farming

23 people who make wells, ie holes bored in the ground from which water is obtained
24 people who give advice about maintaining the quality of the soil
25 people who make or repair roofs
26 people who make a living by fitting and mending water-pipes, cisterns, etc
27 people concerned with construction of roads, bridges, buildings who work for the county, an

administrative area in the country
28 people who measure the shape, position and boundaries of land
29 professional wall-builders
30 people who put on the layer of plaster required on interior walls of houses before painting
31 persons who arrange the buying and selling of land and buildings, *Br* estate agents
32 people who buy and sell
33 animal doctors, *Br* veterinary

surgeons, usually *coll* vet
34 emphatically, sharply, directly
35 one who assesses (fixes the value of) property and income for taxation
36 night butterfly
37 edible mushroom
38 see what happens, *lit* give evidence
39 variety of trees, also known as the Judas tree
40 have flowers, be in blossom

AS YOU WERE

1 department stores where goods are sold at reduced prices

PLAINLY

1 *coll* straightforwardly
2 *coll* was terribly frightened
3 *coll* to try to find out in an indirect way
4 artifices, ways of doing things
5 inclined to, liable to
6 openly
7 *coll* make to feel very embarrassed or surprised

AS YOU WERE

When United States postal service chiefs heard that Carmel, California, had no postal deliveries, they sent investigators there to put matters right.

But the townsfolk — all 4,791 of them — didn't want to be modernised. They liked walking to the post office to pick up their mail and have a chat.

That wasn't the first time Carmel has refused to be modernised. It claims to be the only town in the world without supermarkets, **discount stores**[1], factories, parking meters, car parks or neon lights.

The citizens are determined to keep things just as they are.

Weekend

PLAINLY

We didn't play around with words in the small, rural village I was brought up in. Such questions as: 'How old are you?' 'how much did you pay for it?' and 'how much does your husband earn?' were asked and answered **without messing about**[1].

When I married and moved to a town my husband **grew scared stiff**[2] every time I opened my mouth. It's taken me years to learn how **to fish for information**[3] and to deal with the **ploys**[4] of others. And I'm still **prone to**[5] 'going native' and **blandly**[6] asking a question in company which **shakes**[7] my poor husband absolutely **rigid**[7].
— Mrs L Turner: Bideford.

Woman

Discussion

1 Why are country dwellers often drawn to go and try a new life in a big city? Do they usually find what they are hoping for?
2 What are the differences between life in the country and life in the city? Which do you prefer, and why? Which do you think is better for your physical and mental well-being?
3 What parallels can you draw between the findings of the monkey study and man's behaviour in the country and in the city?
4 What do you think is meant by 'urban collapse'? Do we have any indications that this is already taking place?
5 Why is the idea that life was better in the 'good old days' (*The Problem of the Cities: It's an Old refrain*) so prevalent? What kind of reasons do people usually give to support this theory? Do you agree with them, or do you feel that life is better now than 100 years ago, or do you feel that, in fact, it's more or less the same?

Word Study

A Semantic Fields

1 Living in

	in a town, region or country	in a type of habitation (tree, cave, flat)	in a type of environment (eg city, mountain)	in a house, hotel, hall of residence or locality	permanently	temporarily (while working, studying or visiting)
inhabitant	+				+	
dweller		+	+		+	
resident				+	+	+

Unlike the verb **dwell**, **dweller** is quite common and is usually found in compounds.

EXAMPLES

inhabitant   The **inhabitants** of this rocky, arid region manage to exist by breeding goats whose cheese they can sell.

The island used to support a thriving population of fishermen and their families, but now the only **inhabitants** are gulls and rabbits.

dweller   Many primitive peoples are still cave-**dwellers** as our ancestors were.

Apes, which are tree-**dwellers**, have a highly developed sense of balance and co-ordination.

resident   The local **residents** have formed an action committee to protest about the condition of the streets.

Swallows are summer **residents** in Britain and fly south for the winter.

2 Noisy fights or quarrels

	violent physical fight	non-serious physical fight	verbal quarrel	disorderly behaviour	numerous participants	few participants	noisy
riot	+	+			+		+
brawl	+					+	+
row			+			+	+
rumpus			+	+	+	+	+
scrap		+				+	+

Notice that **rumpus** and **scrap** are not used in formal style.

EXAMPLES

riot   There is always a danger of race **riots** in communities of mixed origin.

What started as an orderly demonstration rapidly turned into a **riot** when police tried to prevent demonstrators from blocking the entrance of the factory.

scrap   Three visiting sailors were involved in a **scrap** with local fishermen who accused them of making improper suggestions to their girlfriends.

brawl   Every Saturday night the police have to deal with numerous drunken **brawls** between supporters of the two football teams.

row   Martin told his parents he wanted to leave school without taking the final exams and a terrible **row** ensued.

rumpus   The **rumpus** above our heads is Jill trying to make ten children be quiet and go to sleep in the same room.

The scandal surrounding the Foreign Secretary has caused a terrible **rumpus** among members of the Government.

Riot and **scrap** are also commonly used as verbs.

EXAMPLES

to riot   The students are **rioting** over the Government's proposals to exclude foreign students from the Universities.

to scrap   Her two little sons are very aggressive and are constantly **scrapping** over something.

3 Giving or getting the use of

	give the use of sth	or get the use of sth	in return for payment	always by written contract	long-term	short-term	usu of ships and aeroplanes
lend	+						
let	+		+				
borrow		+					
rent		+	+				
lease	+	+	+	+	+		
hire	+	+	+			+	
charter	+	+	+				+

All the verbs, except **hire**, collocate with the preposition **to**; all, except **let** and **lend**, can also take **from**. In colloquial style **borrow** is common with **off**.

EXAMPLES

lend   Could you **lend** me £10?

let   They have **let** their house to a visiting professor for the summer.

borrow   I **borrowed** a washing machine from my neighbour while she was away.

I prefer to **borrow** money off a friend than off someone I hardly know.

rent   We **rented** a flat by the sea from friends.

lease   The school **leases** its sports field from the town council.

hire   You can **hire** bicycles by the day from the railway station.

charter   A jet specially **chartered** from British Airways carried the two football teams directly to Brazil.

	rooms	flats	houses	shops	money	dresses	suits	typewriters	concert halls	theatres	coaches	cars	boats	planes	ships
lend	+	+	+	+	+	+	+	+				+	+	+	
let	+	+	+	+											
borrow	+	+	+	(+)	+	+	+	+				+	+	+	
rent	+	+	+	+							+				
lease	+	+	+	+				+	+						
hire					+	+	+	+	+	+	+	+			
charter													+	+	+

4 Being or making suitable

	modify so as to suit new conditions	often changing existing form	retaining existing form	be, or act, according to pre-existing patterns, forms or principles
adapt	+	+		
adjust	+		+	
conform				+

All three verbs collocate with the preposition **to**. Unlike **adapt** and **adjust**, **conform** does not take a direct object. The distinction between **adapt** and **adjust** is not always made, particularly when they refer to people.

EXAMPLE

He just cannot $\left\{ \begin{array}{l} \textbf{adapt} \\ \textbf{adjust} \end{array} \right\}$ to the different life style here in America.

	adapt(ed)	adjust(ed)	conform(ed)	
The novel has been	+			for television.
Two Koala bears which were brought to England	+			easily to their new life in a cooler climate.
My camera can be		+		to take pictures in cloudy or sunny conditions.
You can		+		the height of the cutter depending on the crop.
Many immigrants find it difficult to	+	+	+	to the different social conditions they find in their new country.
Imported electrical equipment frequently does not			+	to our safety standards.

5 Taking hold of

take				
seize	grasp	clutch	snatch	grab

take hold of	suddenly and forcibly	often of sth difficult or elusive	and hold firmly	and hold tightly or convulsively	sth one is eager to keep or retain	quickly	roughly
seize	+	+					
grasp	+		+				
clutch	+			+	+		
snatch	+					+	
grab	+						+

All the verbs are transitive and all can collocate with the preposition **at**, which adds the feature [+ try to]. In colloquial style **grasp** is used figuratively to mean 'understand'.

EXAMPLES

I explained really carefully, but she seemed quite unable to **grasp** what I was talking about.

If he could **grasp** even the basic principles of transformational grammar, it would help.

	take (took) (taken)	seize(d)	grasp(ed)	clutch(ed)	snatch(ed)	grab(bed)	
You must	+						the racket in your right hand and the ball in your left.
The ape	+	+				+	her baby and ran up the tree.
He	+		+				her hand and guided her across the road.
John		+	+	+			the rope firmly and swung himself over the river.
The climber			+	+			at the ledge above his head but was unable to reach it.
An eerie sound made her			+	+			my arm in fear.
He		+				+	her and pulled her out of the path of the truck.
Bobby	+	+			+	+	the apple from his little sister's hand.
The monkey leaned down and	+				+	+	a tourist's hat as he passed under the tree.
The bank robbers	+				+	+	as much money as they could carry and ran off.

6 Organising

	see that sth functions or is done	be in sole charge of	actually do the work oneself	originate work for others	make sure others are fulfilling a task	by using organisational skills
conduct	+		+			
direct	+	+		+		+
manage	+			+		+
run	+		+	+		+
supervise	+				+	

In musical terminology **conduct** means 'direct an orchestra when it is playing', and in this sense only the verb may be intransitive.

	a film	a play	a summer school	a research programme	a meeting	a course in history	a series of tests	research	an experiment	negotiations	a trial	a factory	a shop	an organisation	a publishing company	a business	a theatre	sb's house	classes in biology
conduct				+	+	+	+	+	+	+									
direct	+	+	+	+		+													
manage											+	+	+	+	+	+			
run			+	+	+	+						+	+	+	+	+	+	+	
supervise			+			+	+	+	+										

7 Stealing

	steal	small-sized things —or— small amounts	usu things of little or no value	by quick snatching	never for things of great value (like famous artworks, precious stones, big quantities of gold)	often by underhanded business which appears honest
pinch	+					
swipe	+					
lift	+	+				
pilfer	+	+	+	+		
snitch	+		+	+	+	
rip off	+				+	+

Like **steal**, **pilfer** can be used either transitively or intransitively. All the other verbs are transitive. The differences between **pinch**, **swipe** and **steal** are mainly stylistic (see scale below). **Snitch** is particularly used by schoolboys. **Rip off** may take a [+human] object which denotes the person being stolen from.

EXAMPLE

The car repair firm really **ripped** me **off**.

These words may be placed along a stylistic scale to show how formal or informal they are.

slang			colloquial	informal	formal
rip off	**snitch**	**swipe**	**lift** **pinch**	**steal**	**steal** **pilfer**

	steal (stole) (stolen)	pinch(ed)	swipe(d)	lift(ed)	pilfer(ed)	snitch(ed)	rip(ped) off	
The poor woman	+							food to feed her children.
The bank robbers	+	+						a car to make their escape.
The well-known art thieves	+		+					a Leonardo da Vinci drawing from the National Gallery.
O.K.! Who has	+	+	+				+	my cigarettes?
The students have	+	+		+			+	a large number of books from the library.
Someone has	+	+	+	+		+	+	all my chocolates!
Someone	+	+	+	+		+	+	my new pen from my desk.
Children	+				+			extensively in self-service shops.
People don't feel guilty if they	+				+		+	(from) large organisations.
All the silver was	+						+	while we were on holiday.

8. Likely to do, be or undergo

	likely to do	likely to undergo	likely to be affected by	having a natural or habitual inclination or tendency to	often to inevitable things
apt	+			+	
liable	+	+		+	
prone		+		+	+
susceptible		+	+		
subject		+			

In the sense in which they are found here, these words can only occur as predicates. **Liable, prone, susceptible** and **subject** collocate with the preposition **to**; **liable** and **apt** take a **to-**infinitive.
Note the idiomatic construction **accident prone**.

EXAMPLE
Having broken my arm and my leg in the space of 3 months, I'm beginning to think I'm really **accident prone**.
Notice also that when used attributively **apt** has the feature [+suitable] and **susceptible** [+easily influenced].

EXAMPLES
Can you think of an **apt** quotation for the beginning of my book?
Such a **susceptible** young girl shouldn't be let loose in London by herself.

	apt	liable	prone	susceptible	subject	
Friends are	+	+				to arrive unexpectedly, hoping to swim in our pool.
He is	+	+				to forget that he promised to do things.
The handle is	+	+				to stick, so pull it hard.
Foreigners are		+				to be stopped by the police.
The road is		+		+		to flooding.
My sister is			+	+		to fits of depression.
Young children are more			+	+		to infection than adults.
Most people are				+		to flattery.
People from hot climates are				+		to the cold.
The timetable is				+	+	to change without notice.

B Synonymous Pairs

1 **to inhabit** ⎱ [+to occupy as one's home] ⎰ [+only a region or area] [+with plural subject]
to live in ⎰ ⎱

EXAMPLES
The tribesmen who **inhabit** the region are nomadic.
As a result of irrigation this former desert area is now **inhabited** by thousands of families.
When I **lived** in London, I was never bored.
Do you prefer to **live** in a house or a flat?
We **lived** near the sea when I was young.
Last year I was **living** in England.

2   **to fall down** $\Big\{$ [+stop being $\Big\}$

    to collapse $\Big\{$ upright] $\Big\}$ or [+lose its force or shape]

	fall down	collapse
an argument		+
a (legal) case		+
a platform		+
lungs		+
a person	+	+
a house	+	+
a wall	+	+
a tree	+	

can

3   **pernicious** $\Big\{$ [+harmful] $\Big\}$ [+poisonous]

    noxious

	lies	influence	gas	fumes	wastes	substance	effect
pernicious	+	+					
noxious			+	+	+	+	+

4   **effective** $\Big[$ [+bringing about, or capable $\Big]$

    efficient $\Big\{$ of bringing about, definite $\Big\}$ [+in a fast, skilful or

               results] $\Big]$ economical way]

	remedy	medication	weed-killer	machine	methods	worker	secretary
effective	+	+	+	+	+		
efficient				+	+	+	+

Exercises

1 How does the meaning of the words in bold change in the given collocations?

1 **to earn** respect/admiration/one's living/£5000 a year
2 **to break** one's leg/somebody's heart/the news to somebody/a record/somebody's spirit/the law/one's word
3 **to grasp** a rope/somebody's hand/an argument
4 **to spend** one's money/time/one's leisure
5 **to build** a house/a railway
    to build in a cupboard
    to build up a good reputation/a fortune
6 the roof **leaks**/the news **leaked out**
7 the tent **collapsed**/our plans **collapsed**
8 **susceptible** to flattery/a **susceptible** young girl

2 In each case add a few nouns that can collocate with the given word.

1 adjust   2 pinch   3 run   4 snitch   5 direct   6 snatch
7 adapt to   8 let   9 conform to   10 hire   11 seize   12 clutch
13 be subject to   14 be susceptible to

3 Describe the differences and/or similarities between the following:

1 to delve/to dig   2 to forage/to search   3 to lift/to swipe
4 to manage/to supervise   5 to lend/to borrow   6 to hire/to rent
7 to snatch/to grab   8 riot/rumpus   9 upheaval/change
10 inhabitant/resident   11 thug/criminal

4 What nouns can be derived from the following words?

1 multiply   2 distinguish   3 lodge   4 imply   5 dwell   6 base
7 grow   8 find   9 destroy   10 disturb   11 combat
12 operate   13 dig   14 settle   15 deliver   16 plaster
17 intervene   18 roof   19 forest   20 insecure   21 rich
22 persistent

5 What do you need to be able to do the following?

1 fish   2 plough   3 measure something   4 hunt   5 picnic
6 drive   7 lease a shop   8 compete with somebody   9 send a
letter   10 get into university   11 get a good job   12 build a
house

6 Guess the right word.

1 Even before the houses were completed pr . . . . . buyers were coming to look at them.
2 'En . . . . . to get him to change his mind; it's vital!'
3 The man was r . . . . . from prison after serving his sentence.
4 I ch . . . . . away the bees that were around the pot of honey.
5 Defeated, the reporter had to f . . . . . the fact that he wouldn't get his story in on time.
6 The ra . . . . . carried out by the police produced nothing.
7 The d . . . . . that followed the dam breaking was indescribably frightening.
8 The l . . . . . we'd found during our short holiday in London was in a small back-street hotel.
9 We fo . . . . . among the old curiosities in the attic, until we found what we'd come for.
10 His p . . . . . was to get us out of the house before the visitors arrived.
11 She b . . . . . y informed the hotel proprietress that she couldn't pay the bill as she had no money.
12 He had an el . . . . . way of talking, as though complexity were a quality in itself.

7 Fill in the missing words:

1 She is not . . . . . to the job.
2 We can't do . . . . . a second car.
3 It was all . . . . . talk, nothing really important.
4 I read the letter with . . . . . feelings.
5 They have very strange sleeping . . . . . .
6 At midnight the confusion r . . . . . a climax.
7 The s . . . . . of the axe is broken.
8 The disease . . . . . throughout the continent.

8 Describe the differences and/or similarities between the following:

1 a chat/a conversation   2 a prowler/a thief   3 a barn/a stable
4 an income/a sum of money   5 a creek/a river   6 an upheaval/
a riot   7 a suburb/a town   8 a field/a meadow   9 a mason/
a plasterer   10 to nudge/to push   11 to steal/to pilfer
12 to conduct/to direct

9 In each case add two or three nouns that can collocate with the following adjectives:

1 (an) explosive . . .   2 (an) elaborate . . .   3 (an) efficient . . .
4 (a) fatal . . .   5 (a) wise . . .   6 (a) noxious . . .
7 (a) gigantic . . .   8 (a) thorough . . .   9 (a) complex . . .
10 (a) tedious . . .   11 (a) dubious . . .   12 (a) cheerful . . .

10 Fill in the componential grids.

1

	likely to do *or* likely to undergo	likely to be affected by	having a natural or habitual inclination or tendency to	often to inevitable things
apt				
liable				
prone				
susceptible				
subject				

2

	violent physical fight *or* non-serious physical fight	verbal quarrel *or* disorderly behaviour	numerous participants	few participants	noisy
riot					
brawl					
row					
rumpus					
scrap					

11 Complete these sentences by choosing an appropriate word from those in brackets, altering it grammatically where necessary.

1 You must . . . . . the basic essentials before you can go further in mathematics. (snatch, catch, grasp)
2 There is nothing more . . . . . than having to listen to the same story for the hundredth time! (dull, drab, tedious)
3 On seeing the actress arrive, the boy . . . . . his friend excitedly. (touch, nudge, push)
4 She . . . . . into her memory, trying to remember where, in the past, she'd seen this face. (dig, go, delve)
5 The party . . . . . of politicians, publishers and top journalists. (comprise, compose)
6 The psychiatrist's . . . . . seems exaggerated considering the short time he spends on each patient. (pay, fee, wages)
7 Having made his fortune he now . . . . . in great luxury in a large house in the country. (inhabit, dwell, reside)
8 This once flourishing port is now only . . . . . by monkeys and birds. (inhabit, dwell, reside)

12 Fill in the componential grids.

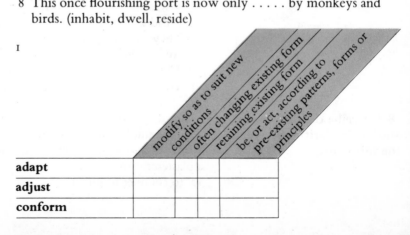

1

	modify so as to suit new conditions	often changing existing form	retaining existing form	be, or act, according to pre-existing patterns, forms or principles
adapt				
adjust				
conform				

2

	person or animal that lives					
	in a town, region or country	in a type of habitation (tree, cave, flat) *or*	in a type of environment (eg city, mountain)	in a house, hotel, hall of residence or locality	permanently *or*	temporarily (while working, studying or visiting)
inhabitant						
dweller						
resident						

Revision Exercises

R1 Which of the given features are included in the meaning of the following words?

1 fastidious   2 salary   3 mock   4 shirk   5 toil   6 avert
7 compassion   8 flounder   9 glisten   10 furtive   11 divest
12 underhand

[+careful not to be seen] [+long] [+sensitive, emotional reaction] [+stumble or struggle] [+not very bright, as from a wet surface] [+helplessly and without progress] [+imposing near perfection] [+prevent] [+usu by cheque] [+intended as a substitute for the real thing] [+share and understand the distress or misfortune of another] [+tiring] [+take away] [+not telling anybody what one is doing or thinking] [+of undesirable things] [+paid monthly] [+usu work or duty] [+not open or straightforward] [+in cash] [+made in close imitation of something else] [+distinction or mark of special privilege] [+avoid] [+work] [+desire to help and spare] [+reflect light] [+deceitful]

R2 Find the words to fit the following descriptions/definitions:

1 a period of paid free time for rest and special study given to a university teacher after a certain length of service
2 wanting more than a fair share or more than it is right
3 respect combined with fear or reverence
4 health of mind
5 pretty, neat and delicate in appearance
6 proposed law, to be presented to a parliament
7 able to glow in the dark
8 a thing or quantity that is changeable
9 mediaeval Christian military expeditions to save the Holy Land

R3 Describe the differences and/or similarities between the following:

1 to dodge/to duck   2 to strip/to divest   3 to boast/to brag
4 to glimmer/to shimmer   5 to belittle oneself/to be modest
6 real/genuine   7 beginning/onset   8 lawyer/solicitor
9 trick/gimmick

R4 Fill in the componential grids.

1	be visible _or_ make visible	spread out objects so that they can be easily seen	often to attract public attention or inspection	give evidence of (eg quality) _or_ lay open, uncover or take away protection	in an ostentatious and boastful manner
show					
display					
exhibit					
expose					
flaunt					

2	bring together _or_ come together	look for and bring back	in a pile or heap, or as if in a pile	often arrange in an orderly way	for a common purpose
gather					
accumulate					
assemble					
collect					
muster					

R5 Guess the right word.

1 The af . . . . . that existed between the two men was difficult to pinpoint.
2 Judging by his peculiar behaviour, I'd say that the man is a bit de . . . . .!
3 The app . . . . . which seemed to come from nowhere was dressed in a suspicious-looking white sheet!
4 The rebellious students returned to their desks but re . . . . . to work.
5 'T . . . . . me once more with violence, and I'll divorce you,' she said.
6 She s . . . . . with disgust at the thought of having to meet the man again.
7 With apparent unconcern she m . . . . . her way through fresh crisp carrots in the cinema!
8 What a f . . . . . man, he can't leave his children alone for a minute!
9 Being somewhat short-sighted, she had this unattractive habit of p . . . . . at people.
10 The ironmonger spread out his me . . . . . in front of his shop.
11 He gave my hand a g . . . . . squeeze.
12 Right from the o . . . . . of that tedious walk Peregrin was complaining about his feet.

R6 With the help of a monolingual dictionary explain the different senses (literal and figurative) of the following collocations:

1 (a) **flat** tyre/bottom/surface/beer/refusal/note
2 (a) **plain** English/food/cooking/talk
3 (a) **dry** wood/clothes/well/bread/wine/book/subject/humour/facts/cough
4 (a) **simple** machine/sentence/food/style/life/peasant/forms of life

5 (a) **rich** furnishings/cake/diet/colours/voice/joke
6 (a) **small** town/sum/business/talk/eater
7 (a) **steady** rate/speed/worker/progress/boyfriend

R7 Which of these words should not be used in formal contexts?

to steal, to pinch, fake, drudgery, to complain, sham, perilous, to brag, clean, shipshape, to shift, to change, to crow, to advance, to grouse, to crash, to squat (meaning: to sit), to pilfer, apt, mock, phony, fussy, work, to astound, to bellyache, to spurn, to decline, to flabbergast, to lift (to steal), bogus, prone, grind, toil, scrap, spurious, ghastly (very unlikeable), to reject, to acquire, to turn down.

R8 Describe the differences and/or similarities between the following:

1 to bicker/to wrangle   2 to complain/to grumble   3 to advance/ to further   4 to astound/to surprise   5 to smirk/to chuckle 6 cunning/shrewd   7 affluent/opulent   8 meagre/scanty 9 folk/people

R9 In each case provide three or four nouns that can collocate with the following adjectives:

1 steady   2 lenient   3 bogus   4 occupational   5 drab   6 sly 7 affluent   8 potent   9 shrewd   10 permissive   11 even 12 tidy   13 meagre   14 counterfeit   15 austere   16 mock

R10 Fill in the following grids:

1

	an attack	a blow	an accident	evil	disaster	suspicion	one's eyes	one's gaze
ward off								
avert								

2

	a lover	sb's attentions	sb's offer	a request	an invitation	sb's proposal	an application	a candidate	a gift	sb admittance
spurn										
decline										
turn down										
reject										
refuse										

3

	a plant	an old tradition	old feelings of hostility	a castle	a painting	somebody to health	law and order	peace
revive								
restore								

R11 Choose the word that best fits the context. Modify its form where necessary.

1 The judge . . . . . his verdict on the case. (proclaim, declare, pronounce)
2 We . . . . . in line before marching into school each morning. (collect, muster, assemble)
3 They . . . . . the dying soldier long enough to learn where the enemy was hiding out. (revive, resuscitate)
4 There was nothing . . . . . in his behaviour, but we could tell that he didn't like us. (open, overt)
5 He was . . . . . to begin a new contract and I could not persuade him otherwise, so I'm afraid we have lost him. (reluctant, unwilling)
6 He was . . . . . to the point of being rude. (disagreeable, ghastly)
7 I would not advise anyone to drive on those . . . . . snowy roads, and particularly not a beginner. (risky, hazardous)
8 One could already . . . . . what she would be like when she was older. (forecast, predict, foretell, prophesy)
9 Danger was . . . . . only by a matter of seconds. (prevent, avert, forestall)
10 He was always . . . . . about addressing letters. (carefree, reckless, careless)
11 '. . . . . yourself' she said, as she squeezed herself in beside me. (change, alter, shift)
12 The girl's dress was the first thing that . . . . . him to her. (lure, tempt, attract)
13 . . . . . ing with rage, she turned and left the room without a word. (quake, shake, quiver)
14 The court showed a lot of . . . . . in dealing with a woman who had stolen money to buy food for her children. (compassion, sympathy)

R12 Solve the crossword puzzle.

Across

1 small clear spaces in a wood (6)
5 sb who likes and follows closely, for example, football (3)
7 The huge elephant walked with p . . . . . steps along the road. (9)
10 smile unkindly or foolishly (5)
11 take firm hold of (5)
13 popular domestic animal which catches mice (3)
14 When wood becomes diseased and weak, it is said to . . . . (3)
16 sense of honesty and sincerity to others and oneself (9)
20 place where something was or will be (4)
21 Butterflies f . . . . . from flower to flower. (4)
22 lost, esp of domestic animals (5)
23 empty, as in 'null and . . . . .' (4)
25 suggestion that one will do sth for sb (5)
26 Don't worry about me, I'm . . . . . right! (3)
29 search everywhere, very carefully (*coll*) (5)
31 break sth fragile, eg a glass into small pieces (5)
33 mental hospital (*of*) (6)
35 sweet smelling liquid people put on to make themselves attractive (5)
36 opens, discloses, reveals (7)
39 The fire engine arrived just in time to a . . . . . disaster. (5)
41 make sb feel left out and different from the main group (8)

42 Her children are so rude and naughty, they really ex . . . . . me! (10)

43 run away together to get married secretly (5)

44 quick to notice (5)

45 In the country the p . . . . . of life is much slower than in the town. (4)

47 not what it claims or pretends to be (begins with 'to encourage a horse') (8)

48 thin or narrow (4)

49 person who is mad (*of*) (7)

50 good quality which brings praise (5)

Down

1 looks for a long time, and unceasingly, at sth (5)

2 man's best friend (3)

3 bang the door (4)

4 sand or mud carried by moving water and left at the mouth of a river (5)

6 You like crosswords, don't you? . . . . ., I don't! (2)

7 hole dug in the ground (3)

8 first version of a piece of writing, to be changed or amended (5)

9 We like . . . . . new house very much. (3)

10 of the back (6)

12 dizzy (5)

15 Very heavy rain is t . . . . . . (10)

17 complain by muttering in a low, indistinct voice (6)

18 keeping oneself distant from everybody else (5)

19 redirect light or energy from its original path (7)

22 influence sb to change their ideas or a course of action (4)

24 Your baby is . . . . . good as gold! (2)

26 In calculating our journey time, we need to make a . . . . .

for unexpected delays like traffic jams, accidents, or bad weather. (10)

27 dale (anagram) (4)

28 of uncertain status or meaning (10)

30 The river is very full and has . . . . . its banks, causing a flood. (5)

32 the children who live at number 22 are this (9)

34 Tensions between members of a family are often resolved by r . . . . . . (4)

37 pulls a covering off sth, eg wallpaper from a wall (6)

38 He hasn't said anything direct, but I i . . . . . from his behaviour that he doesn't want to help us. (5)

40 Tomatoes are r . . . . . when they turn red. (4)

46 He didn't see the p . . . . . in the road, and fell right into it! (3)

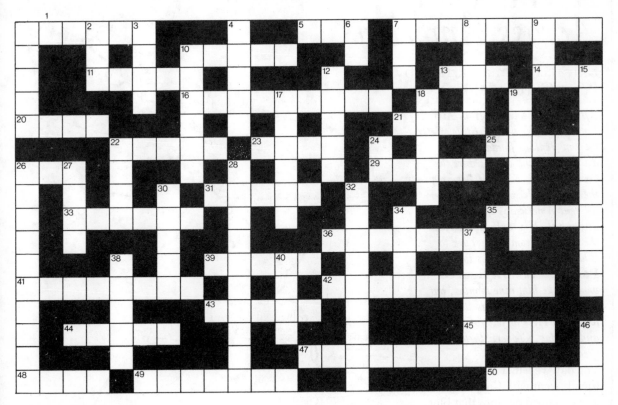

Unit 10 **A walk across America**

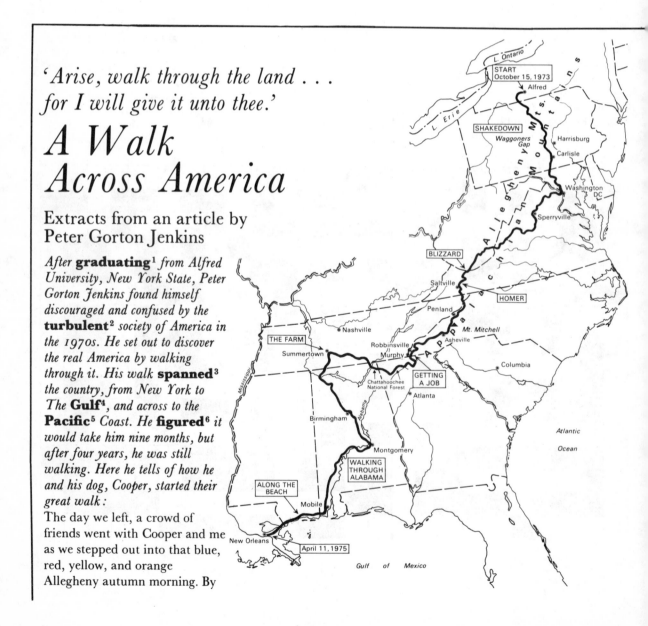

'*Arise, walk through the land . . .
for I will give it unto thee.*'

A Walk Across America

Extracts from an article by
Peter Gorton Jenkins

*After **graduating**[1] from Alfred
University, New York State, Peter
Gorton Jenkins found himself
discouraged and confused by the
turbulent[2] society of America in
the 1970s. He set out to discover
the real America by walking
through it. His walk **spanned**[3]
the country, from New York to
The **Gulf**[4], and across to the
Pacific[5] Coast. He **figured**[6] it
would take him nine months, but
after four years, he was still
walking. Here he tells of how he
and his dog, Cooper, started their
great walk:*
The day we left, a crowd of
friends went with Cooper and me
as we stepped out into that blue,
red, yellow, and orange
Allegheny autumn morning. By

A WALK ACROSS AMERICA

1 *Br* get a degree (obtained first university qualification which in GB and US takes 3–4 years and gives its holder the title of Bachelor (of Arts, of Sciences), usually known as BA, BSc etc Also used in US for leaving secondary school with a qualification
2 disorderly, violent, hard to control
3 to cross from one end to the other
4 Gulf of Mexico
5 Pacific Ocean
6 *Am* reckoned, estimated
7 went for a long walk
8 pine trees, evergreen trees with needle shaped leaves
9 *coll* moved in a certain direction
10 equal
11 plural of goose, a kind of waterbird
12 a kind of bird of prey
13 a kind of bird of prey
14 passed by as bullets of a gun
15 dash off as fast as a rocket
16 the sound made by leaves blown in the wind
17 muscles used to city life
18 cord made from the intestines of sheep, etc used for the strings of violins, tennis-rackets, etc
19 at a stretch, without interruption
20 make a plan, map, or diagram
21 uncultivated areas
22 variety of wild animal
23 regularly and in order, *lit* according to the season
24 *Br* reached, got to
25 Washington in the District of Columbia, capital of the US
26 traffic made by people commuting to and from their work
27 *Br* choked, was unable to breathe
28 the smoke from the exhaust pipe of cars, buses, etc
29 a road encircling the city, *Br* ring-road
30 forms or bends into a loop, a curve that crosses itself

the time we'd **hiked**[7] 30 miles and made our first night's camp in the northern Pennsylvania mountains, only my brother Scott and Charlie Keane, a friend, remained. We had a ceremonial fire and herb tea and slept better than kings under wise old **pines**[8].

Next morning Cooper and I **headed**[9] south on Pennsylvania road 449. We were alone. The walk had begun.

Fast as we walked, we were no **match**[10] for the great flocks of **geese**[11] migrating south over our heads, though somehow they transmitted their spirit to us.

We spent eight windblown hours in 1,479-foot Waggoners Gap just north of Carlisle, Pennsylvania. Thousands of **hawks**[12] and **falcons**[13] **bulleted by**[14] only a dozen feet above our heads.

Cooper came alive when the sun went down and the animals came out to be chased. Watching him **rocket**[15] into the darkness after a mysterious **rustle**[16], I remembered how he and I had trained for this walk for 4½ months, running hundreds

of hours uphill and down and turning our **suburbanized**[17] muscles into the **catgut**[18] and piano wire you need, man or dog, if you're going to walk 20, 30, 40 miles a day for months **on end**[19].

Instead of following a detailed route on a map, I would **plot**[20] our way by asking directions from farmers, hunters, police, anyone we met. When practical, we would go by the **wilds**[21] and back roads. I had promised myself to obey two rules. One is an Indian law that says, 'With all beings and all things we shall be as relatives'. The other is my own: 'Disturb the land no more than a **deer**[22] would do in passing through.'

Everything flowed **seasonally**[23] for fifteen 16-hour days until we **hit**[24] **Washington D.C.**[25], and **commuter traffic**[26]. I **gagged**[27] on **exhaust fumes**[28] getting past the **beltway**[29] that **loops**[30] the city, then wandered among the great marble buildings – outward symbols of the inward America I was seeking.

But already there was a cold breath of winter in the air, and I felt that same southward pull that **impels**[31] the geese and hawks. We took the first country road we could find toward the wilds of the Appalachians.

Our first snow **flurry**[32] hit us five miles west of Sperryville, Virginia, making the footing **slick**[33] as we hiked through the late-autumn forest up toward Skyline Drive.

Unexpectedly, I heard a car struggling up the other side of this killer mountain. It was a silver and white VW bus. The driver **pulled to a stop**[34]. I asked how far it was to a store and food.

'Oh, three or four miles,' he said. It was nice to hear a human voice. He reached back into his VW and, one by one, brought out five giant red apples. They seemed to glow with an inner **ruby**[35] light. Sitting on a rock after the good Samaritan drove off, I shared the fruit of Eden with Cooper. This priceless gift from that unknown man totally renewed my body, mind, and spirit. I sang all the way to that country store.

The Mountain Man
In Virginia, Gorton Jenkins' **wanderings**[36] *led him to the home of someone said to be*

America's greatest living mountain man – his name is Homer Davenport. The local people warned him to be careful, because Homer doesn't like strangers on his mountain . . .

But I went. Rural Route 2 goes half those 12 miles, then ends. The last six miles were torture. Homer's front **sidewalk**[37] is a rocky mountain stream with **a trail**[38] **fading in and out**[39] and mud, mud, mud!

After several miles of **head-down**[40] **trudging**[41]. we came to a sharp bend in the stream. In those pure woods I felt another presence. Cooper barked once – a rarity – and then stood still as

stone – also a rarity.

I looked up. And there he was – looking for all the world like a prophet on his way down from the holy mountain. Fifty feet away stood an ageless old man with white shoulder-length hair. Something electric passed from his eyes to mine and back again.

He had an empty sack over his shoulder. He **nodded**[42] back down the mountain.

'**Goin'**[43] down to fetch some **meal**[44], **flour**[45], and salt,' he said. 'Join me if you like.'

I would have followed him anywhere. So it was back down the mountain again, then back up – me with my 45-pound **pack**[46] and Homer with his 30

---

31 pushes or drives forward
32 sudden gust of rain, hail or snow
33 slippery
34 stopped
35 a red precious stone
36 going about from place to place without any special purpose or destination
37 *Br* pavement
38 path
39 appearing and disappearing
40 bending forward, face down
41 walking wearily or with an effort

42 bowed the head quickly as a sign of agreement or as a greeting
43 in speech only, the *g* in *ing* words may be dropped, particularly in US
44 coarsely ground grain
45 the fine meal (powder) made from wheat and used for making bread
46 bag with straps, carried on the shoulders, often with a frame, *Br* rucksack
47 a rough length of wood as it comes from the tree

48 articles which have been thrown away, usually of metal
49 a hole in the ground
50 made with a spade
51 short for rac(c)oon, a small, flesh-eating animal of North-America
52 *fig* went through the motion of swallowing (taking food down the throat) as the result of a feeling of discomfort in the throat, ie revulsion
53 *coll* to cook, to produce things to

pounds of supplies. It was all I could do to keep up with him.

Just below the peak of this 4,400-foot mountain is Homer's 'mansion' – a cabin of **logs**[47] and **scrap**[48], about 30 by 15 feet, with its back end built right into the mountainside. His fireplace is a **pit**[49] **dug**[50] into the living earth. While we warmed our hands by the fire, he began 'boilin'' up some **coon**'[51].

Being a vegetarian, I **swallowed**[52] hard at the thought of that boiling raccoon in the fireplace pot. I didn't realize Homer intended it only for his dogs.

Homer **whipped up**[53] some hot **corn**[54] bread, **canned**[55] **applesauce**[56], and homegrown yellow **beets**[57] the size of **cantaloupes**[58]. He laughed **hoarse**[59] and loud when he realized I thought the coon was for me. With a swift **slice**[60] of his **bowie knife**[61] he cut a **chop**[62] from a quarter of lamb hanging from a **beam**[63], then handed me a straightened **coat hanger**[64] and pointed to the fire.

'Cook up a chop, son,' he said. 'Freshest meat you'll ever have.'

My vegetarians days were over. I never ate a more satisfying meal. We talked until 3 a.m., exchanging details of our lives like two collectors **trading**[65] rare old coins. Then I slept on

ashwood[66] **shavings**[67].

From Homer's mountaintop, it took us seven days – mostly in heavy snow – to reach Penland, North Carolina. There I enjoyed some indoor warmth, conversation, hot tea, and **bell-shaped**[68] Christmas cookies with my old college friend Jack Neff and his family. Jack was teaching **pottery**[69] at the Penland School of **Handicrafts**[70].

A strange contrast

Cooper and his master began their New Year on the top of Mount Mitchell. Travelling on, they found a complete contrast in the city of Asheville, North Carolina. Gorton Jenkins gives his impression of the city:

It was the first sizable city we'd hit since Washington, D.C. We went right through the middle of town, for a time walking side by side with **scurrying**[71], dark-suited businessmen. If I looked strange to them in my **stained**[72] and **sweaty**[73] walking **garb**[74] and pack, they looked no less strange to me in their three-piece business suits with those strange **ribbons**[75] of colored cloth around their necks, separating their heads from the rest of their

bodies. I was glad this rush hour was theirs, not mine. Cooper and I headed out of that **extra-terrestrial**[76] scene and back to the wilds of mother earth.

His second family

*Gorton Jenkins was running short of money, so he **backtracked**[77] up and down country roads from one small town to another looking for work. Finally someone told him there might be the chance of a job in the town of Murphy, so he and Cooper headed off there. He takes up his story again:*

I had $15 left when, after a 36-mile hike in cold, damp weather, Cooper and I walked into Murphy on a Friday evening. I passed some lighted basketball courts where a **bunch**[78] of black teenagers were playing. They came over when they saw me and Cooper, asked the usual questions, then invited me to play. I couldn't resist.

Later, exhausted, we camped out for the night in their neighborhood across the railroad tracks. Two of the teenagers, Eric and Bruce, invited me to their home for a southern meal next day. And that's how I met my second mother, Mary Elizabeth Lloyd.

She was standing there in the door of the **house trailer**[79]

---

eat quickly	62 one rib of animal and the meat
54 maize	attached to it, for eating
55 tinned	63 a long, thick, heavy piece of wood
56 stewed apples	used to support a floor or roof
57 kinds of plants either eaten as	64 a thing to hang coats on

eat quickly
54 maize
55 tinned
56 stewed apples
57 kinds of plants either eaten as vegetables or used to make sugar from (beet-sugar as opposed to cane-sugar)
58 a kind of melon
59 rough, not clear
60 movement made to slice or cut into thin, flat pieces
61 a strong hunting-knife

62 one rib of animal and the meat attached to it, for eating
63 a long, thick, heavy piece of wood used to support a floor or roof
64 a thing to hang coats on
65 exchanging
66 wood from the ash, a tree with hard, tough wood
67 thin slices of wood cut off with a plane or knife
68 in the shape or form of a bell
69 the art of making earthenware pots, or the pots themselves

70 skills of making things with the hands
71 hurrying with quick, short steps
72 covered with stains, dirty marks
73 damp with sweat or perspiration
74 style of dress
75 long narrow strips of material
76 not of the earth
77 retracing one's steps
78 group
79 a kind of caravan used as a permanent home

home in the leafy depths of Smokey Hollow. She told me later that when she first saw my **scraggly**[80] red beard, she thought, 'Uh-oh, what have the boys brought home to dinner this time?' But when she saw how Cooper liked me, she figured I must be worth her trust. Dogs don't lie. Soon we were **immersed**[81] in a dinner of rich corn bread, forever-**simmered**[82] **turnip greens**[83], ham **chunks**[84], freshly caught **perch**[85], **bream**[86] and catfish, and rivers of **Kool-Aid**[87].

In the middle of the meal, Mary Elizabeth rose and announced that she believed God had sent me to test their faith and henceforth I was one of the family. Bruce, 15, immediately volunteered his bedroom, saying he would sleep on the spring-protruding **couch**[88] in the living room.

For the next several months I lived with my family in Smokey Hollow and worked **sawing**[89] logs at a **veneer mill**[90].

Weekends I would usually go wandering with Cooper through the mountain wilds, coming back Sunday morning to attend Mount Zion Baptist Church, where Mary Elizabeth's 73-year-old father Pau Pau was a deacon. He would put me in the front **pew**[91], and there I would sit, the only grain of salt in a

shaker[92] of black pepper.

The time came to leave. My good-byes with Mary Elizabeth and the family were more **gut wrenching**[93] than any of the trip so far. I had enough money to get down to the Gulf Coast – I hoped – and so I headed into Georgia.

Somehow I had **envisioned**[94] Georgia as all flatness and dust and red clay, but here were the sweet green mountains of Chattahoochee National Forest. I was rock-climbing at a survival school called Wolf Creek Wilderness when a couple of fellow climbers told me about something that would turn my plans upside down. It was the Farm – a spiritually oriented agricultural commune in Tennessee.

The Farm

Although it wasn't on his planned route, the Farm sounded interesting. Gorton Jenkins felt a kind of **call**[95] *so he and Cooper turned their steps towards Tennessee. It took them two weeks to reach Summertown, where the Farm is located. Here he describes what it is and what it does.*

What is the Farm?

I learned that it's a place where some 1,100 people have come together to lead a simple, devoted, intensely spiritual way of life.

Back in 1967, in San Francisco, a college teacher named Stephen Gaskin had begun teaching free classes dedicated to the expansion of the human potential – mental, physical, and spiritual. By 1970 his Monday-night classes were **magnetizing**[96] some 2,000 students. Stephen then **recessed**[97] the classes in order to make an **extended**[98] trip around the U.S.A. in a bus. Some 250 of his students decided to go along, and for four months their spiritual caravan **roamed**[99] from coast to coast, visiting colleges, churches, small towns – always looking for a piece of the American landscape that might become their own promised land. They found it in south-central Tennessee. **Pooling resources**[100], they made a **down payment** on 1,000 acres of Tennessee red dirt, and soon some 400 young people – artists, students, college graduates, high-school dropouts, businessmen and women, rock musicians – landed **en masse**[102] on Lewis County, Tennessee. A **Martian**[103] landing party could not have been much more astonishing to local folk.

But these 'Martians' soon proved that they were not here to **dawdle**[104] but to work, and work hard. They became farmers, real farmers – even if their life-style, by Tennessee

80 shaggy, unkempt, untidy
81 enjoying, *lit* covered with water
82 boiled or cooked gently
83 the leaves and stems of turnips cooked as vegetables
84 thick, solid pieces
85 a kind of fresh water fish
86 a kind of fresh water fish
87 a kind of soft drink (trade name)
88 a kind of sofa
89 cutting wood with a saw
90 a factory or workshop where

wood is covered with a thin layer of finer wood
91 an enclosed seat in a church
92 a container in which something is shaken
93 *coll* very moving and sad, *lit* causing pains in the guts or intestines, *Br* would say heart-breaking
94 seen or foreseen in the imagination
95 attraction, a feeling towards or in

favour of something
96 *fig* attracting as a magnet does, influencing by personal charm, moral or intellectual power, etc
97 a brief stopping of work, business, etc, temporarily ended (for school or college courses, courts of law)
98 long
99 wandered, travelled here and there without a particular destination
100 putting their money and other

country standards, was a bit **offbeat**[105]. Tomatoes, cabbages, sweet potatoes, hot peppers, beans, watermelons poured from the soil of the Farm and helped **buoy**[106] the local economy.

After initial suspicions and misunderstandings, the folk of the Farm soon became recognized as good neighbors by most of the people of Lewis County.

Upon my arrival I was allowed **to partake of**[107] the Farm's life – working and eating and meditating.

Six weeks passed. I started **staring**[108] down country roads. October came – marking a full year since the walk from Alfred, New York, had begun. Once again I heard the soul-moving **honks**[109] of migrating geese high above. I decided the time had come to leave.

Once the decision was made, my spirits **soared**[110]. Soon I would be back out on the road again with Cooper.

Reaching the Gulf

At last the two weary travellers reached the coast of the Gulf of Mexico at the city of Mobile, renowned for its parks, trees and flowers:

The whole city seemed like a pink, white, and red fantasy. Equally exciting were the live oaks standing like **moss**[111]-bearded prophets above the **petty**[112] affairs of men. I was so **enamored**[113] of these wood giants – and so out of money – that I got a job with the city **trimming trees**[114]. Cutting dead branches off a **regal**[115] live oak made me feel like a privileged barber trimming the hair of a king.

I fell in love with Mobile, the most beautiful city I had ever seen, and the one that seemed to me to have struck the best balance between nature and urban man.

And so I reached the Gulf Coast. Now I had come as far south as I could go. I particularly loved the sea air, all salt and vaguely fishy and filled with magical, **soul-stirring**[116] vapors that no mountain wind can surpass for perfection. I **swung**[117] westward along unending **beaches**[118] that led across the misty, marvelous coastlands of Alabama and Mississippi.

After all the **landlocked**[119] miles I had walked, it was pure poetry to go **barefoot**[120] at the water's **foamy**[121] edge.

I glanced behind myself down the long Mississippi **shoreline**[122]. I could see my two footprints trailing behind me into the misty milk-blue infinity. Those footprints in the sand, in a way, were my own signature. I liked the fact that the waves would soon wash them away.

Facing back toward New Orleans, I quickened my steps.

National Geographic

---

asset together in a common fund
101 in instalment buying, the initial payment on a purchase
102 *French* adverbial phrase meaning many people doing something together
103 from the planet Mars
104 waste time, go slowly
105 *sl* unconventional, out of the ordinary, not conforming to social norms
106 buoy up, keep up or support

107 *of* take part in
108 looking steadily with wide-open eyes
109 cries of the wild goose
110 rose, *lit* fly high into the sky
111 a variety of small green plant
112 small, unimportant
113 in love
114 *Am* pruning trees, ie making neat and tidy by removing uneven or irregular parts
115 royal

116 exciting
117 turned
118 the shores of the sea or of a lake
119 surrounded by land
120 with bare feet, without shoes or stockings
121 like foam, covered with foam, a mass of white bubbles
122 the line or contour of a shore

Discussion

1 Is doing a walking tour through the countryside the only way to 'know' a country? Describe any experiences you have had which characterise your country, and make you feel you know it well.
2 What sort of attitude to 'civilisation' and city life does the author seem to develop during his walk? Do you agree with him, and why?
3 Have you had any experiences of kindness from total strangers similar to the gift of apples from the unknown driver? Describe them, and try to say what effect this kind of event has on you and your feelings to your fellow human beings.
4 If you were going to do a walk similar to this one, would you do it in your own country or another one? What are your reasons?

Word Study

A   Semantic Fields

1 Different kinds of limits

	dividing line between two countries	or part of the surface of sth along its limit	part not written on at two sides of a page	or line dividing off that part	narrow strip of land beside a road	line or part of a line marking the limit of sth	often circular or curved	upper limits, usu of a container when full	flat part which extends round the face of a hat	of water, esp when deep	usu with a steep/vertical side	usu outdoors and natural	dividing line between two areas of land	the limits of sth
border	+	+												
margin			+	+										
verge					+									
edge						+								
rim						+	+							
brim								+	+					
brink						+				+	+	+		
boundary													+	
bounds														+

Notice that the use of **brim** in the first sense is restricted to the expressions: **full to the brim**, **brim-full** and **to fill sth to the brim**. In their literal senses, **verge** does not take an **of**-adjunct and **brink** seldom does.

Bounds is always used in the plural. It occurs in a limited number of phrases, the most common of which are:

beyond the bounds of $\begin{Bmatrix} \text{reason} \\ \text{imagination} \end{Bmatrix}$

within the bounds of $\begin{Bmatrix} \text{reason} \\ \text{possibility} \\ \text{probability} \\ \text{credibility} \end{Bmatrix}$

out of bounds   (places forbidden, according to rules or regulations, usu to soldiers or schoolchildren)

EXAMPLES

the $\begin{Bmatrix} \text{park} \\ \text{village} \\ \text{pub} \\ \text{river} \end{Bmatrix}$ is **out of bounds**

to know no bounds

his $\begin{Bmatrix} \text{ambition} \\ \text{enthusiasm} \\ \text{perseverence} \\ \text{patience} \\ \text{kindness} \end{Bmatrix}$ **knows no bounds**

EXAMPLES

The **border** between two countries.
The left hand **margin** of a page.
The **edge** of a lake.
The **rim** of a cup.
The **brim** of a hat.
The **brink** of a ravine.
The **boundary** between two fields.

The meaning of some of the nouns can be extended in the following way:

border	[+imaginary line between two things]
margin	[+difference between two sums of money] or [+amount of error allowed]

$\left.\begin{matrix} \textbf{verge} \\ \textbf{brink} \end{matrix}\right\}$ $\begin{Bmatrix} [+\text{point just before beginning sth}] \end{Bmatrix}$

	between sanity and insanity	between humour and stupidity	for error	of tears	of a nervous breakdown	of collapsing	of disaster	of war	of economic collapse	of a new discovery
the border	+	+								
the margin			+							
on the verge				+	+	+	+	+	+	+
on the brink							+	+	+	+

Notice also the expression **a profit margin**.

2 Land beside water

	point where land meets sea or lake	or area of land near to the sea	or land bordering a river or canal
shore	+		
coast		+	
bank			+
–side	+	+	+

Shore is often found in the plural.

In the sense in which it occurs here, **–side** is always used in compounds.

EXAMPLES

on the lake **shore**; the **shores** of Lake Ontario; the western **shores** of our country

the west **coast**; on the south **coast**; the Atlantic **coast**; off the **coast** of Mexico

the south **bank** of the Tyne; on the **banks** of the Mississippi

at the sea**side**; on the lake**side**; on the river**side**

Riverside is more common as an attributive adjunct and **seaside** and **lakeside** may also be used in this way.

EXAMPLES

a **riverside** restaurant; a **seaside** holiday; a **lakeside** cottage

3 Groups of animals, birds and insects

	number of creatures of one kind	living together	or kept or travelling together	animals or birds	usu wild or domestic cattle	usu dogs or dog-like animals	animals	insects	only bees when forming new colony	only lions	only geese	only fish
flock	+	+	+	+								
herd	+	+	+		+							
pack	+	+	+			+						
troop	+	+	+				+	+				
colony	+	+						+				
swarm	+								+			
pride	+	+								+		
gaggle	+	+									+	
shoal	+	+										+

The use of some of these terms may be extended to humans.

EXAMPLES

flock   Jesus Christ and his **flock** (Christians)
I think I'd better take my **flock** home. (children, *coll*)

swarm   **Swarms** of people descended on the stores for the first day of the winter sales. (large numbers, *coll*)

gaggle   A **gaggle** of giggling girls filled the platform and spoilt our quiet goodbye. (*coll*)

	sheep	birds	cattle	deer	goats	horses	buffaloes	elephants	dogs	wolves	monkeys	ants	bees
flock	+	+											
herd			+	+	+	+	+	+					
pack *of*									+	+			
troop											+		
colony												+	+

4 Going from place to place

going	on foot or by other means	quite a long way or short distance	without any special purpose or destination	for pleasure	usu in the country	without any definite destination	in an unhurried manner	relaxed
roam	+	+	+	+		+		
ramble	+	+		+	+			
wander	+		+			+	+	
stroll	+	+					+	+

All these words can be used with prepositions and **stroll** must be.

EXAMPLES

In the evening we
{ **roamed** / **rambled** / **wandered** / **strolled** } round the old town. / through the meadows.

He **roamed** the streets not knowing what to do.
The boys went **rambling** in the hills all day.
We **wandered** into a part of the town we had never seen before.
Could you just **stroll down/along** to the baker and get me some bread?

5 Wasting one's time

	not strain oneself *or* waste time	waste time	stay standing in one place	usu in a public place	for no apparent reason or no apparent reason	spend more time than is necessary or usual in doing sth	by playing around with irrelevant and unimportant things	in a silly way
idle	+	+						
loiter			+	+	+			
dawdle						+		
dally						+	+	
dillydally						+	+	+

All five verbs are intransitive and all, except **idle**, collocate with the preposition **over**. **Dally, idle** and **loiter** are also transitive and collocate with **away**. **Dawdle, dally** and **dillydally** are colloquial.

Note the special expression **loitering with intent**, which in English law means 'being in a place with a view to committing a crime'.

Note also the use of **idle** in **the motor is idling** (just running, not doing any work).

	idle(d) (ing)	loiter(ed) (ing)	dawdle(d) (ing)	dally(ing)	dillydally(ing)	
We	+					away the days in reading, swimming and making music.
I	+					over breakfast and the morning papers until almost lunch time.
The large numbers of unemployed have nothing better to do than	+	+				away their time in the streets and bars.
Why are you		+				here in the corridor? Go and do some work!
I get so irritated when the children			+			over their food!
If you don't stop			+		+	we will never get this job finished.
He is just				+	+	in the orchard instead of picking apples as he should be.
No			+	+	+	! We have at least a two-hour walk ahead of us.

6 Being in the air

	fly		hover	glide
flit		soar		

	operate a glider or	move through the air or	cause to move through the air	travel in a plane with an engine	lightly and quickly with wings	in a series of brief flights from place to place	smoothly	without using any energy	rise upwards	stay in one place in the air
fly		+	+	+						
flit		+			+	+				
glide	+	+					+	+		
soar		+							+	
hover										+

All the verbs are intransitive and **fly** and **glide** are also transitive.

	fly (flew) (flown)	flit(ted) (ing)	glide(d) (ing)	soar(ed) (ing)	hover(ed) (ing)	
The plane	+					over the sea.
The birds have	+					away to the South.
I often	+					to Brussels for the weekend from London.
Sometimes he	+					his brother's plane but he was not a qualified pilot.
A brick	+					across the street and struck me on the arm.
At night bats	+	+				in and out of the church.
The bees	+	+				from flower to flower.
Birds	+	+				around catching insects.
The plane's engine failed but the pilot managed to	+		+			it down to the airfield.
A bird	+		+			gently past my window.
The seagull	+			+		up into the blue sky.
Gliders can	+			+		in a rising air current.
The eagle				+	+	above its nest before landing.
A cloud of dust					+	over the town.
The rescue helicopter					+	above the drowning man.

When **fly**, **flit** and **hover** are used figuratively, they are colloquial.

EXAMPLES

I **flew** round the house, trying to finish the chores in time to come and meet you.

For about two years now he has been **flitting** from job to job but he can't find anything that suits him.

Stop **flitting** about the room – sit down and relax!
He **hovers** around me when I'm working as if he thinks I'm incapable of doing anything myself.

7 Looking

look				
stare	glare	gape	peep	peek

	fixedly	with wide open eyes (as in astonishment or curiosity)	angrily or fiercely	with the mouth open (as in wonder or curiosity)	quickly; often so as not to be noticed	through a small opening or from behind sth	stealthily
stare	+	+					
glare			+				
gape	+			+			
peep					+	+	+
peek					+	+	

All the verbs collocate with the preposition **at**; **stare**, **peep** and **peek** may take **into**. **Peep** and **peek** are colloquial.

Notice that only **peep** (and, of course, **look**) may be used in an imperative construction.

EXAMPLES

stare   Don't sit there **staring** into space, get on with your work!
We **stared** in surprise at some strangely-dressed people in the street.

glare   The boxer **glared** at his opponent.
Why are you **glaring** at me in that unpleasant way? Have I done something wrong?

gape   When I told him the news he didn't reply, but just **gaped** at me in sheer amazement.

peep   The boys hid behind the hedge and **peeped** at the girls swimming.
Peep into the bedroom and see if the baby is still asleep.

peek   I just **peeked** into the kitchen to see what was for dinner.
Two little faces were **peeking** at me from behind the curtain.

Either **peek** or **peep** may be used in the last four examples.

8 Being unimportant

	over-concerned with unimportant details	or unimportant	or showing lack of effort	or very small	or weak	of poor quality	or ungenerous	having hardly any value	often contemptible
petty	+	+							+
trivial		+							
trifling		+					+		
paltry		+	+	+				+	
puny				+	+				
measly				+		+	+		

Measly is colloquial. **Trifling**, **paltry** and **puny** are not usu found in formal writing.

	mind	officials	offence	objections	considerations	problems	preoccupations	affair	person	conversation	matter	loss	accomplishments	attempt	donation	salary	present	helping of ice-cream	child	little puppy
petty	+	+	+	+	+	+	+	(+)	+											
trivial			+	+	+	+	(+)	+		+	+	+	+							
trifling			+	+	+	+					+									
paltry			+	+	+	(+)	+				+	+	+	+	+	+				
puny									+										+	+
measly																+	+	+		

B Synonymous Pairs

1 to begin
to set out | [+ on a journey] or [+ sth long or difficult]

EXAMPLES
Although we **set out** very early, the journey was long and we didn't arrive till midnight.
When I **set out** to learn English, I didn't realise how difficult it would be.

2 to outdo
to surpass { [+ do better] } [+ than someone else] [+ go further] [+ in degree, amount or quality]

Outdo only takes a [+ human] object.
EXAMPLES
Mr Smith has **outdone** everybody by raising ten times more money than the rest of us.

My sister really **outdid** her boastful friend when she was invited to Buckingham Palace to meet the Queen.

This new law **surpasses** everything we have so far seen for sheer impracticability.

This candidate **surpasses** all the others in the brilliance of his playing.

3 **to lose**
to fade | [+slowly] [+brightness] ⇒ [+lose] [+slowly] [+distinctness] [+usu of sound and memory]

EXAMPLES
Brightly-coloured material **fades** easily in the sun.
As the sun set, the light rapidly **faded**.
The sound of singing gradually **faded** as the procession moved away.
Childhood memories **fade** as one grows older.

4 **to trim** { [+reduce in size by removing] } [+small amounts] [+uneven or unwanted parts]
to prune [+of plants] [+certain parts] → [+considerably reduce in size by taking out unnecessary parts]

	the hedges	the edges of a picture	off the rough edge of sth	one's beard	sb's hair	a budget	expenditure	an article	trees	rose-bushes
trim	+	+	+	+	+	+				
prune						+	+	+	+	+

Exercises

1 Explain the meaning of the following in your own words:

1 a log   2 a dropout   3 a vegetarian   4 a ruby   5 pottery
6 applesauce   7 a petty mind   8 the margin for error
9 full to the brim   10 a measly salary   11 out of bounds
12 on the verge of war   13 heart-breaking   14 for years on end
15 to backtrack   16 to go barefoot   17 to flit from job to job
18 to prune an article   19 to strike a balance between two things
20 to hike

2 Match appropriate features with the following words:

1 roam   2 verge   3 dawdle   4 coast   5 stroll   6 brink
7 loiter   8 rim   9 bank   10 dillydally   11 brim   12 bounds

[+often circular or curved] [+walk in an unhurried manner]
[+by playing around with irrelevant and unimportant things]
[+narrow strip of land beside a road] [+upper limits, usu of a container when full] [+without any special purpose] [+flat part

which extends round the face on a hat] [+in a silly way]
[+the limits of something] [+area of land near to the sea]
[+relaxed] [+spend more time than is necessary or usual in doing
sth] [+a short distance] [+for no reason or no apparent reason]
[+line or part of a line marking the limit of sth] [+usu of water]
[+go on foot or by other means] [+land bordering a river or
canal] [+quite a long way] [+stay in one place]

3 In each case add two or three nouns that can collocate with the given adjective:

1 petty   2 turbulent   3 puny   4 sharp   5 paltry   6 hoarse
7 holy   8 trivial   9 scraggy   10 spiritual   11 measly   12 fresh

4 Find words to fit the following descriptions/ definitions:

1 a mass of white bubbles
2 a long, narrow strip of material
3 a bag strapped to the back, used by people on a walking holiday
4 a large, imposing house
5 an adolescent aged between thirteen and twenty
6 articles which have been thrown away, usu of metal
7 to cover with, or put under the surface of, water or other liquid
8 to regularly travel a long distance (usu at least from one town to another) to and from work

5 Fill in the componential grids.

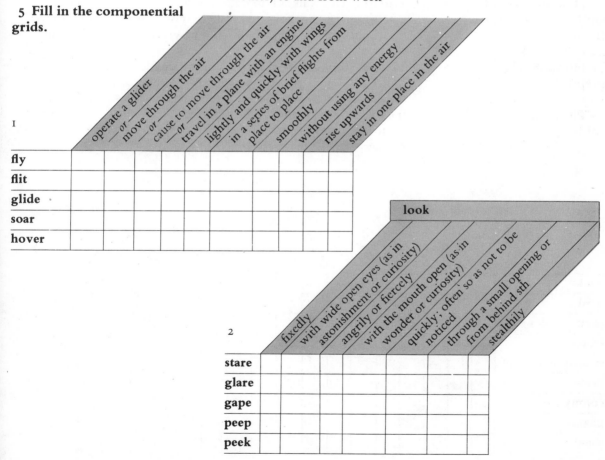

6 Guess the right word.

1 In the utter blackness of the night, his cigarette g . . . . . like a red-hot coal.
2 The teacher was quite ho . . . . . from shouting at his pupils all day.
3 There was a fl . . . . . of excitement and confusion as the company prepared itself for the arrival of the King.
4 If you tighten the dog's collar much more, you're going to c . . . . . him!
5 The r . . . . . of her dress could be heard as she crept towards us in the dark.
6 When the wind strengthened, the sea became tu . . . . . and uninviting.
7 In the dampness of the forest we found many places where soft and closely-packed m . . . . . had taken root.
8 He pulled up on the ve . . . . . and asked the hitch-hikers where they were heading for.

7 Explain the literal and metaphorical senses of each of the following words:

1 verge   2 flock   3 border   4 fade   5 margin   6 prune   7 brink   8 swarm

8 Describe the differences and/or similarities between the following:

1 to trudge/to walk   2 to nod/to bow   3 to scurry/to hurry
4 to simmer/to cook   5 to bustle/to move   6 to envision/to see
7 a chop/a rib   8 a pit/a hole   9 a pew/a seat   10 rustle/sound

9 Fill in the right preposition(s).

10 Fill in the collocational grids.

1 . . . the banks of the river   2 . . . the seaside   3 to stare . . . somebody   4 to glare . . . somebody   5 to set . . . to do something   6 to peep/peek . . . the kitchen   7 to stroll . . ./. . . to the baker   8 to roam . . . the old town   9 to idle . . . breakfast   10 to idle/loiter . . . one's time   11 . . . the brink/verge . . . disaster   12 . . . the coast

1

	cattle	geese	deer	goats	elephants	lions	dogs	sheep	birds	wolves	fish	ants	bees	monkeys	horses	buffalo
flock																
herd																
pack																
troop																
swarm of																
pride																
colony																
gaggle																
shoal																

2

	a tablecloth	a hat	a cup	a playground	a wheel	a precipice	a bed	a roof	a lake	a nervous breakdown	a new discovery	economic collapse	disaster	collapsing	tears
border															
margin															
edge															
rim *of*															
brim															
boundary															
verge															

3

	off the rough edge of sth	the hedges	trees	rose-bushes	one's beard	sb's hair	a budget	an article	the edges of a picture	expenditure
prune										
trim										

11 Choose the word that best fits the context. Modify its form where necessary.

1 The party . . . . . across the lawn to meet us, champagne in hand. (roam, stroll, ramble)
2 We sat on the . . . . . of the precipice and admired the awe-inspiring view below. (edge, rim, verge)
3 We . . . . . in the foyer, hoping to catch a glimpse of our favourite opera singer. (dawdle, idle, loiter)
4 The arrow . . . . . into the sky, and was lost from view. (fly, hover, soar)
5 The moth . . . . . from candle to candle. (fly, flit, glide, hover)
6 The wasp . . . . . over the jam-jar before it finally settled on the rim. (flit, soar, hover, glide)
7 I . . . . . at myself in the mirror, trying to see if I looked any older. (peak, stare, gape, glare)
8 His jaw fell open, and he could only . . . . . in amazement at the incredible sight before him. (peek, stare, gape, glare)
9 He had a . . . . . mentality, always making issues over unimportant details. (petty, trivial, measly)
10 She . . . . . herself by breaking her previous world record. (outdo, surpass)
11 Everyone jumped into the swimming pool except Peregrine, who stood shivering on the . . . . .. (brim, brink, rim)

12 Look at the text again.

If you are learning British English, pick out the American spellings in 'A Walk Across America' and give their British equivalents (without looking at the list!)

13 Look at the text again.

The author of 'A Walk Across America' has a personal style which depends mostly on unusual collocation, eg 'blue, yellow, and orange . . . morning', 'hawks and falcons bulleted by'. Find as many examples of this as you can and say why they are 'unusual'.

Revision Exercises

R1 Find the cover term for the following words:

EXAMPLE: grubby, filthy, grimy, **dirty**

1 drudgery, grind, labour, toil   2 seize, grasp, snatch, grab
3 hazardous, perilous, risky   4 dodge, duck, evade, shirk
5 bellyache, grouse, moan, grumble, whine   6 solicitor, barrister
7 stare, glare, gape, peek   8 grin, smirk   9 bicker, squabble, wrangle   10 flit, soar   11 giggle, chuckle   12 quake, shiver, quiver, shudder, tremble   13 pilfer, pinch, swipe, snitch, rip off

R2 Match words from group a with suitable words/ phrases from group b

a   1 stray   2 weird   3 odd   4 enigmatic   5 uncanny
6 announce   7 declare   8 proclaim   9 pronounce
b   sb to be the winner, that the price of the meat will rise, sb dead, sb king, experience, dogs, cattle, animal, smile, times, circumstances, jobs, person

R3 Name the things you can:

1 conduct   2 adjust   3 hire   4 dodge   5 charter   6 inflate
7 let   8 reveal   9 share with sb   10 quote   11 ward off
12 plough   13 forestall   14 rent

R4 Describe the differences and/or similarities between the following:

1 to shirk/to evade   2 to avert/to ward off   3 to expose/to flaunt
4 to impress/to sway   5 to muster/to gather   6 to announce/
to pronounce   7 wages/salary   8 shiny/luminous   9 uncanny/
weird   10 plain/simple   11 liable/prone   12 effective/efficient

R5 Give the opposite of the following words/ expressions:

1 to take off (a plane)   2 to look up to   3 to accept   4 to damage
5 to catch (a train)   6 to retard   7 to lend   8 to hide
9 spiritual   10 immune   11 huge   12 outward   13 important
14 abundant, ample   15 stealthy, furtive   16 changeable
17 flexible   18 authentic   19 smooth   20 barren   21 severe
22 indifference

R6 Find words to fit the following descriptions/ definitions:

1 outbreaks of disorder, disturbances of the public peace
2 people who roam the streets to find what they can
3 people who buy and sell
4 people who measure the shape, position and boundaries of land
5 people who make a living by fitting and mending water-pipes, cisterns, etc
6 night butterflies
7 professional wall builders
8 people who put on the layer of material required on interior walls of houses before painting

R7 Which of the given words/suffixes will pair with 'work', which with 'sea'? What is the meaning of each of these compounds?

1 . . . er 2 able 3 less 4 man 5 side 6 mile 7 load
8 shop 9 sick 10 food 11 day 12 shore 13 weed 14 shy
15 gull

R8 Guess the right word.

1 She sat down on the drawing pin and quickly l . . . . . in the air with pain.
2 Arriving in this foreign country, she was h . . . . . by the fact that she couldn't speak the language.
3 The pr . . . . . sneaked around the house, gently trying the doors and windows.
4 The boy who d . . . . . our newspapers is on holiday.
5 The q . . . . . for gold led people in America to give up house, job and family.
6 With regret we had to d . . . . . their invitation as we were going out that evening.
7 When she arrived at her d . . . . ., she breathed a sigh of relief.
8 We would eat at o . . . . . hours of the day, regardless of time.
9 The weather s . . . . . y grew worse as the day wore on.
10 She lived in a rather poor, dr . . . . . district of the town.
11 He g . . . . . at her, realizing that at last he had found Miss Right.
12 The sh . . . . . g door-knocker gave the final touch of smartness to the house.

R9 Give the British equivalents of the following words and expressions:

1 public transportation 2 attorney 3 sidewalk 4 elevator
5 apartment 6 automobile 7 checker-board 8 veterinarian
9 real estate broker 10 pack 11 belt-way 12 to trim (trees)
13 to raise (crops) 14 to hit (a place) 15 to gag

R10 The following nouns have been used in the texts in compounds/set phrases as modifiers to other nouns. List those compounds/set phrases.

1 lunatic 2 bedside 3 foot 4 heart 5 water 6 death
7 motor 8 finger 9 shop 10 insurance 11 snow 12 land
13 estate 14 neon 15 car 16 mountain 17 farm
18 telephone 19 tax 20 health

R11 Choose the word that best fits the context. Modify its form where necessary.

1 Could you just . . . . . the picture with your hand while I bang in a nail to fix it to the wall? (bolster, support)
2 She could . . . . . English better than she could speak it. (grasp, comprehend, understand)
3 A . . . . . man knocked at the door and asked most politely which was the route to Elvington. (odd, strange)
4 The case involved the safety of the state, and as such, all the relevant documents were . . . . . . (secretive, stealthy, clandestine, secret)
5 It was a . . . . . old bird, sleeping during the day and pottering around at night. (mysterious, uncanny, weird)
6 He . . . . . his address frequently. (change, amend, shift)

7 Because of the increase in serious crime, it was decided to reintroduce the death . . . . .. (punishment, penalty)

8 We . . . . . her reasons for not wanting to go. (protect, shield, defend, guard)

9 Because she had once broken his heart, John . . . . . seeing Mary whenever possible. (dodge, shirk, avoid)

10 The . . . . . sound of the rain on the window drove us nearly crazy with frustration. (dull, drab, monotonous)

11 She . . . . . my friendship thinking she could find better elsewhere. (decline, spurn, refuse)

12 For miles around us there was nothing but . . . . . countryside, with not a plant or tree in sight. (dry, arid)

13 The news was a great shock but in a few moments she . . . . her thoughts and started to pack a suitcase. (gather, muster, collect, assemble)

R12 Describe the differences and/or similarities between the following:

1 to adapt/to conform   2 to strip/to denude   3 to chase/to hunt   4 to lease/to rent   5 to clutch/to grab   6 to pilfer/to rip off   7 to fall down/to collapse   8 to condemn/to decry   9 to direct/to supervise   10 scrap/brawl

R13 Test your collocational competence.

1

	a blow	a falling branch	a speeding motorcyclist	the police	military service	taxes	the issue	one's head	out of doing sth	a question	work	one's duty	one's responsibility
dodge													
duck													
evade													
shirk													

2

	trip	person	character	driving	investment	attempt to escape	spender
adventurous							
reckless							

3

	arrangement	experience	discovery	business	deal	profession	trade	occupation
profitable								
lucrative								

4

	village	little house	garden	kitchen	room	study	office	clothes	worker	person	household	appearance	habits	work	mind	handwriting	queue of people	demonstration	presentation of the facts
tidy																			
neat																			
orderly																			

5

	judge of character	assessment of the situation	politician	diplomat	move	person	way of going about things	smile	nature	plot	trick
shrewd											
sly											
cunning											
crafty											

R14 Complete the story.

design, job, salary, vacancies, work, stability, wages, self-confidence, fussy, diversified, managerial, glamorous, executive, secretarial, drab, clerical, to query, to strip off, to shirk, to avert, to struggle, to accommodate, to aim, to amend, to fight

'Having separated from my husband, I was looking for a 1 . . . . . Of course, there were plenty of 2 . . . . . for shop-assistants, but the 3 . . . . . were low, and I was looking for something a little more 4 . . . . .. It's not that I'm 5 . . . . . or 6 . . . . . menial 7 . . . . ., but having 8 . . . . . at night school to pass a few exams, it would have been a wry comment on my success if I ended up in some 9 . . . . . 10 . . . . . or 11 . . . . . job. On the other hand, I wasn't 12 . . . . . at 13 . . . . . or 14 . . . . . status, with a 15 . . . . . in the upper-income bracket! No. I was looking for an opening into some kind of social work; there at least one could count on the work being 16 . . . . . and full of human interest. An interesting job is the best medicine for mending a broken heart!

I'd 17 . . . . . for years to keep my husband, but, once I realised that I couldn't 18 . . . . . the inevitable, I was pleased when the separation came. Of course, I miss the 19 . . . . . which marriage involves, but I've tried to 20 . . . . . for that loss by building up my own 21 . . . . ., or rather, let me 22 . . . . . that by saying my own self-reliance. It's of course impossible to 23 . . . . ., in one go, all the trappings of marriage, and I would even 24 . . . . . the advisability of doing so. And anyway, it must be in the 25 . . . . . of things that my life turned out this way.'

R15 Solve the crossword puzzle.

Across

1 A . . . . . of geese crossed the road in front of me. (6)

3 look in amazement, often with the mouth open (4)

5 a written legal agreement concerning property, ownership (4)

7 curved upper edge of a container, eg cup (4)

11 make a sudden attack on sth (4)

13 walk slowly and in a relaxed way, for pleasure (6)

14 meeting for the 1st time (9)

15 unorganised fight between a small number of people, often in the street (5)

18 winged insect which flies at night (4)

21 small and weak in growth, not likely to survive (4)

22 disorderly, noisy meeting of people (6)

24 Stars t . . . . . in the sky. (7)

26 supernatural power, people believe in (3)

28 unexpected and direct refusal (6)

29 I label (anagram) (6)

31 This glass is very full, try not to s . . . . . water over my papers! (5)

33 support and strengthen sth which is weakening, eg morale, confidence (7)

37 bring sb back to life (11)

38 an enclosed seat in a church (3)

39 She must stay in bed, she is quite seriously i . . . . .. (3)

40 Puts M (anagram) is impossible to solve. (5)

41 Quickly and quietly look into, eg a room, so as not to disturb. (4)

42 line marking the limit or edge of sth (3)

Down

1 very small organism which causes disease and infection (4)
2 He managed to g . . . . . the child's hand and pull her out of the way of the car. (4)
4 Sb who is over-concerned with unimportant details is p . . . . . (5)
6 what you do with food (3)
7 duck's beak (4)
8 small, or of poor quality (*coll*) (6)
9 stumble helplessly in deep mud, or water, or snow (8)
10 raw (anagram) (3)
12 Des and Tiny together make your future! (7)
13 Little boys enjoy having one. (5)
16 touch sb with one's elbow to attract attention (5)

17 The television picture isn't very clear, can you a . . . . . the brightness control? (6)
19 small round smooth stone (6)
20 be enough: ie scuff (anagram) (7)
23 fly high in the sky (4)
25 Pigs love to w . . . . . in mud. (6)
27 sb who buys and sells things (6)
30 stay standing in one place, for no particular reason (6)
32 fasten 2 sheets of paper together with a paper-c . . . . . (4)
33 One man does this in cricket. (4)
34 You must pass a t . . . . . if you want to drive a car. (4)
35 think about sth in a relaxed way (4)
36 pat (anagram) (3)
37 tear material or paper (*coll*) (3)

Index

Words are listed according to Unit (number in **bold** type) followed by the page number.

The authors and publishers wish to thank the following who have kindly given permission for the use of copyright material:–

Academic Press Inc. and Dr. Peter L. Benson for extracts from the *Journal of Experimental Social Psychology*, September and December 1976; Associated Book Publishers Ltd. and Harper & Row Inc. for extracts from *King Solomon's Ring* by Konrad Z. Lorenz, © 1952, published by Methuen & Co. Ltd.; Associated Catholic Newspapers Ltd. for an extract from *The Universe*; Associated Newspapers Group Ltd. for extracts from *Weekend* magazine; Blond & Briggs Ltd. and Harper & Row Inc. for an extract from *Small is Beautiful: Economics as if People Mattered* by E. F. Schumacher. © 1973 by E. F. Schumacher; The British Council for a job advertisement; Church and World, International Center for Research and Communication, Brussels, for extracts from *Prospective* GRO/501/75 and POP/108/73; William Collins Sons & Co. Ltd. for extracts from *God Bless Love*, compiled by Nanette Newman; W. H. Freeman and Co. for adapted extracts from *Scientific American* articles 'Urban Monkeys' by Sheo Dan Singh, July 1969, and 'The Social Order of Japanese Macaques' by G. Gray Eaton, October 1976; Hodder & Stoughton Ltd. and Bantam Books Inc. for an extract from *The Search For Psychic Power* by David Hammond, © 1975; Jonathan Cape Ltd. on behalf of the Estate of Robert Frost and Holt, Rinehart & Winston Inc. for the poem 'Fire and Ice' by Robert Frost from *The Poetry of Robert Frost* edited by Edward Connery Lathem, © 1923, © 1969 by Holt, Rinehart & Winston, © 1951 by Robert Frost; London Express News & Feature Services for extracts from the *Daily Express* and the *Evening Standard*; John Murray (Publishers) Ltd. and Houghton Mifflin Co. for an extract from *Parkinson's Law* by C. Northcote Parkinson; National Geographic Society for extracts from the article 'A Walk Across America' by Peter Gorton Jenkins from the *National Geographic Magazine*, March 1971; Newsweek Inc., International Editorial Service, New York, for extracts from *Newsweek*; The Observer Ltd. for an extract from the *Observer Magazine*, March 1977; Random House Inc. for an extract from *I Can Sell You Anything* by Carl P. Wrighter; The Reader's Digest Association Ltd. for extracts from *Reader's Digest*; Reed Employment Ltd. for an advertisement in *The Times*, March 1977; Rodale Press Inc. for extracts from *Organic Gardening and Farming* magazine; Routledge & Kegan Paul Ltd. and Doubleday & Co. Inc. for extracts from *The Second Sin* by Thomas Szasz, © 1973; Routledge & Kegan Paul Ltd. and Holt, Rinehart & Winston Inc. for an extract from *The Sane Society* by Erich Fromm; Ivor Smullen for the item 'Spot Cheque' published in *Weekend* magazine, May 1977; Stanbrook Publications Ltd. for an extract from *Family Circle*, May 1977; The Statesman & Nation Publishing Co. Ltd. for an extract from the *New Statesman*, September 1969; Syndication International Ltd. for extracts from the *Daily Mirror*, and *Honey*, *Woman's Own*, *Woman* magazines; D. C. Thomson & Co. Ltd. for extracts from *The Sunday Post*; R. & C. Vintners for the Veuve du Vernay advertisement featured in the British *Cosmopolitan* magazine; World Future Society, Washington for extracts from *The Futurist*, February, June and December 1976; Yardley of London Ltd. for their advertisement 'Come closer seeing is believing' featured in the British *Cosmopolitan* magazine, May 1977; Ziff-Davis Publishing Co. for extracts from *Psychology Today*.

Every effort has been made to trace all the copyright holders, but if any have been inadvertently overlooked the publishers will be pleased to make the necessary arrangement at the first opportunity.

The authors and publishers wish to acknowledge, with thanks, the following illustration sources.

All drawings by George Craig

Map by Dorothy Robertson

Photographs: Aerofilms Ltd.; Australian News and Information Bureau; Barnabys Picture Library; Jim Brown bill; Central Office of Information; Cutex; Richard Musman; Peter Newark's Western Americana Picture Library; U.K.A.E.A.; R. & C. Vintners; Yardley Ltd.

UNIVERSITY OF CAMBRIDGE
RESEARCH CENTRE FOR ENGLISH
AND APPLIED LINGUISTICS
KEYNES HOUSE
TRUMPINGTON STREET
CAMBRIDGE CB2 1QA